GIAP

VOLCANO UNDER SNOW

by the same author

Twice Around the World

Not Ordinary Men

GIAP

VOLCANO UNDER SNOW

JOHN COLVIN

SOHO

Published by
Soho Press Inc.
853 Broadway
New York, NY 10003

The moral right of the author has been asserted

First published in England by Quartet Books Ltd.. in 1996

Library of Congress Cataloging-in-Publication Data

Colvin, John.
    Giap : volcano under snow / John Colvin.
        p.   cm.
    Includes bibliographical references.
    ISBN 1-56947-053-7 (alk. paper)
        1. Võ, Nguyên Giáp, 1912-   . 2. Vietnam—History, Military.
    3. Vietnam—Politics and government—20th century.   4. Generals—
    Vietnam—Biography.   5. Vietnam. Quân dôi nhân dan—Biography.
    I. Title.
    DS560.72.V6C65 1996
    355'.0092—dc20
        [B]   95-26280
                                                                        CIP

10 9 8 7 6 5 4 3 2 1

for Mark and Zoë,
my dear and patient children

Contents

Acknowledgements

I am indebted to Tom Hartman, and to Leo, without whom nothing much might *ever* have happened: to Naim Attallah and Jeremy Beale: to Richard Stolz and Cameron La Clair in Washington: to Brigadier Johnny Ricketts, Sir Christopher Mallaby, Sir Robin Renwick, Mark Milburn, Jean Romain Désfossés: to Robert P Richardson of the Defence Intelligence Agency Washington, Colonel Paul Gaujac of the Service Historique of the Armeé de Terre at the Chateau de Vincennes, the late Richard Bone, Head of Library and Records Department at the Foreign and Commonwealth Office: the staffs of the Public Records Office at Kew, the School of Oriental and African Studies Library at London University, the Imperial War Museum, the Centre des Archives de la France d' Outre Mer at Aix-en-Provence, and Messrs Pham and Dung of the Mayor's office in Hanoi. I am particularly indebted to Monsieur Jacques Decornoy for permission to use material which forms a substantial part of Chapter XXVI.

I am above everything grateful to Peter Simpson-Jones and Victor Colville, indeed to all my friends and colleagues, living and dead, of the golden days so many years ago in Saigon and those, later and more sombre, in Hanoi, Ambassadors Dhawan, Ranjit Sethi, Francois de Quirielle and his wife Anne; Mr Geoffrey Livesey. For endless hospitality in Saigon or in Vientiane I am indebted to Sir Peter Wilkinson, the late Sir Fred Warner, the late Joe Ford and the late Alexis Forter.

My thanks are especially due to Gaye Briscoe who translates my hieroglyphs into the King's English.

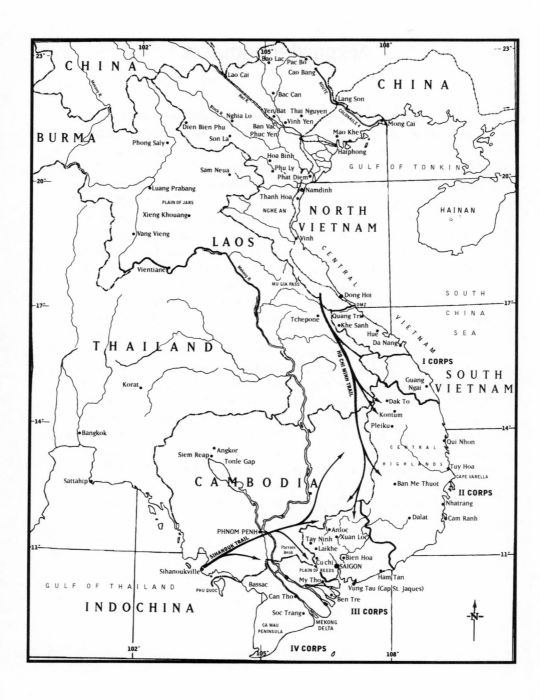

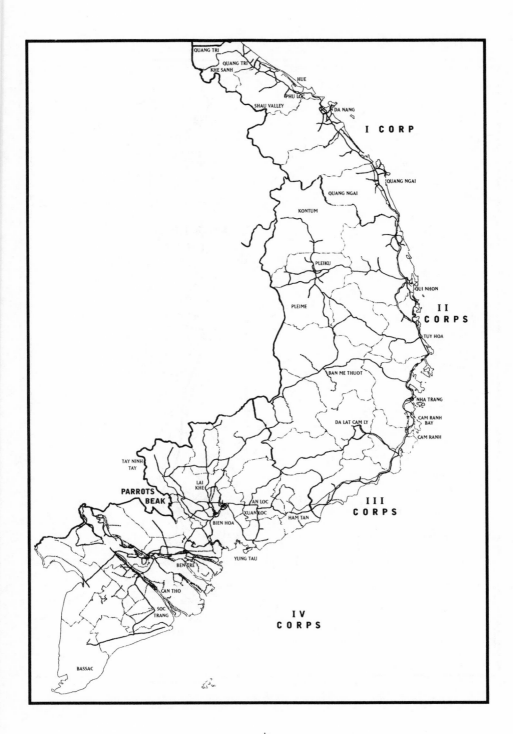

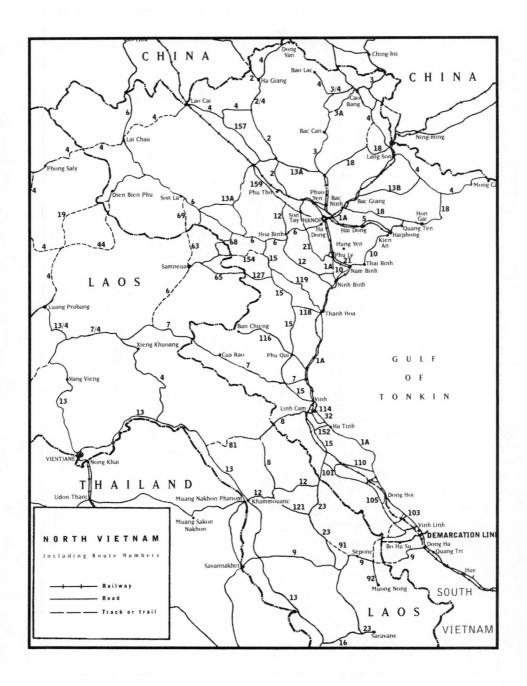

Prologue

Vietnam, together with Cambodia and Laos, is geographically part of Indochina. Rice cultivation remains the principal occupation in the plains and deltas, most successfully in the South. The hills and plateaux have been, hitherto, almost exclusively the home of tribes – Muong, T'ai, Nung, Man, Meo – practising slash-and-burn agriculture, although settlement there by plainsmen has been more recently encouraged. Minerals, especially coal but also wolfram, zinc, tin, manganese, and so on, are found in commercial quantities.

Apart from the tribes, the largest ethnic minority in the South, despite massive emigration after the Vietnam Wars, is still the Chinese, fulfilling their customary South-east Asian function of merchants, traders and entrepreneurs. In the past few years, however, the Vietnamese have demonstrated increasing skill in these roles. There are also residual traces of the Cham and Khmer, seriously reduced in the eighteenth and ninteenth centuries by the southern march of the Vietnamese, the latter themselves the racial product of unions in neolithic times between T'ai from China and indigenous 'Indonesian' tribes.

The mythical Vietnamese kingdom of Van Lang became, at least in legend, Au Lac, a province of the Han Empire from 100 BC for a 'Thousand Years'. The country achieved independence from China by force of arms in AD 938, its capital at Hanoi, and with institutions based on Chinese patterns. Vietnam under the Ly and Tran dynasties defeated Sung and Mongol (Yuan) Chinese invasions – the Mongols three times – in the eleventh and thirteenth centuries, while the founder of the Le dynasty, Le Loi, drove out a temporary Chinese occupation of his country in 1428. The first native rebellion against the Chinese was much earlier, that of the famous Trung sisters in AD 43. Opposition to Han rule was continual and, on at least one occasion, was led by another woman, Trieu An who, like the Trung and many other Vietnamese, killed herself when defeated.

After Le Loi, Vietnam was 'divided' between the Mac, the Trinh in the north and the Nguyen in the south. A rebellion under the Tay-Son in 1789 brought about civil war. Order was restored by the

1

Nguyen, who had already undertaken the conquest of the south. Their leader, under the title Gia Long, proclaimed himself emperor at Huë in 1802, thus uniting Vietnam, as it is today, for the first time under one ruler. The dynasty then went on to conquer much of Cambodia.

In the nineteenth century, France repelled in India by the British, chose Indochina as her area of colonization in Asia, securing Vietnam by 1885 chiefly through a series of amphibious operations under naval command. (Subsequent governors-general were often admirals). By 1893 Vietnam, Laos and Cambodia had been combined to form French Indochina or the *Union Indochinoise*. In 1884 China recognized a French protectorate over the Viet Empire.

The French introduced considerable economic development, in rubber and other crops, in minerals, roads and railways. But productivity, as opposed to production, remained low in the paddi-fields, while increased taxes on small farmers at a time of inflation and slump severely damaged and estranged the peasantry. Excellent French educational institutions were not widespread. They were thought to subvert ancient tradition, and were not accompanied by sufficient opportunities for high and medium level employment amongst Vietnamese. Resentment grew.

The economic contribution of the French was marred by official exploitation and corruption, and repression of almost all mani-festations of nationalism led inexorably to the predominance in political life of the Communist Party of Indochina over less ideological and less secure nationalist parties. In 1941 the Communist Party led by Ho Chi Minh founded the Revolutionary League for the Independence of Vietnam, otherwise known as the Viet Minh. By 1945 the Viet Minh had secured American aid from Chungking and, after the Japanese mounted their anti-French *coup d'état* in March, they were the single most effective body in Vietnam when the Japanese surrendered, commanding – because of enforced French impotence – most of the organs of state throughout the country. The emperor, although temporarily to become their chief political advisor, abdicated in their stead.

The man, under Ho Chi Minh's direction, who carried Indochina from colonialism to independence was Vo Nguyen Giap, later awarded the nickname of Volcano Under Snow by the Hanoi propagandists. In the process of securing statehood for his country and its neighbours, Giap defeated the armies of both France and the United States of America.

His wars, like all wars so far, were won not just by machines but by the men engaged. When speaking of the siege of Kohima in the Burma campaign, an officer of the 4th Battalion, the Queen's Own Royal West Kent Regiment, said, 'It was the men who did it. We couldn't have done it without the men.' But, out of earshot, Sergeant Clinch of the battalion's HQ Company, contradicted him: 'No, it was the officers. We never had a bad officer.' A 'B' Company sergeant said, 'It was *our* officer who did it . . .'

This unity, demonstrated in a single battle, albeit one not dissimilar from Rorke's Drift or even Thermopylae, was matched not only in one shining encounter but consistently from 1945 to 1975 in the People's Army of Vietnam. While that cannot excuse disgusting treatment by North Vietnamese military of French or American prisoners, the example set in training and in the field by Senior General Vo Nguyen Giap and his subordinates was an essential factor in the formation of this victorious Army.

That example was imposed through three concepts. The first was supervision of the 'fighters' by cadre superiors watching for signs of low morale which might lead to malingering or desertion. The second was criticism and self-criticism, which, curiously, soldiers seemed to regard as a sort of mutual affection and an eventual source of self-pride. The 'three-man cell' formed the third leg of this tripod.

The political officers were described as 'gentle, affable, friendly', universally liked and respected, the 'mothers' or brothers of the fighters. Their task, that of morale motivation, was the most important political duty, and the political task was more important even than the military. A man had to know what he was fighting for.

His 'war aims' were proclaimed as independence, the departure of the Americans, liberation, an end to 'exploitation, the oppression of the weak and contempt for the poor'. Most men had hazy ideas about politics, even about the difference between Communism and Socialism. They did not claim to be 'democrats'. They knew that they were 'revolutionaries', that they 'fought for Vietnam'. There was universal detestation of the 'American invader', a determination to 'live greatly and die gloriously', to 'realize a revolution'. Their slogan was 'We are the People'.

Under Giap's guidance, they believed that a combination of

military and political means, in a collaboration between the USSR, China, the East European countries, the 'American people', the DRV and the NLF, would defeat the United States and South Vietnam. They denied even the possibility of victory by the Republic of Vietnam (RVN) or of Democratic Republic of Vietnam/National Liberation Front (DRV/NLF) defeat.

They sought to eliminate or at least to overcome the fear of death, as opposed to Western determination to perform honourably when frightened of death. 'One must accept death, so that the younger generation may grow up in liberty . . . we wanted to see our loved ones, but we knew that the country was invaded, that the South was dominated by the Americans, so all we could do to rejoin our people sooner was to fight the war.'

Before operations, troops were often invited to discuss the plans. Orders were not always executed cheerfully, but they were always executed. There was never disobedience, although malingering sometimes occurred, as did defection. Cadres did not demand anything which was too difficult for the fighters to do. All orders were aimed at safeguarding the troops. The soldiers, although disliking sudden, rapid movement to new positions after battle or air attacks, and 'feeling lonely and depressed' in jungles, did not complain. This attitude was much encouraged by cadres. 'You should endure hardships today in order to have a happy future.' But the leaders listened and tried to work out a solution to problems of uncertainty or doubt.

Even when units had fought as many as eight or ten battles in six months, or had lost in killed, wounded and captured up to 80 per cent of their strength, 'fighters' continued to express 'confidence in their leaders and in the ultimately favourable outcome of the struggle'. When the prospect of a long war became painful to the men, or when disappointments came – such as the failure of the uprisings during Tet 1968 – the cadres tried hard and successfully to raise morale. The soldiers recovered enthusiasm and strictly obeyed orders.

Viet Cong prisoners claimed that 'education and indoctrination', not conventional punishment, were used to discipline defaulters, a process including criticism within the three-man cell.

Perseverance in the long struggle had many causes: hatred of the Americans and, to a lesser extent of the Army of the Republic of Vietnam (ARVN); belief in a self-governing and independent Vietnam.

These persistent attributes differed not only from those in the Army of the Southern Republic, with its incompetent and often cowardly officer class, but from the Chinese People's Liberation Army (PLA) in Korea. The PLA's morale in June 1951 had been low enough to demand the presence at the Korean front line itself of senior Chinese officers, in order to prevent breakdown and desertions. 'The high command could not control its troops.' Chinese soldiers had been badly trained, inadequately equipped and lacked all confidence in their commanders' doctrine. They were, except in numbers, the inferiors of the People's Army of Vietnam (PAVN).

The latter was the equal of Field Marshal Slim's 14th Army, although lacking that formation's dour insouciance and driven by a doomed ideology.

Tran Hung Dao, who defeated the Mongol armies in the thirteenth century, is remembered by two maxims. They guided Giap from the beginning. The first was: 'The army must have one soul, like father and son in the family. It is vital to treat the people with humanity, to achieve deep roots and a lasting base.' The second was: 'Defeat the greater with the lesser.'

Giap believed that military action within the revolutionary line should incorporate political, diplomatic and economic theory and practice. He believed also in the offensive, in 'central' thrusts with maximum resources against the American Army, not in a reversion to guerrilla warfare or a withdrawal to the inaccessible mountains. He regarded the North as 'the great rear area for the supply of the southern battlefield', and the Socialist countries as the essential bases for the support of the North: since the North was the begetter of the southern battlefield, the first claim was disingenuous. He saw that willpower was the paramount weapon of Vietnam, as it was the major weakness of America, and, at an early stage, he grasped that in the United States media lay the last battleground. It was there that the 'lesser would defeat the greater'.

Guerrilla warfare, in its wide expansion into the countryside, had been the political, then the military *fons et origo* of victory, sealing the mountains and plains to the enemy. But not for ever, or not uniquely. Methods changed with the situation, tactical or strategic. Politics was both the key and the objective. 'Revolutionary armed strength was as strong as the revolution itself.' Giap's total war included guerrilla action, mobile warfare, uprising, main-force battle, political action at home and abroad through 'foreign friends', often concurrent and all under unremitting political, 'moral' and military direction.

The general knew that only protracted war could contain the immense technological superiority of the United States forces. Initially against the enemy bases, mainly in the rear, the ultimate objective was nevertheless a general insurrection brought about by simultaneous 'civil' and military means. And although Giap recognized the importance of the human will, he also acknowledged that military success was eventually dependent on fire-power. He enlisted help from the Socialist countries in building élite forces to meet the requirements of modern warfare, particularly against American air and ground fire-power.

Small, well-armed groups became the *forces de frappe*, concentrated against US and ARVN bases in order to overcome mobile, larger enemy forces, defeating 'greater with lesser'. According to Vo Nguyen Giap, the objective of 'people's war' was *to gain surprise and time* through the maximum economy of force. Anti-aircraft defences also multiplied, as did the whole underground infrastructure.

'Every operation must produce an increase in strength . . . extension of war in time is obtained by the brevity of actions and by limitations on the numbers of troops, in attacks on points selected for shock value . . . It follows that every operation must produce an increase in strength.'

Historians might attribute Giap's eventual triumph less to his own merits than to the faults and *faiblesses* of his adversaries. While Hanoi fought total war under totalitarian control, the French and American democracies operated under crippling restrictions.

The quality, for example, of the French Expeditionary Force was conditioned by prohibitions on service overseas by metropolitan conscripts, and the consequent use of less reliable colonial troops. The United States, in its war, considered itself prohibited, until 1972 under Nixon's presidency, from the strategic use of air-power against ports and marshalling yards, thus permitting to the DRV the import of those armaments which procured their final victory. (The stepping-up in summer 1967 of *Rolling Thunder* was too temporary to form an exception.) America, similarly, excluded from its objectives the employment of ground troops against the territory itself of the DRV; perhaps it was well that it did.

And both Paris and Washington, in the end, fell victim to the weight of their own public opinion, a factor which hardly had to be addressed at home by Hanoi, buoyed up by the conviction that neither colonial reconquest nor Western 'neo-colonialism' were any longer possible.

As a historian, Giap studied Sun Tzu and the campaigns of both Napoleon and of the early Vietnamese commanders against Chinese and Mongols. His only military training was, however, at Tsingsi with the Chinese in the 1940s and with the OSS Mission in Vietnam in 1945. General Nguyen Son, once commander in northern Annam and for twenty years an officer in the Chinese Red Army, including service in the Long March, described him as a 'military illiterate, his rank deriving from his political importance'.

The judgement contained elements of prejudice, including jealousy. Giap's military prowess, nevertheless, was not hindered by the errors of his enemies, including French strategic miscalculation in 1954 leading to defeat at Dien Bien Phu.

US mistakes were even more substantial. President Johnson was unable to decide on the aims or methods of the war, or to summon up public support in the strategic void in which he and his advisors had doomed themselves to wander. Washington consistently failed to establish agreement on the character of the war – whether insurgency, conventional war or a combination – and to define clear US military and political objectives. The initiative, in consequence, passed to the PAVN, who applied protracted war to the US diet of 'quick fixes' with their effects on corrupt Saigon governments.

No effective decisions were taken, despite the solid success of the Marine Combined Action Platoons in the enclaves, on pacification as opposed to attrition. Vietnamization also was unsuccessful, not so much because of Saigon's weakness, but because the aims for which it was originally designed – counter-insurgency and internal security – were overtaken by conventional warfare as NVA forces in the South moved to Phase III after the American withdrawal. Airpower, because it was 'graduated', failed in its objectives of interdiction and coercion, even reinforcing Hanoi's political will; when attacks against ports and 'marshalling yards' were adopted in 1967, they produced virtual collapse in the DRV.

It must also be said that Giap himself was soundly defeated by the only opponent whose talents matched his own, General de Lattre de Tassigny. Because Giap lacked a vocational formation and because, for once, he discounted Sun Tzu, in 1951 he launched direct attacks on 'an Army drawn up in calm and confident array, with banners in perfect order'.

De Lattre defeated him three times, at Vinh Yen, Mao Khe and the Day River, inflicting 20,000 Viet Minh casualties. He built a line of fortified posts to protect the Red River delta and, in November, seized Hoa Binh on the Black River, and also formed a battery of large mobile groups for pan-Indochina service. But seven months after the Day River, he died of cancer, succeeded by Raoul Salan, a subtle colonial officer but of less *élan* or vision. De Lattre was a good, dashing general. Had he lived, however, one must still ask whether Paris and the US would have supplied him with the resources to move with panache further from the strategic defensive, to lure Giap into definitive defeat.

At the start in 1940, partly because he had only a few men, Giap preferred guerrilla to conventional warfare. On moving to Bac Bo, he showed his great organizational skill for the first time in achieving material self-sufficiency for his little group, as well as in producing written propaganda including a newspaper. By 1941 he had a force of 100, by 1944 he was even considering pan-Vietnamese guerrilla warfare – sharply countermanded by Ho – and in 1945 he carried out the Viet Minh's first small armed actions against the Japanese.

In August 1945 he led his troops into Hanoi. By late 1946 the Viet Minh Army numbered 60,000 men, most of whom Giap took to the hills of Northern Tonkin, where they trained, consolidated and expanded. Already his guerrillas were able to harass the French in their fixed positions, ambushing patrols, blowing bridges from valleys and caves in the jungle-covered limestone mountains over an area of 7,000 square miles. Here in the Viet Bac in 1947 he survived, although with severe casualties, three major French combined operations. The French then chose to retain only the *forts* on Route 4, otherwise concentrating on the plains and coast bordering China and on the Red River delta. By causing them to abandon most of the mountains, Giap obtained time to plan and to develop his forces, thus scoring his first strategic success.

Politics, he decided, must have precedence over military action. Fair administration would produce popular support, and hence strengthen popular will, which would, in turn, lead to the military strength necessary to beat France. 'The Army is dependent on the people'. The Viet Minh, in its guerrilla and propaganda operations, was now in the second Phase, preparing for the counter-offensive or war of movement, leading to the third phase of revolutionary war.

General Alessandri in 1950 disapproved of the French withdrawal from the Viet Bac. He proposed to lead fifty battalions against the Viet Minh on their own ground, before the North Vietnamese were ready to move. He lost the argument, in Paris, with his superiors. Immaculate and terrible Franco-Vietnamese battles followed along the tops of knife-edged ridges and in vile valley bottoms along Route 4, won by Giap's soldiers newly trained and equipped by the Chinese People's Liberation Army. The French lost the frontier with China and everything besides; Hanoi trembled, but it was then that de Lattre arrived.

After the great man died, Giap retook Hoa Binh, not attempting direct assault, as in 1951, but exploiting the heights, artillery surveillance of the Black River and a sabotaged main road (Route 6), admirably forcing dispersal of French reserves in the Delta to meet his divisional attacks at Hoa Binh. It was on the Black and Red Rivers, too, that he demonstrated his genius for logistic supply over distance by Soviet trucks and the recruitment of huge numbers of porters; it is possible that even de Lattre would have been seen to have over-reached his grasp.

Robert O'Neill believes that, as a result of this battle, Giap had virtually destroyed French capacity for operations beyond the Red River delta in Tonkin. It was now for Giap, not for the French, to lure the 'enemy' on to territory where he could force a settlement of the war on his terms, military or political.

A number of actions, nevertheless, took place before this could occur. In *Lorraine*, Salan captured much equipment, but lost 500 men. Giap lost 1,000 men in yet another direct assault, on Na San, but fatally persuaded General Navarre that the French could stand similarly at Dien Bien Pha. He guessed that the French would move troops west of the Black River to oppose a Viet Minh drive on Laos and therefore created a series of diversions. These included harassment in the Delta, battalion-strength attacks in Laos and on towns in the Central Highlands, all depriving Navarre of the reserves that he should have deployed at Dien Bien Phu . . . 'The enemy found himself face to face with a contradiction: without scattering his forces, it was impossible for him to occupy the invaded territory, in scattering his forces he put himself in difficulty.'

There must have been Chinese advice at Dien Bien Phu. But Giap's control, of strategy first and last, of tactics, deception, morale, artillery and anti-aircraft fire, entrenching, mines and, above all, of supply, shows him – even given French error – to have been a good general. The battle also demonstrated, in its concordance with the Geneva Conference, rare political perception, which was directly responsible for the end of the Indochina War on as favourable terms as Hanoi could obtain from its friends and enemies. Those 'friends', fearful of United States intervention, refused to allow Vietnam to pursue the enemy further and to take the whole country by military means, obliging Giap to switch to the slow but certain processes of protracted war. He, and Ho Chi Minh, his master, also counted on reunification through the ballot box at the pan-Vietnam elections envisaged as a result of the Geneva Conference for 1956.

Diem and the Republic of Vietnam refused to participate in elections. Viet Minh terrorism, and the violent Saigon reaction, started. More than 5,000 RVN officials were assassinated and kidnapped between 1957 and 1961. Hanoi started to infiltrate cadres in 1959 to join those who had stayed behind in the South and, in 1960, established the National Liberation Front, or Viet Cong, as the Lao Dong's creation in the South. Giap said that the North was 'the revolutionary base for the whole country' while, by 1963, the NLF had grown to 100,000 men, who, in 1964, were ordered by Giap to 'cut South Vietnam in two' in the central highlands.

In response to that and to the Tonkin Gulf incident, the bombing of the North began and the first US troops landed. In the meanwhile, Giap had concerned himself with the development of a modern Army (PAVN), able to fight both conventional and guerrilla war, supported by a huge militia. He preached people's war to the (Southern) National Liberation Front (NLF), 'that gigantic creation of the masses, highly developed and invincible people's war . . . absolutely superior to atomic war'. The Viet Cong became the most effective guerrillas in the world, numbering 200,000 in 1965 and 350,000 by 1967, at a time also when the North Vietnamese Army in the South, which controlled the VC, had reached 150,000. To support the VC and the PAVN, Giap built the astonishing Ho Chi Minh Trail, later to become a 'super-highway'.

Giap, with Soviet and Chinese help, constructed as efficient an anti-aircraft defence as was possible in North Vietnam. Morale was nowhere completely destroyed, although material damage was severe, at least in the industrial field. In the South, he gave precedence to mobile and guerrilla war over positional warfare. He knew that the key to victory lay in destroying the will and enthusiasm of the American people, not through confrontations with superior technology, but by incessant sword-thrusts in offensive mobile operations. American operations, for their part, caused enormous Communist casualties, but held little ground. The PAVN and the VC everywhere came back within hours or days. Pacification was hardly ever assured: given the US strategic defensive and Hanoi's strategic offensive postures, perhaps it never could have been.

The Tet offensive of 1968 did not achieve its military objective of 'general uprisings'. In purely military terms, it demonstrated the loyalty and competence of the ARVN and their United States allies. It pointed out the weaknesses of Hanoi's intelligence and planning, perhaps most significantly, the Communists' deficiency in politico-military diagnosis. But none of these things mattered compared with the disruptive effect of television reportage on the opinions of the American people. Mr and Mrs John Doe had thought that they were winning. They had been told so. 'Our biggest victory, however,' said Giap 'was to change the ideas of the people of the United States. Johnson was forced to decrease military activity and to discuss with us round a table how to end the war.' In March 1968, the president cancelled nearly all the US bombing effort against North Vietnam.

Giap 'had wanted to carry the war into the families of America' and that is what he did. 'More and more Americans renounced the war.' Negotiations between the DRV and the US began in May 1965 and went on for years. After the unsuccessful North Vietnamese spring 1972 offensive, well fought by ARVN and by much diminished American forces and, finally defeated by Nixon's 'Christmas bombings', a Peace Agreement was signed in Paris on 27 January 1973.

This unsatisfactory document permitted the retention in South Vietnam of existing PAVN soldiers, but nominally precluded further PAVN infiltrations. (Hanoi instantly breached their undertakings, from all directions – north Vietnam, Laos and Cambodia.) All US troops, already much reduced anyway under the process of Vietnamization, were required to leave the country, although, before going, the United States supplied quantities of fuel, guns, aircraft and other armaments to the Saigon régime, to be replenished as required.

In June 1973, however, Congress cut off funds for all US military activity in Indochina. 'The floodgates of Watergate had opened.' Short of equipment, spare parts, oil, ammunition, and deprived by Congress of the support by the B-52s which President Nixon had promised them, the ARVN, with its incompetent maintenance, was unable to resist Giap's sixteen or more massed divisions in their drive to ultimate, total victory.

On 11 March 1975, Ban Me Thuot was taken by General Van Tien Dung. Rout began in the central highlands; Nha Trang and then Da Nang fell; Saigon, the lovely, corrupt, flower-hung child of France, surrendered on 30 April. Vietnam, for the time being, was one, united in the last resort by a great military organizer and leader. Giap's revolutionary vision embraced political consequences beyond the grasp of 'good generals', accessible only to one whose posts combined military and political direction. To combine the roles of minister of defence and commander-in-chief may not be open to democracies. That it was open to a totalitarian state is one of the reasons why two democracies were defeated in Indochina.

'But there is a great irony in the fact that the North Vietnamese finally won by purely conventional means, using precisely the kind of warfare which the American Army was best equipped to fight.' The American Army, however, had gone home. 'In their lengthy battle accounts which followed Hanoi's great military victory, Giap and Dung barely mentioned the contribution of local forces.' Although aided by the partisans of the Viet Cong operating under Hanoi's control, the war was waged and won by the invading People's Army of Vietnam in conventional battles. Vietnamization was unsuccessful, not only because of Saigon's weaknesses, but because the aim of counter-insurgency – itself secondary – was overtaken by conventional warfare just as the Americans themselves withdrew.

In the words of Commander-in-Chief Pacific's political adviser, the US had attacked the secondary, not the primary target. 'We had responded to Hanoi's simulated insurgency, the VC, rather than to its real but controlled aggression across the international frontier, as a bull charges the toreador's cape, not the toreador', thus losing the support of the American people. And to enlist that support, furthermore, war should have been formally declared by Congress as early as 1965. But that is another story.

The absence of US military and political objectives, therefore, led to the loss to the enemy of any initiative except tactical initiative.

Prologue

Publicly expressed official fears of nuclear war and of the involvement of China in a land war similarly led the United States into what Colonel Harry Summers, in *On Strategy*, described as 'an untenable strategic position where the enemy's territory was inviolable, while the territory of our ally was open to attack.'

1
End of One War . . .

Japanese troops had entered French Indochina in 1941 at much the same time as Japan had attacked Pearl Harbour and British and Dutch colonies in the region. Their strength was increased thereafter in order to exploit the country as a centre of resources and communication, and as a military base against China and the countries of South-east Asia. Actual government was left in Vichy or Pétainist hands until, on 9 March 1945, fearful of an allied invasion and believing that the local French government was creating a Gaullist resistance to their occupation, Japan took full powers.

Then on 10 August 1945, after the US nuclear attacks on Hiroshima and Nagasaki and accumulating Japanese defeats at sea, on land and in the air, imperial Japan surrendered to the Allies, including the French. ('*La France, aideé de ses allies,*' as de Gaulle notoriously said, '*a gagné la guerre*')

The Potsdam Conference of July 1945 had allocated to the Chinese the tasks of disarming the Japanese and liberating allied prisoners of war in Indochina north of the 16th parallel; and to the British those responsibilities south of that parallel.

Supreme Allied Commander South-east Asia, Admiral Lord Mountbatten, selected General (later Sir) Douglas Gracey to lead the Southern or Saigon Commission as commander allied land forces, Saigon. Gracey, his narrow head and long nose above a small moustache, the white Kukri flash of his own XXth Division sewn on both upper arms of his battle dress, was the victor of the Shenam Saddle, one of Field Marshal Slim's most distinguished commanders. Because of a shortage of aircraft and shipping, among other reasons, he did not initially bring his whole division, only about 1,800 men in a brigade including companies of Jat, Gurkha, Dogra, Punjabi and Hyderabad regiments under British officers, some Indian and British artillery units, with a company of Free French troops. Reinforcements came later.

He was a good man, a good soldier and, on a sound but not invariable British model, a non-political one, later becoming commander-in-chief of the Army of Pakistan. Unfortunately, this attitude did not prepare him for the situation on the ground when his Dakota landed at Tan Son Nhut airport. Here he was met by a reception committee from the Provisional Executive Committee of the South which, under Viet Minh Communist domination, had taken over the Mairie, Palais du Government and other offices, as the Nam Bo (South) branch of Ho Chi Minh's Provisional Government National Liberation Committee. The Japanese had remained 'neutral', instructed by the Allies to keep order until the British arrived. The French had been confined to barracks and to their houses at the time of the March coup and, with a few exceptions parachuted in during August, remained there. Bao Dai, emperor under Japanese rule since March, and the United National Front, the non-Communist opposition, had both yielded authority to the Viet Minh.

The reception committee said, 'Welcome and all that sort of thing.' Douglas Gracey 'promptly sent them about their business'. But all along the road into Saigon there fluttered the yellow star on a red ground, even today the flag of the Socialist Republic of Vietnam. Posters on the walls and buildings abused the French while ostensibly welcoming the Allies. The Viet Minh flag was similarly prominent on the public buildings of Saigon, although often flanked by Union Jack, Hammer and Sickle, Stars and Stripes, and the sun in blue square on red ground of Chiang Kai Shek's China.

Gracey and his Burma veterans in their bush hats, whether in barracks, tents or the Hotel Continental – whose kitchen miraculously transformed British rations of spam, tinned vegetables, dried eggs and reconstituted potatoes – found themselves in a mini Communist state established as a *fait accompli* without a by-your-leave to anyone. In this French provincial town in the tropics, with its pretty villas, tree-lined streets and boulevards, cream and pink Haussmann or *fin de siècle* Francois I or Henry IV-style public buildings, the experience was unusual. The Mediterranean charm of Saigon seemed to disallow totalitarian brutality. One might have been in Aix-en-Provence.

Gracey had been plainly instructed by Mountbatten that the restoration of French rule over what was now the self-proclaimed Democratic Republic of Vietnam (DRV) was *not* one of the Commission's objectives. Anyway his forces were not large enough even for the tasks allotted him of disarming and repatriating the Japanese. The rapid collapse of law and order now required him to demand the assistance of Japanese troops, precisely those whose early return to their islands had been the prime British objective. Their response, until Field Marshal Terauchi was brought to order, was not always whole-hearted.

The religious sects Cao Dai and Hoa Hao* fought against the Viet Minh, the Viet Minh under Tran Van Giau forcibly put down the Trotskyites and, although the Viet Minh widened the Committee of the South by including the nationalist parties, or some of them, dissent within was substantial. On 2 September a demonstration near the cathedral – like a construction in Asia imagined by Butterfield – got completely out of hand. Some Vietnamese were killed, but French men, women and children were massacred and houses looted. French government plans for Vietnam, devised earlier that year – a federal Indochina in a French Union with greatly improved rights for Vietnamese – were judged inadequate by revolutionaries who had already, or so they thought, secured independence. The indigenous press assaulted the colonial power, Viet Minh and Binh Xuyen adherents pillaged, burned and looted French houses and property, non-Chinese Vietnamese withdrew labour. Tradesmen dealt with the French clandestinely, if at all. The markets, frequently lethal for Europeans, were sniped and grenaded, and the dwellings of French citizens had to be protected by Japanese troops. French citizens were abducted, tortured, held as hostages, murdered. Roads were blocked and wells poisoned.

American commentators were filled with righteous indignation at Gracey's reaction but it was unlikely in these circumstances of sudden and terrible violence that *any* British general would not have tried to protect these victims, the families and homes of a French ally whose morale and, hence, ability to function in the grand alliance, particularly in the chaos of post-war Europe, it was also British policy to restore. Gracey ordered a curfew, banned the press, imposed martial law and released French paratroops from the Saigon goal. At the same time, the 11th Infanterie Coloniale ceased to be interned in the barracks to which they had been confined by the Japanese in the *coup d'état* in March, which had overthrown Admiral Decoux's government and seized French institutions.

---

* Both these had paramilitary establishments led by war lords and religious fanatics, the Hoa Hoa militia numbering about 50,000, dedicated to anti-communist nationalism and a degree of regional autonomy.

These steps, although genuinely intended to restore peace to a situation close to anarchy, could not have been perceived as being in the interests of the Committee of the South and of Ho's republic. Ho Chi Minh did persuade the general to relicense newspapers on a selective basis, but attacks on light, power and other utilities continued.

The general's objectives were simply the restoration of law and order, the control of Field Marshal Terauchi's Southern Armies Headquarters, the location, care and repatriation of allied prisoners of war, and the disarming of 60,000 Japanese soldiers.

Neither the United Nations nor the United Kingdom recognized changes of sovereignty which had taken place by force during the war, as had the Viet Minh's assumption of power. Nevertheless, Gracey was determined to avoid involvement in political affairs, to ensure that his division was not used to reinstate French government by force, or to fight unless attacked. It was precisely to avoid charges of interference in the internal scene that he rejected requests for interviews from the Viet Minh, preferring that they should be conducted by High Commissioner Cédile who, unfortunately, could not or would not comply.

After six days in the country, Gracey concluded that the Viet Minh, nominally installed in office through Japanese connivance on 13 August, were not in control of security, and through 'inactive mob rule', without legal process or effective administrative services, were a potential menace to his own small force and to the safety of French civilians. He was not, of course, discouraged in this view by the stout, bespectacled Cédile, his hair *en brosse*, or by Colonel Rivier, General Leclerc's representatives. Without re-establishment of French services, Gracey foresaw complete breakdown, but he was perfectly aware that neither the Annamites nor most Cochinchinese had anything but contempt for the Vichy French, particularly after the March *coup d'état*, from which, incidentally, they themselves had secured Japanese arms and *matériel*.

On the night of September 22/23, Gracey's troops, immediately relieved by French units, took over all the Saigon police comm-issariats, the Treasury, the Mairie, the Palais du Gouvernment, the power and radio stations, the Banque d'Indochine and the Yoko-hama Bank. Unfortunately the 11th Infanterie Coloniale, despite the assurances of Rivier, was undisciplined. And the intemperate violence of French civilians – including a disgusting public lynching on the

Place Norodom – provoked Vietnamese reaction. There followed severe clashes near the Arroyo Chinois, around warehouses in the Messagerie Maritime docks, at Gia Dinh, Phu Lam, attacks on factories, the power station and rubber stores, even a three-hour Franco-Vietnamese battle on the Boulevard Gallieni. Sniping was fairly widespread and at least one frightful massacre of French women and children took place, in the Cité Heraud, while the Japanese, for the last time, stood idly by.

The supreme allied commander, with reservations, supported his subordinate. The French under Leclerc had refused to take over until the end of November when the 9th Colonial Infantry Division was due to arrive. By that time the British could, without Gracey's actions, have become much more gravely involved. (To have handed the problem to Terauchi and the Japanese would have been wholly unacceptable.) Until then, the French on the ground could not have handled prisoners of war, law and order, and the disarming of the Japanese, but Mountbatten believed that Leclerc, now in Singapore, should be encouraged to assume law and order at the earliest possible date. In the meanwhile, Gracey continued with his duties, progressively disarming the Vietnamese to prevent further looting and attacks against the French. There was to be no molestation by the Viet Minh; looters, robbers, saboteurs or persons attempting to fire public buildings were to be shot; the safety of the markets was to be assured.

Reinforcements from 3/1 and 4/10 Gurkhas for XXth Division entered the port. On 5 October, General (later Marshal of France) Leclerc (Jacques Philippe de la Hautecloque), hero of the Second Armoured Division (2me DB) and the relief of Paris, arrived by air, followed shortly by the Massu group of the 2me DB (Second Armoured Division) and a Foreign Legion battalion, in red forage caps and white kepis respectively. (Units of the 3rd and 9th Colonial Infantry Divisions were to arrive later.) Negotiations under Gracey's truce between the Viet Minh and Leclerc achieved no result. Military operations began. On 3 November the French occupied My Tho and Tay Ninh. They cleared the Viet Minh from the north, south and north-west suburbs of Saigon. Most Japanese guards had been disarmed, but some were still stationed in Dalat and Nha Truong to protect civilians. By the end of January nearly all British forces had departed from French Indochina. The Indian troops were glad to go home, describing the Viet Minh, because of the latter's murderous conduct, as 'bushmen'. As late as 7 December an Indian Army convoy had taken casualties in officers and men from grenade and sniper attacks.

The first Vietnam War had begun. In Cochinchina the French initially made great military progress. The towns were in their hands and, although the countryside was unsafe, they began to move out towards the doomed reconquest of Annam and Tonkin. There was, from the beginning, no way in which any human agency could have prevented the *déroulement* of the two tragedies that shook the world nine and twenty years later. In 1947, however, refusing the posts of commander-in-chief and, later, of high commissioner, General Leclerc recognized that the old colonialism could not be reimposed, but that rigidities on either side precluded compromise on a French union.

Events, although reaching the same conclusion, developed quite differently in Hanoi. As the Second World War approached its end, a Liberation Army platoon of the Quang Trang detachment of the Viet Minh was sent to escort Ho Chi Minh to a large house in Hang Ngan Street, one of the thirty-six ancient streets of Hanoi. Vo Nguyen Giap and Truong Chinh drove out of the city to meet him in Phu Gia along an old dyke bordered with guava trees, through villages in which red flags fluttered, until they reached Ho's headquarters at Tan Trao, 'Seat of Power', sixty miles from Hanoi.

When they had last seen him, Ho had looked like an old Nung minority peasant. Now, in his brown pyjamas, he looked a low-lander. But when Truong Chinh accompanied him into Hanoi on the litter upon which, because of fever, he was being carried, Ho was the leader-designate of the National Liberation Committee and the Provisional Government. Offered the second floor in Hang Ngan Street, he preferred to share the first – himself on a collapsible canvas bed – with Vo Nguyen Giap. 'So I am really the president?' he said to his compatriots.

He ate with the others, then a fifteen minute nap in an armchair after lunch. He met the Politburo at six in the morning. He typed his own letters. When some soldiers wrestling broke a table, he did not punish them, only told them to wrestle on the grass. He made his driver read in idle moments, and sent back presents which he considered undeserved.

On 2 September, the old man, with his 'broad forehead, bright eyes, high-collared khaki suit and white rubber sandals,' took the rostrum in Ba Dinh Square. The square was covered with red bunting, flags, lanterns, flowers on all the roofs and trees and on the shores of the lakes. Victims of famine and of floods which, in the absence of French maintenance, had destroyed dykes and inundated six provinces, had staggered into the capital to die of cholera or starvation, their corpses loaded into dust-carts for carriage to communal graves outside the city. But on Ba Dinh Square, as Ho delivered his famous oration, the militia in white shirts and blue trousers armed with swords, scimitars and clubs, women in medieval costume, yellow turbans, bright green sashes, listened and cheered him to the echo. Ho paraphrased the American Declaration of Independence, conscientiously amended for him by Major Archimedes L.A. Patti, the naïve representative in Hanoi of the US Office of Special Services (OSS). Afterwards Military Order No. 1 of the Insurrection was reissued: 'March south and attack the towns and cities'.

This officer's 'infantile anti-colonialism' did much to delude the unfortunate Vietnamese into believing that their movement, the Viet Minh, was regarded in Washington as the rightful government of French Indochina and the consequent recipient of complete American political and economic support. Nothing was to prove further from the truth. At the same time, Patti's presumptious, unhelpful and prejudiced opposition to the mission of Jean Sainteny, French commissioner in Northern Indochina, did much to ensure that Sainteny had no early opportunity to introduce an alternative policy to that of Ho Chi Minh and his Marxist colleagues, a policy of Franco-Viet reconciliation and independence without the bloodshed of the next thirty years.

It is certainly true that Sainteny did not receive adequate recognition from Paris either, when it would have been most significant. It is also the case that, apart from their manipulation by Ho Chi Minh and his colleagues, the American Mission at Hanoi was too small and lacked the authority to exercise effective influence on either the Japanese or the Vietnamese. Some days elapsed before they could even secure proper access to, let alone liberate, allied prisoners of war. Neither their groups, nor those of the unfortunate Sainteny and Messmer, compared in any way with the strength of Douglas Gracey's XXth Division in the South. It was fortunate for the Anglo-French entente that the British had a worthy representative at Hanoi in Lieutenant-Commander Peter Simpson-

Jones, a veteran of Narvik and Madagascar, later head of Lucas in Paris and of the British Chamber of Commerce, celebrated in Hanoi for his enormous amphibious vehicle (DUKW). Two assassination attempts were made against this officer who was, for his part, responsible for the rescue of many French hostages; he became a friend of Ho Chi Minh and of Sainteny and Leclerc.

But on 2 September, the day that President Ho announced the independence of Vietnam, the advance party of the Chinese equivalent to Gracey's troops arrived by air in Hanoi. Generals Lu Han and Hsiao Wen commanded 150,000 – 180,000 men, some of whom were disciplined troops, with military bands, carrying well-maintained American weapons. The bulk, in particular some of the Yunnanese (Lu Han) irregulars, were pale and haggard in their yellowish uniforms, even carrying shoulder poles with baskets and accompanied by women and children, their legs often swollen with beriberi. (The 93rd Division for their part, were nothing but professional smugglers.) By mid-October, to the resentment of the Vietnamese, Chinese technicians were supervising, if not operating, the PTT, railways, broadcasting and radio stations, even the buses, while bleeding the country by an exchange rate grossly weighted in China's favour.

Nevertheless, although the Chinese were deeply divided between Kuo Min Tang and Yunnanese, none of them supported reinstatement of French rule. Instead they worked through pro-China Vietnamese political parties in the Republic of Vietnam, which was quite unlike the situation south of the 16th parallel. On 22 September, General Lu Han refused to recognize General Alessandri as de Gaulle's representative. (Alessandri, after the 9 March coup, had brought 6,000 French troops out of Indochina in a daring march into China.) On the same day, he refused office facilities to Sainteny.

On 6 March 1946, however, in order to avoid a permanent Chinese take-over of Vietnam, Ho Chi Minh agreed to the less horrid alternative in an agreement with Commissioner Jean Sainteny under which France recognized a 'free state with its own government, parliament, army and finances, part of the Indochinese Federation and the French Union'. In return, 25,000 French troops (then under General Leclerc) were permitted to return to Tonkin on condition that none would remain in Vietnam after 1952, except for guards on any bases that might then exist. By March the Chinese had satisfactorily disarmed over 32,000 Japanese and, in agreement with

Paris, agreed to remove their forces from Vietnam on relief by the French Army on 31 March 1946. (The 'Celestials' did not, in fact, all depart before 31 October.) In exchange, the French renounced pre-Second World War rights and privileges in China itself, and awarded China benefits in the port of Haiphong.

Later that year there was severe fighting between the French and the Viet Minh under Giap in Haiphong. Serious Viet Minh attacks on the French and their installations in Hanoi led to the occupation of Hanoi on 19 December 1946 by Leclerc's units. Repression of the population followed and hostilities spread to the rest of Tonkin and northern Annam. Ho Chi Minh and his Politburo fled to the countryside.

In the North, too, the war had thus now begun.

Only in Laos and Cambodia had events taken a relatively peaceful course. Parts of both countries had been sequestered by Siam in 1941 under Japanese instructions after weak French ground forces had been beaten in Cambodia by the Siamese. (The latter's Navy was, however, defeated by the French.) A small French detachment was sent to Phnom Penh in September 1945 under a Colonel Murray as British commander, with orders to disarm the Japanese. General Leclerc visited the city in October and arrested San Ngoc Thanh, the Japanese puppet prime minister, bringing him to Saigon with the tacit approval of the Cambodian king, Norodom Sihanouk. It was not, however, until the Chinese occupation forces left Laos in March 1946 that General Alessandri was able to enter that state and, in a series of engagements, defeat the Free Laotian Government (Vissarak), restoring King Sisavang Vong.

In November 1946 Siam returned the areas in Laos on the east bank of the Mekong and the three Cambodian provinces taken in 1941 to Laos and Cambodia.

Meanwhile, in Saigon the bars and restaurants reopened – Brodard, L'Amiral, Bodega, Reine Pédauque, Tout va Bien – some on the Rue Catinat, the inclined main street of that colonial city, so close in atmosphere to a Provençal town. In the Continental, with its huge verandah and loggia, the 'boys' in their immaculate whites served *fine-à-l'eau*, rice wine and pastis. Above them in the high bedrooms the fans would start to turn slowly over the mosquito nets. The 'boys' lit the lamps on the tables below; Monsieur Loi, the rotund and genial director began to circulate among his clients . . . In later years the statue outside of the parachutist, automatic weapon at the ready, would relentlessly threaten the National Assembly, surrounded by beggars, cripples, tarts and pimping children. The flamboyants, tamarind, teak and rubber trees, the scent of burning leaves, the noises of the knife-grinders, ice-cream vendors, soup sellers . . . a little remains – the cuisine, the echo of France, the elegance and sensuality of the women; a memory of lost time.

II
Formation of a Revolutionary

The village of An Xa (xa means 'village' in Vietnamese) is in Quang Binh province, just north of the 17th parallel along which Vietnam was divided between Communists and non-Communists after the 1954 Geneva Agreements. It lies north of Huë, the imperial capital on the Perfumed River, and of Da Nang (Tourane), later a vast American base, which later still sheltered units of the Soviet Pacific Fleet. The capital of the province is Dong Hoi, with its citadel and curious oval enclosures once forming a fortress. The village is in the middle of Route 1, 'the street without joy,' where dreadful battles were to be fought between French and Viet Minh.

In 1910 An Xa consisted of a number of hamlets containing closely-built farmhouses behind bamboo 'screens' or stockades, under the shade of areca, banana and coconut palms. Bougainvillea, purple and scarlet, ran wild. The lantana palms, water-palms unlike most of those in Manipur and Assam, were used for thatching houses. Fruit trees grew, custard-apple, berries blue and red, sapodilla. Lime, fragile castor-oil, guava, mango and grapefruit trees were cultivated in less prolific, more inexpert mode. Maize, chillies and varieties of cabbage and spinach were tended on dry, sandy land away from the paddi.

Ducks were kept, sometimes in ones and twos by individual families, sometimes in larger numbers on the pond or on flooded paddi. Hundreds of chickens pecked around the houses, frequently entering them, as pets or scavengers. Pigs were raised, either for early sale in the markets, or for local killing and eating, usually at feasts and ritual occasions in the village. Cattle and buffalo were rarely kept for consumption or labour, but Vietnamese like beef as well as pork and chicken, and will eat it when it is not too expensive. Fish was plentiful, often caught by young boys in vase-shaped wicker traps or heavy fixed nets from streams, irrigation ditches and ponds. An Xa is close to the sea and the catch included crab, prawns and other seafood. Frogs were plentiful. Norman Lewis reports the shooting, much further south, of mallard, silver pheasant, 'wild cocks', black-winged stilts, and peacocks. Hornbill abounded.

The man destined to deal with the consequences of the events in North and South Vietnam in 1945 was born in this humid, tropical village: Vo Nguyen Giap, whose names mean 'Military Literary Champion at the Imperial Contest'. His father was a farmer owning two acres of rice, but also a respected scholar, a mandarin of the second class, who taught his son at home personally before the latter went to the village school. The system of mandarins had been inherited, in this Confucian society, from China. Examinations were the key, and the young Giap's future was planned by his parents within that framework.

Giap's father, however, is claimed by Giap himself to have been active in anti-French politics, while his grandfather was a rebel commander during the revolt of Ham Nghi, the boy-emperor of the 1890s. Giap's father, according to the general, was murdered in a French prison after his arrest in 1919 on conspiracy charges. In conversation with a British officer, Giap added that one of his two sisters also died then, from illness contracted in a gaol from which she had just been released.

Another source, however, has alleged that Giap's father did not die until 1947. While minister of the interior, Giap visted him, but the father refused to see the son: 'He has betrayed the moral ideals of the nation by his employment with a foreign ideology [Communism] whose sole purpose is the destruction of nationalism, family tradition and religious philosophy.' In 1947 the French arrested his father at the home of Father The, priest of An Xa, and demanded he denounce his son publicly: for several weeks they forced him to appeal on the radio to Giap to lay down his arms. That year, he died of torture and despair.

In 1919 Giap was only nine years old. He was an attractive child, this Annamite, without the narrow, malign features of many Tonkinese, round, smiling, cheerful, with a broad nose and high domed forehead. Later he would have a widow's peak.

The Vo (a name meaning 'military') family house was wooden, with a thatched roof. It had a small granary, a tool shed, a stable for the few animals they kept, and was surrounded by a little land inside a bamboo hedge. The interior of the house contained an altar to the ancestors, with its *lares et penates*, photographs of grandparents, candles, flowers, oranges and joss-sticks. Behind the building, reeds and rice were dried. Shrubs and flowers grew in large green and brown earthenware cylindrical jars. Around the altar the family would sit with visitors. The floor was earth. No step in the house's construction had been taken without rigorous attention to the principles of *feng-shui*, the Chinese science of geomancy, fire, water, metal, earth and wood, and the prohiibition of access to evil spirits.

In the village there were several small shrines and a pagoda, the shrines red-tiled, with dragons, lions and flowers. A temple (*dinh*) housed the guardian spirit of the village and Emperor Gia Long's rescript thereto: it was used for rituals and was closed to the public except for quarterly celebrations. The building had a dragon roof and, within, several altars, lacquer tablets, and gold and red sacred boxes decorated with the phoenix and the twelve weapon symbols. It was not the Buddhist pagoda nor a temple of the Taoist or Cao Daist sects, but it formed a central point for the village. The four annual ceremonies lasted several days each. Offerings of rice and pork, tea and rice wine were made. Feasting took place, followed by a procession carrying a spirit boat, much kowtowing, a sorcerer's shamanist dance, the sacrifice of a pig, and ending with the launching of the boat. Other ceremonies were similar, but varied in detail.

A few lacquer pictures hung on the walls of the Vo family house. Furniture varied from a sort of blackwood, sometimes with a marble or mother-of-pearl top, to French maple manufactured on licence in Huë. The tables, once mats were laid upon them, became *k'angs* or sleeping platforms. At least one large framed looking-glass was set into a clothes cupboard, and daguerreotypes stood on available flat surfaces. The ornaments were brass candlesticks or bowls, and the ceramics were 'bleu d'Huë', that somewhat blurry and livid blue glaze. The blinding white light of the fizzing kerosene lamps, while the old women chewed their betel-nut round the *k'angs*, appreciably increased the airless night temperatures of 90–100 degrees Fahrenheit. Dead butterflies proliferated.

Formal dress, worn at rituals and ceremonies, included a round black turban cap, white trousers and a short black frock coat for men, and for women the white *ao dai*, a long white silk dress slit from waist to knee over billowing trousers, the most erotic garment in Asia. (Some of the French claimed it as *their* invention, designed to mask Vietnamese bow-legs.) Black shorts or trousers under a conical white straw hat were worn when working in the paddi. Women in and around the home wore a short white shirt and black trousers. Bicycles were still rare in the villages of 1910; within the village people walked or trotted carrying a yoke across their shoulders from which two baskets hung containing produce or equipment. Shoes were little worn except at services and celebrations.

Giap had only been to Dong Hoi, and visited Huë once as a small boy before he left home and his mother in 1924, with, he has said, 'tears in his eyes', for the (French) Lycée Nationale, Quoc Hoc College, in that town. Entry had been secured with the help of a respected French Catholic missionary called Father René Marinot, a family friend. In 1968 Huë was to be destroyed after the violent three-week incursion by Giap's own troops of the People's Army of Vietnam (PAVN) and the National Liberation Front (NLF or Vietcong) in the Tet offensive. In 1924 it was a place of considerable beauty, containing the Imperial City, with its yellow and green tiled, triple-arched gates, dragons and flaming pearl on the summits and eaves, pavilions and temples with glazed panelling in high relief, all within high walls and surrounded by a moat. Before the Temple of the Generations stood Emperor Gia Long's massive bronze urn and the eight other urns of the Nguyen nobility. Nearby were the Gold Water Pond and the Esplanade of Great Welcome where Ho Chi Minh's father, who was one of the nine Nguyen mandarins, stood with his peers before following Emperor Ham Nghi's resistance against French rule in the 1880s.

Also within the Imperial City stood the Forbidden Purple City (now a vegetable garden), an enormous series of structures covering some twenty-five acres and accessible only by the imperial family, their entourage, staffs and concubines. The King's Knight, a vast tower, has gone with all else and, as the Nguyens invariably refused French archaeologists permission to research the city, reconstruction would be difficult even were the authorities to sanction it.

The throne room was here, with its steep, pink, tiled roofs, their eaves held by scarlet pillars, the five-toed imperial dragon on the roof tops and angles. The sides of all the buildings were screens or folding doors in crimson and yellow. These colours were repeated inside, on the throne itself; the pillars were of scarlet and gold. Lakes filled with lotus and bordered with frangipani surrounded the courts.

The imperial tombs lay along the Perfumed River, Gia Long's covering over 7,000 acres. All were large, and some were guarded by standing grey stone figures, bearded and robed, on the terraces and courtyards. (The guardians were sometimes accompanied by stone horses.) The concept of the 'Valley of the Dead', mirrored that of the Ming tombs near Peking vandalized during the Cultural Revolution; worn by time, neglect and incompetent maintenance, the Huë tombs are now in worse condition than their Chinese models. One Buddhist pagoda with white and yellow stupas dated back to the seventeenth century. Another, the Hillock of Heavenly Sacrifices, served the same imperial purpose as the Temple of Heaven in Peking.

Thousands died during the North Vietnamese occupation of Huë in 1968. After it was recaptured by the Army of the Republic of Vietnam (ARVN), mass graves were found containing up to 2,800 civilians executed by the People's Army and the Viet Cong – mostly Catholics, including women and children, massacred in cold blood. Giap himself regarded Catholics as French lackeys, traitors to the motherland.

Ho Chi Minh, then known as Nguyen Ai Quoc, had attended a government school in Huë, the 'College of the Sons of the State', for one year. This school was coterminous with the Lycée and was the Alma Mater not only of Giap, but also of Ngo Dinh Diem, later president of South Vietnam, son of Ngo Dinh Kha, 'founder' of the college. The Ngo family originated from the market-town of Dai Phong, close to Giap's natal village; Diem and Giap spent several evenings together, possibly pillorying set topics such as 'Our country was called Gaul and our ancestors were the Gauls'.

It should be remembered that while the French were sluggish in introducing their own educational systems in the colony – in 1918 a reactionary governor-general even closed Hanoi University – there had also been native opposition on cultural grounds to French schools. After 1910 this diminished and, in the face of French obstinacy, the Vietnamese had started to build their own schools; they were soon closed by the authorities and the teachers imprisoned. After violent rioting, this policy was rescinded. It was then that the Lycée and other French schools for Vietnamese were opened.

The rioting, and the Scholars Movement which organized it, operated under the cover of demands for tax reduction. (This was preceded by the Monarchist movement in the late nineteenth century which, however, took a military form and had little to do with the man in the street). Because, at least in the South, the French then gave more political representation to the Vietnamese, the first nationalist parties were not created until the 1920s. Some of these, such as those led by Phan Boi Chau (Phuc Quoc) and Phan Chu Trinh, were reformist, collaborating where convenient with the French. They were frequently pro-Japanese. Others, including the Vietnamese People's Party (VNQDD), were more militant, using strikes, bombs, mutiny, violence and terror.

The Communists in 1925 were represented by the Revolutionary Youth League or Association (Thanh Nien) founded by Ho Chi Minh in Canton, the centre for Vietnamese of the extreme left. Ho's pseudonym at that time was Ly Thuy. His attachment under Borodin to the Soviet Communist Mission with Generalissimo Chiang Kai Shek at Whampoa in no way deterred him from betraying Phan Boi Chau to the French. Ho received 100,000 piastres for arranging his naïve friend's arrest in Shanghai, after which a Hanoi court sentenced Chau to hard labour for life, commuted to house arrest in Huë by a more liberal governor-general. Ho 'justified' this treason by 'the consequent accretion of funds to "the Movement"' and by 'the anti-French hatred which Chau's arrest stimulated in Vietnam'.

His policy at that time reflected the teaching of his Soviet employers in tactically rejecting force in favour of propaganda, peaceful demonstration, industrial action. In that sense, although in few others, his view had coincided with those of Phan Boi Chau in Huë.

Giap as a teenager had not yet met Ho Chi Minh. Under the influence of the Private Schools Movement, he began to visit Chau in his home, learning lessons on political organization and international affairs. At the same time he acquired a copy of Ho's 'Colonialism on Trial' which, although a fierce polemic, did not depart from the Bolshevik line of a two-stage initially bourgeois, nationalist revolution under 'workers' control.

Several student strikes took place in the three or four years of Giap's first stay at the Lycée. (He had also worked as a messenger for an electric power company.) After a major 'quit-school' demonstration in Huë, he was expelled and obliged to return to An Xa under 'close administrative supervision'. Here he was recruited into the Tan Viet Nationalist Party by a friend from Huë. This party consisted largely of Social Democrat intellectuals, although it had a left wing, that joined by Giap, which in 1927 had become the Indochinese Communist Union, one of the three Communist parties then existing in Vietnam. Giap took the literature supplied by the

Tan Viet into the countryside, and, to avoid observation, climbed a tree to read pamphlets written by Ho and by the 'World League of Oppressed Peoples' formed in Canton by Ho himself.

Giap has said that Ho's formulation of a 'just, fair and classless society, the possibility of happiness for all mankind' changed his life. 'Colonialism on Trial' thrilled him, and filled him with hatred for the colonial system. (Curiously, his own province, Quang Binh, even in 1930 at a most revolutionary period, was described by the Sûreté: 'Absolute calm reigns here. The inhabitants seemed opposed to communist teachings, although some arrests were made following distributions of tracts'). His political position shifted from simple nationalism to whatever aspect of Marxist Communism the USSR was then advocating, which happened temporarily to coincide with the direction of the Tan Viet. He was, anyway, only fifteen years old and more useful in Vietnam than in Canton, where most older students and other dissidents had fled to escape the tentacles of the Sûreté, the French security service. He soon left the village again for Huë to act in a minor clandestine role fitted to his youth.

The Revolutionary Youth League (Thanh Nien) had by this time established a sounder footing in Vietnam and drew to its ranks those most resentful at the policies of the moderate parties. These recruits were frequently, as elsewhere, rich, well-educated young men, seduced by the 'scientific' and messianic message of the 'faith'. In 1927 the extremists in the league formed the Indochinese Communist Party (ICP). Its rival, the VNQDD, was based more firmly in the lower-middle class, and even the proletariat, than the Communist Party and was certainly more violent. Equally certainly, it was worse organized and, since it was not 'cellular', more vulnerable. The VNQDD was broken up by the French in the 1930s, not to reappear again before 1945, when it returned under Chinese auspices. In 1946 it was penetrated and destroyed by the Viet Minh.

Giap would not have been able to resume his political life in Huë had he not received permission from the authorities to return to the Lycée. In the light of the alleged fate of his father and his sister, and after the disciplinary action taken against himself, this measure seems to indicate a remarkably negligent or liberal attitude on the part of the Sûreté. Another explanation may lie in Hoang Van Chi's statement that Giap – and Dang Thai Mai, whose daughter became Giap's second wife – were the protégés of Louis Marty, director of the Political Affairs and General Security Services of Indochina.

Such considerations, not infrequent in colonial societies, may have been strengthened by subsequent events. On May Day 1930 large demonstrations against the executions of the Yen Bay nationalists, were fired on by the French and several Annamese were killed. The Communists then attempted to establish organizations, or soviets, on a very considerable scale, columns of up to 800 men in Nghe An province ('Nghe An Soviets'), which were put down by the authorities including the Foreign Legion. The temporary collapse of the entire movement followed. Giap was sentenced to two years imprisonment, but he served less than one, allegedly for good behaviour, although, according to Giap, it was really because of 'insufficient evidence'. (Truong Chinh, later Secretary of the Lao Dong party, on the other hand, who was sentenced to twelve years at about this time, was not released for six years. Pham Van Dong, later to become prime minister, was in prison from 1926 to 1932.

Giap, on his return to Huë, appears to have undergone a complete transformation, working extremely hard and taking the first part of his baccalauréat from the Lycée. He then moved to the Lycée Albert Sarraut at Hanoi for one year, under a liberal French professor of philosophy named Marcel Ner, before entering the Faculty of Law at the University. At the Lycée he was described by one teacher as smiling, courteous, 'a charming youth, eagerly searching for truth'. Owing to his extra-curricular journalism on behalf of the Revolutionary Youth League, which he had joined in 1930, he had no time to acquire a PhD nor a Certificate in Administrative Law. He did, however, gain a degree in Law and Political Economy at the Faculty of Law in 1937, with the aid of a French professor named Quirian, American by birth, who wanted Giap to complete his education in France.

As to journalism, he worked for *The News* (*Tin Tuc*), *The Current Situation* (*Thoi The*) and for two Communist French-language papers, *Nôtre Voix* and *Le Travail*, some of which at various times carried articles by Ho Chi Minh under one of his pseudonyms, P.C. Lin. The government in France at this time was that of the Popular Front under Léon Blum, tolerant to the left at home and, to a lesser extent, throughout the empire. But Giap told a British informant that in these 'tolerant' years, his brother's wife, who had been indoctrinated in the USSR, was arrested in Saigon on her return, tried and executed – a trio of deaths in Giap's immediate family attributable to French colonialism. His own survival is thus yet more mysterious.

In 1938 he married Nguyen Thi Minh Giang ('Thai'), the daughter of his landlord in Hanoi, a professor at Hanoi University and a member of the Communist Party of Indochina. Their own daughter, Hong Anh (Red Thought), was born in May 1939. Despite earnings from journalism, Giap could not afford to continue his studies for a doctorate, and from 1938 to 1940 he taught history and geography as a paid teacher at the Thang Long Private School under Huynh Thuc Khang. He and his wife had frequent encounters with the director of the school, Ton That Bien, an anti-Communist, who was liquidated in 1945 when Giap had become minister of the interior, together with Bien's father-in-law, the intellectual Pham Quynh. (In 1938, however, under the nationalist influence of Ngo Dinh Diem and Phan Boi Chau, Giap was as much a supporter of the exiled Prince Cuong De in Japan as of Communist doctrines.) Among his friends were also Pham Van Dong, a mandarin's son from Annam and a journalist who worked for *Volonté Indochinoise*, and another journalist, Tran Huy Lieu, who later became the Viet Minh minister of information.

III
From Quiet Homes and Small Beginnings

In Yunnan, Ho Chi Minh decided in April 1940 that the time had come to withdraw from Vietnam the leaders of the Indochina Communist Party, Pham Van Dong, Vo Nguyen Giap and, by 1941, Truong Chinh. In France, the French Communist Party had been banned after the signature in 1939 of the Nazi-Soviet Pact by Ribbentrop and Molotov. The arrests that followed there would certainly have been later matched in the colonies. Furthermore it seemed probable that the Japanese would soon have to occupy French Indochina in order to cut the railway from Hanoi to China and control the Haiphong – China shipping lanes, leaving only a Burma Road which itself had been temporarily closed by the British in 1940 under Japanese pressure. It was unlikely that the invading Japanese would spare Vietnamese Communists.

These leaders, and those already in China and the USSR, were deeply immersed in the teachings of Marx, Engels, Lenin, Stalin and Mao Tse-tung. Unlike the more "elitist" nationalist parties, who focused on the inner circle of native nationalist capitalists and functionaries, the Communists concentrated on the construction of a mass base in the cities and the countryside which would support eventual armed struggles. Ho had the right, after June 1940, to expect that the defeat of the French in Europe would gravely reduce the effectiveness of French forces in Asia.

Giap by this time had shown himself to be an able, intelligent and articulate revolutionary, well adapted for leadership. He was little read and completely untrained in any military matters, but he was a natural political strategist, animated by theories which, in those years, attracted the hearts as well as the minds of idealistic and emotional young men throughout the world. These theories were of equality, liberty, the elimination of "squalid" profit, an end to class and to exploitation, and the projection of a centralized Utopia. He was only twenty-nine when, saying goodbye to his wife and child by the Grand Lac in Hanoi, he slipped out of the town at the beginning of a hot, humid May weekend in 1940. He and Pham Van Dong took separate *cyclo-pousses* (rickshaws) to a safe house in the suburbs. Next

33

morning they secured "hard" seats in the train which ran beside a Red River in spate to Lao Kay in the north-west, crossing the river there on a bamboo raft and, after changing trains, walking into China. His wife was soon arrested and sentenced to fifteen years' imprisonment in the Maison Centrale, Hanoi Central gaol, the notorious 'Hanoi Hilton', later to hold American pilots.

As to his frame of mind, many years later when expounding his views on colonialism to a French official, Giap said how much he had resented the racism of a French woman placing orders in a shop. A group of Vietnamese customers patiently waited: 'Serve me at once, the peasants will wait.' Giap said that he had been among those peasants. He had never forgotten it. Nor had he forgotten the absence of freedom of the press, of assembly, or of travel . . . different legal guarantees for Vietnamese and French, deep material inequalities, jobs for French in preference to Vietnamese. 'Is it supportable to be a stranger in one's own country?'

It is strange but not unbelievable that he should have omitted from such a catalogue of complaint the death of *seven* of his family. Apart from his father, Giap's first wife, according to him, died of maltreatment in the prison, the Maison Centrale, and his second sister was guillotined by the French. According to rumour, another sister, his sister-in-law and her husband were all killed by the French. There is no doubt, however, that despite a good knowledge of the language and of French culture, and despite a certain French dapperness in dress, he burned for the removal of French rule with the militancy of a Robespierre. (It is probable that his wife's death was the greatest single factor in this racial hatred.) In its place, he would put socialism and independence, land to the tillers in a free country where workers would work hand-in-hand with peasants for the common good.

Pham Van Dong already knew Ho Chi Minh. It was not until after changing trains at Lao Kay and evading police searches on both Vietnamese and Chinese railways by hiding in lavatories that Giap at last made contact with Ho. Dong was present at their first meeting. Giap has said that he recognized Ho, who was calling himself 'Comrade Vuong' and wearing a grey hat and European suit, at first sight as Nguyen Ai Quoc and P. C. Lin, without having previously seen more than a photograph. He instantly acknowledged him as paramount leader. 'He had a very special humanism', a simplicity and pragmatism that appealed to the future general.

Ho shortly despatched Giap to study military and political matters at the headquarters of Mao Tse-tung's People's Liberation Army (PLA) in Yenan. Giap never reached it because Ho, believing that, after the fall of Paris to the Germans, there might be advantage in returning Giap to Vietnam at an early date, recalled him to Kweilin. Ho's messenger found him at Kweiyang. The journey back to Kweilin, although aided by the Chinese PLA, was a long one. Here he and Pham Van Dong held discussions with the Kuo Min Tang (KMT) commander about the possibility of Chiang Kai Shek's troops entering Indochina to be deployed against the Japanese. But as fighting had broken out locally between Mao's Red Army and the KMT, Ho ordered Giap to Tsingsi to examine co-operation between the nationalists there and 'a few Vietnamese' under the aegis of two officers called Truong Boi Chong and Ho Ngoc Lam.

In Nanking Ho Ngoc Lam had already founded a group called the Vietnam Independence League. In Kweilin in the autumn of 1940, the League decided to merge with the Communists, whose strength had been increased by refugees from Vietnam who had contacted Giap and Truong in Tsingsi. Giap studied the Chinese language as well as the methods of the People's Liberation Army, formulating the latter in a pamphlet entitled 'Chinese Military Affairs'.

Inside Vietnam, nationalist and Communist groups operating with clandestine Japanese support from bases in the mountainous North and in Cochinchina, raised rebellion against the French in a campaign which lasted from September to December 1940, but was ultimately suppressed with severity.

Giap, in Tsingsi and other towns and villages in China north of the north-eastern Tonkin border, was 'administered' by the 4th and 10th Route Armies, who provided communications, stationery, literature, etc. Legend would have it that in the mess he was so bad a cook that his comrades would tolerate him in no other capacity than that of *plongeur*. In any case, he spent most of his time perfecting his role as political standard-bearer and activist and in learning the military profession in all its aspects, strategic and tactical. He also edited a newspaper and ran a more detailed magazine, containing theoretical pieces. Ho Chi Minh found them repetitive, turgid and much too long – so he told Giap, to little effect.

In 1941 Giap's first military recruits, forty members of 'cadres' of the Communist Party, the original soldiers of what would become the Viet Minh, began training in guerrilla warfare, based on the tactics of the People's Liberation Army and of earlier nineteenth-and twentieth-century resistants in Tonkin itself.

Both Buttinger and Hoang Van Chi maintain that Ho Chi Minh was in Moscow until early 1941, and took no part in any of the events recorded here as occurring in 1940. Robert O'Neill and Brigadier Macdonald, the latter after talking to Giap in 1990, believe that Ho returned to Vietnam itself in February 1941 to prepare for the Eighth Central Committee Congress of the Indochinese Communist Party from 10 to 19 May. Ho had previously despatched a member of his staff to select caves and other hidden bases in the Cao Bang hills to which the groups training under Giap in China would be sent. KMT cooperation north of the Tonkin frontier with the Vietnamese Communists had become closer than with the other Vietnamese groups, Dai Viet, VNQDD or the Phuc Quoc, which had earlier mounted an uprising at Langson. In the Japanese, the KMT and the Viet Minh had a common enemy.

The Eighth Congress was held in the mountains in a bamboo hut; everyone wore hill-tribe indigo – stained clothing. It decided to create the Vietnam Doc Lap Dong Minh (VIETMINH), or Vietnam Independence League, subsuming Truong Boi Chan's organization of the same name and to expand guerrilla action to connect three Vietnamese provinces on the south-west frontier of China.

Giap's trainees had been augmented by the arrival in Yunnan of Communists escaping from French prisons where precautions had become greatly relaxed in the face of the common Japanese enemy. But the Viet Minh forces were still minuscule. Giap arrived almost alone, borne in a hammock among the Tho, Nung and Man tribes in the deep jungle and forests surrounding the limestone cliffs pierced with innumerable caves and grottoes. From Lao Kay to Cao Bang to Langson, these peoples were accustomed to deserters, smugglers, outcasts, malefactors. Although Giap, like the outlaw, had nothing to offer but his labour in the maize fields, they gave him food and shelter, water and wild bananas. The days and the weeks passed. First tolerated, he became accepted, then heard. As soon as he could guarantee a few devoted groups, the rest followed quickly. Soon the village lodged, fed and supplied him and his men, forming also intelligence networks in the surrounding hills and valleys. (His deputy was a Tho, Chi Van Tam with Hoang Quoc Viet, a friend of Truong Chinh, as political commissar and hardened theoretician.)

Other 'comrades', only a handful, performed the same tasks.

When the whole region was won, they disappeared into clandestine bases. Giap took refuge entirely alone in a cave which he had discovered on a forested mountain, the location known only to him. He reached it via a river-bed, climbing among rocks, in rushing water, coming down from time to time to meet his contacts, give orders, find supplies, command his *réseaux*. His little band wore conical hats covered, as were their 'uniforms' and puttees, with cloth dyed a dark blue; they wore white belts.

He found it extremely exciting, this life of a hunted man, adventurous, secret, and victorious. Lacouture has told us that, like secret societies, guerrilla fighting is well-suited to the romantic Vietnamese temperament. By the damp, cold autumn of 1941, the Viet Minh were well enough equipped with arms and medicine not only to evade French reconnaissance in the mountains, but also to defend themselves if need be, if not to conduct active guerrilla operations. They moved their bases continually, according to need and to the pressure of French patrols, but relocated their headquarters to Lam Son, where from 1942 to 1943 they were able to coordinate the Indochinese Communist Party committees in Cao Bang, Langson, Backan and Thai Nguyen. By this time, the Viet Minh – perhaps one hundred strong in 1941, although subsequently badly reduced at Bac Son – had been much augmented.

Fifty people a month were being trained at Lam Son to use handmade swords, rifles *and* tactics, but these courses could not securely absorb the growing numbers of recruits. Instruction was devolved to trainers in the Bac Bo, mainly in Cao Bang province, but also in China, isolated from French and Japanese eyes. The movement had to start somewhere. The leadership decided that it should begin with political indoctrination of the masses, concentrating on Vietnamese nationalism and the destruction of French colonialism, inspired preferably but not essentially by Marxism/ Leninism. Ho aimed at the political mobilization of peasants, youth, women and the minorities.

No one, whatever their class or age, was too insignificant to contribute, including active soldiers of the French Indochina armies. All would be led by cadres of probity, and a sanctimonious morality, the brothers and sisters of the peasants and workers, teaching their pupils in bamboo huts, creating 'ink-stains' which would spread into areas where the will of the people eventually overwhelmed the power of the governing institution. This was the 'liberated zone'.

In September 1941, in an attempt to suborn the non-Communist nationalist parties, the Viet Minh (Vietnam Independence League) issued its first programme. This called for the establishment of a 'democratic' Vietnamese republic, independent of either France or Japan, for the unity of all opponents of French Indochina, and for the departure of both French and Japanese.

The non-Communists, for the most part conscious of Communist domination of the Viet Minh, were not seduced, regarding that body as just another enemy of independence and one more dangerous in the long term than either the Japanese – by whom some groups were supported – or the colonialists. The Chinese also opposed the declaration, preferring an anti-French opposition guided by pro-Chinese and anti-Communist parties, Dai Viet or VNQDD.

In late 1941 the KMT, despite their earlier collaboration with the Vietnamese, instead of accepting Ho Chi Minh's offers of intelligence support, arrested him and held him in various prisons for over a year, sick, with criminals, in chains, covered in boils and sores. (Giap and Pham Van Dong believed him dead.) Ho Chi Minh, legendarily, wrote the following verses at this time:

Although they have tightly bound my arms and legs,
All over the mountains I hear the song of birds,
The forest filled with the perfume of spring flowers.
Who can prevent me from enjoying these,
Taking a little of the loneliness from the long journey?

Tungchun gaol is much the same as Ping Ma:
Each meal a bowl of rice gruel, the stomach always empty,
But water and light is here in abundance,
Each day the cells twice opened to let in fresh air.

But none of the nationalists grew to be the least use to the KMT capital at Chungking, and the KMT gradually began to realize that the Viet Minh's contacts in Vietnam itself were better than any other party's. At Liuchow, in October 1942, in a back-door attempt to exploit them, the Chinese nationalists held a congress of ten Vietnamese groups, including the Communists, which led to the formation of the Dong Minh Hoi or Vietnam Revolutionary League. The league was led by an old Tonkinese non-Communist (Nguyen

Hoi Than), who received a monthly salary of 100,000 Chinese dollars: it was in continual dissension.

Neither the Viet Minh nor the Indochinese Communist Party would have anything substantive to do with the league. The Chinese, in despair, released Ho Chi Minh from prison in exchange for the salary allocated to Than and Ho's agreement to collaborate with the KMT Nationalist Army. This agreement, needless to say, was of a purely tactical nature, to be terminated when Ho found it convenient. Within Vietnam, Giap continued to mix propaganda with a merciless terrorism, forcing the French security forces to maintain a permanent state of alert.

Viet Minh planning was not hindered by Japanese support provided through the Kempeitai – the Japanese secret police, under a businessman named Matusita whom the French had expelled before the war – for such non-Communist anti-French groups as the exotic religious movements Cao Dai and Hoa Hao and for political parties like the Phuc Quoc and the various branches of the Dai Viet. The French security sources in their turn found it easier to suppress these organizations than the more effective Viet Minh. The latter, by the end of 1943, was alleged to control greater areas of some northern provinces than did the French themselves.

In 1943 Giap was told by Truong Chinh that his wife Thai, to whom he was devoted, had died of illness or maltreatment in the Hanoi gaol. He himself, although he remarried, said afterwards that his life had been ruined, and it may well be that this was the moment when his determination to end colonialism developed a specific element of hatred for the colonialists themselves. The general's daughter, however, survived and took a physics doctorate, winning in 1987 the Soviet Kowolenska prize in that discipline.

Lengthy French operations against the Viet Minh, some of them effective, increased in 1944. Armed dissidents were wounded and killed, their local supporters – the 'sea' in which the 'fish' swam – arrested and relocated. Giap stepped up brainwashing operations to strengthen Tonkinese determination to resist. He expanded terror against actual or potential French collaborators. He mounted very small-scale harassing patrols and ambushes. He sequestered in caves and other hide-outs prominent tribal and other supporters until French pressure should ease. From his mountain fastness, he thought himself able to create and control some Communist cells in Kontum, Pleiku, even Can Tho, My Tho, the Parrot's Beak and the Mekong delta, in order to dissipate French conventional military strength in forced reactions to hundreds of 'flea bites'. Perhaps it was this confidence that prompted him to declare a pan-Vietnam guerrilla campaign commanded from his base in the Bac Bo.

Ho Chi Minh, however, because so little of the country was ready for a general guerrilla campaign, decided to countermand Giap's decision: 'Stealth, continual stealth. Never attack except by surprise. Retire before the enemy has a chance to strike back.' Instead, a conference attended by Truong Chinh, Giap, Van Tien Dung (later to succeed Giap as minister of defence) and others, decreed the establishment of the 'Armed Propaganda Brigade for the Liberation of Vietnam', the first main-force unit of the People's Army of Vietnam, of which the Tho, Chi Van Tam, was an important cadre. The brigade had three 'teams', with a total of thirty-four members, including three women.

Because Ho wanted a visible victory, the teams – the Tran Hung Dao platoon, named after the thirteenth-century general who beat the Mongols – attacked two French posts at Khai Phat and Na Ngan on Christmas Eve, two days after the conference. ('What champions we are, only one meal a day and two battles.') The attackers, quintessential *franc-tireurs*, Giap with a Homburg hat and no shoes, wore Franco-Vietnamese uniforms during the action itself; they killed two French lieutenants and captured arms and ammunition. Deception played its part, the group pretending to bring in three bound 'Man Communist' prisoners to secure entry to the post of Na Ngan. The colonial troops surrendered. A later attack by a company of 120–140 men appears to have resulted in withdrawal after Giap was wounded in the leg. (At Na Ngan the successful ambush produced sixteen rifles, while at Dong Mu four sharp-shooters came over to Giap's party.)

This brigade then took over a body called the National Salvation Army formed from tribal levies. Below the brigade, in order of battle terms, came the District Armed Groups and, below them, the paramilitary Village Self-protection Groups. Command, as in all Communist organizations, was executed solely and exclusively from brigade, a considerable restriction on the initiative of lower formations. Their arms, training and finance came from several sources. Much was stolen from French armouries or, less often, taken in battle. The Japanese presented them with weapons *en clandestinité*. The American 'Deer Team', which was parachuted into Thuyen

Quang province, and another with ammunition and weapons, gave infantry training to some 200 or 300 Viet Minh leaders. Another US unit, under Major Allison Thomas, operated with Giap's men against Thai Nguyen. Several other joint attacks took place against Japanese targets.

Cao Bang, Langson, Bac Kan, Thuyen Quang, Ha Giang, Lai Chau and, possibly, Lao Kay contained guerrilla bases by March 1945, as Giap spread his groups wider. These bases he incorporated as a 'liberated zone'. His 5,000 troops became the Liberation Army, with himself as general. Their instructions were rigid: to do nothing that would offend the peasants among whom they were stationed, and to do everything to attract their respect and affection; to create the 'sea' which nurtured the 'fish' – to indoctrinate them, to 'raise their political consciousness', so that they would then act as guides, spies, nurses and service corps. Two more actions followed, one against a small Japanese post in the mountains and another, a month before the Japanese surrender, against a larger post of forty-five men belonging to the Japanese 21st Division in the Red River delta at Tam Dao, mounted with a strength of 500 men. Both were successful in causing casualties and acquiring equipment. But the motive was cosmetic, in advance of the enemy's capitulation.

Giap had constructed the first (defensive) phase of revolutionary warfare – the underground organization, the infrastructure and the political mobilization – to be later synthesized with the second – guerrilla warfare – and with the third – concentrations – in cities, mountains, jungles, deltas and lowlands.

The French, unlike the Americans, had always rejected offers of cooperation from the Viet Minh against the Japanese. (Indeed, it does not seem likely that Ho Chi Minh would really have welcomed dilution of his aims by even covert association with the colonial power.) But by 9 March 1945, the date of the Japanese *coup d'etat* against the French, the latter's Tonkin commander, General Sabattier, was at least considering field cooperation with Giap's troops against the occupiers. Had the French responded earlier, the Viet Minh might not have been the only body in Indochina perceived to have rescued pilots, run guerrillas and intelligence agents against the Japanese, and to have communicated with the people there. Others, including the French, of course, did so, but received little credit.

Franco–Viet Minh cooperation did, however, take place on a

small scale between Giap and Pierre de Pontich, inspector of the Indochina Police Guard in Tonkin, who for four years had been responsible for anti-Viet Minh operations. On 21 March he decided to organize anti-Japanese resistance. Giap sought to work with Pontich, ostensibly 'to maintain French prestige and to safeguard French interests in Indochina.'

The Catalan Pontich, with his shaven head, reviewed Giap's team of forty men and women, first armed only with a Thomson sub-machine-gun and three Colt revolvers. Giap refused to speak of political problems and confined himself to the anti-Japanese struggle. He was given 165 Remington rifles and forty carbines in a mediocre state of repair in exchange for an intelligence contribution to Pontich; he did not ask for money, but sought revolvers and grenades. He demanded a formal 'military alliance', which was not granted.

'What a pleasure,' Giap told Pontich, 'to be able to show myself publicly in my native land, and with so human and sympathetic an adversary. You have been looking for me for a long time, haven't you?' Then, he added, 'You have arrested the Mandarin Tam, who has been helping the Japanese?' Pontich admitted that this was so. A firing squad – six of his men and six of Giap's – executed the mandarin.

Despite forty-eight hours of discussion thereafter, joint guerrilla action against the Japanese – for lack of the formal written alliance which Giap sought – did not go much further. Giap claimed to be in close liaison with the US Mission in China and to have crossed the Sino-Vietnam border frequently in the face of Japanese and French surveillance. He told Pontich that he had passed back across the frontier into China a number of US airmen shot down by the Japanese.

Giap believed that a US invasion of Indochina was imminent. He feared that it might come before his groups had established their political base. He wanted an accord with the French, and he wanted joint action against the Japanese, 'to revenge the massacre of the French at Nguyen Binh' – four Frenchmen who had escaped from that disaster were training his men. But, in fact, he sought to avoid Japanese reprisals against his vulnerable organization. The Japanese, for their part, saw no advantage in attacking a potential ally against their French enemy.

When Pontich parted from Giap, the former's Vietnamese

orderly, Chu, warned him that Giap was a particularly evil Viet Minh cadre.

'Thank you, Chu. I know,' said Pontich.

In March 1944 the KMT had 'formed' the Republican Government of Vietnam at a conference in Liuchow, devising a government-in-exile in which the Viet Minh, as well as all the other Vietnamese parties, had a place. The Chinese hoped that the Viet Minh would be thus submerged. But all the other parties' representatives remained in China when the Vietnamese delegation returned to the Bac Bo. So on 10 August 1945 when the Japanese capitulated, the Viet Minh was the only organization – in a country where the French had been effectively imprisoned – with a programme, arms, a reputation, territorial authority and a legitimacy, however spurious. Chiang's manoeuvre had failed.

A People's Congress in Thuyen Quang on 16 August 1945 declared a provisional government in the shape of the National Liberation Committee of Vietnam, with its own Army of Liberation, some of whose soldiers soon moved into the cities, including Hanoi. The emperor resigned, giving way to a Viet Minh committee. The latter claimed, with brillant untruth, to be the Vietnamese arm of the allied armies.

General Vo Nguyen Giap, with perhaps 3,000 soldiers and 1,400 'police', entered Hanoi at the head of the 'People's Army of Vietnam'. He thus fulfilled two of the targets of the Indochinese Communist Party declared by Truong Chinh to have been formulated at a National Congress on 13 August 1945: 'to take over the power in the hands of the Japanese and their puppets, and to receive *as the authority in control of the country*, the allied forces coming to demobilize the Japanese'. The Viet Minh were unable to execute the third demand: 'to guide the rebels so as to disarm the Japanese before the arrival of the Allies in Indochina.' They did, however, manage to hide from the Chinese 'demobilizers' the arms the Viet Minh had acquired from the Japanese, and they also bought a great many American lend-lease weapons from the Yunnan Army.

In the meantime, Giap had absorbed into his forces a number of Japanese soldiers, particularly Kempeitai troops, all led by a Colonel Mukayama from the staff of Japanese 38th Army, who were prominent in the revolt at Hanoi against the French on 19 December 1946, and who were granted Vietnamese citizenship and awarded false papers. Mukayama was killed in a battle with French paratroopers at Chenchu in December 1947.

IV
Beginning of the Next War . . .

We have watched the course of events in Saigon, the brutal Viet
Minh attacks on civilians, and their precipitate removal from power.
But what went wrong in Hanoi between Giap's triumphant arrival
and the tragedy of 19 December 1946? According to Jean Lacouture,
in 1945 the Viet Minh had even placed orders for tricolor flags to be
borne by French delegates who would enter the city side by side
with them. But soon they were to treat the colonists with
frightening severity.

France, indeed, would have been a valuable balance for the Viet
Minh against the latter's rivals, the Dai Viet and VNQDD, 'good
French radical socialists', a role which Ho Chi Minh had earlier
envisaged for the Americans.

Jean Sainteny, for his part, while seeking a negotiated return for
his country to Indochina and acknowledging Vietnam's right to
independence, sought a military presence as a basis from which to
negotiate. In this he was fully supported by General Leclerc, in
preference to an attempt to split the Viet Minh or play the Viet
Minh off against the pro-Chinese parties. Both worked for 'a
privileged relationship between the new state and France.'

Ho's declaration of independence in Ba Dinh Square on 2
September had viciously attacked 'the gang of French colonists',
repudiated the régime and all its privileges and treaties. On 25
November, the Central Committee identified 'the French colonist
aggressors' as the main enemies. But Ho also seems to have taken
account of the Chinese menace, the potential benefits of French aid
in the development of his country, the approaching arrival of
Leclerc's troops. In September 1945 he told Jean-Michel Hertrich:
'France and Vietnam became wedded a long time ago. The marriage
has not always been a happy one but we have nothing to gain by
breaking it up.' And, to P. M. Dessinge, another journalist: 'We
want to – we *must* – reach a private settlement.'

Giap had been appointed minister of the interior after liberation.
Without ruling out a settlement, he spoke of Vietnam's power to
force France's hand, and of a scorched-earth policy. 'The way he

said it,' said Lacouture, 'nodding that huge head with its huge brow! His eyes blazed and his voice was like a slap in the face.' Ho's language was quite different. Later, Giap was to compare the agreement of 6 March 1946 with the Treaty of Brest-Litovsk and with the Soviet plan to gain time to strengthen the Soviet Army and political power.

The Chinese KMT armies in Tonkin did their best, without taking direct power, to support the Vietnamese nationalist parties, not the Viet Minh, in Hanoi and in the provincial capitals in which these parties had been given authority, during the Kuo Min Tang's southwards march. (History, the Chinese thought, precluded a complete takeover by Chiang Kai Shek.) Giap and the Viet Minh propaganda minister were for a short time actually kidnapped in December 1945 by supporters of the Dong Minh Hoi, the pro-Chinese group. Only after the elections of January 1946, which allotted to the nationalists seventy seats not earned by the electors' votes, were the ministers released. To placate his opponents further, Ho then dismissed Giap as minister of the interior and installed him instead as head of the Committee of Military Commissars, effectively minister of defence.

With similar motives, he disbanded the Indochinese Communist Party, a deceptive measure which convinced the innocents, who did not notice the foundation on the same day of the 'Association for the Study of Marxism.'

Negotiations, beginning with an unhappy visit by Giap and Jean Sainteny (Commissioner for Tonkin) to General Leclerc in Haiphong, took place continually thereafter. (On the first occasion Giap refused to meet Leclerc's aircraft at Gia Lam, telling Ho that he would be in tears of rage and shame. 'Go home and cry all night. In the morning, go and meet the Frenchmen,' ordered the president, smiling narrowly.) The Viet Minh's first objective was the removal of General Lu Han's pirate armies as soon as possible, in other words to ensure that they were a temporary, not a permanent feature of life north of the 16th parallel. The French and Chinese governments in early January – in exchange for the end to French 'rights' in China – signed an agreement replacing the Yunnan 'locusts' by the French Army.

The return of a French Army that did not have the prospect of long-term victory in Indochina nor the likely permanent support of the metropolitan government was a more attractive option to the

Viet Minh than the presence – temporary or permanent – of 250,000 unruly Chinese, with an exchange rate ruinously disadvantageous to the economy of North Vietnam. Ho told his people that neither he nor they wanted another thousand-year Chinese occupation. Giap added that the agreement was the only alternative to open combat with the French, for which the Viet Minh were unprepared: they needed time to become stronger.

The Paris–Hanoi Agreement of 6 March 1946 was the consequence of the Paris–Nanking Accord allowing the return of French troops to the North in exchange for French recognition of the Republic of Vietnam within the French Union. The question of Cochinchina was to be settled by referendum. (This agreement was, of course, not enough for Ho, as it was too much for many Frenchmen in Paris and for the high commissioner for Indochina, Admiral Thierry d'Argenlieu, a former monk once described by a member of his staff as 'the best mind of the twelfth century'). But the Chinese left eventually, although they stayed in Laos until the opium harvest.

Ho, under the name of Nguyen Ai Quoc, had attended the 1920 Socialist Congress at Tours, and had studied in Moscow at the University of the Toilers of the East, afterwards working for the Comintern. He founded in 1925 the Revolutionary Youth Association of Vietnam and, on Comintern instructions, ran the Congress of Vietnamese organizations which led to the establishment of the Vietnamese Communist Party. He worked for Michael Borodin in Canton, at the Anti-imperialist League in Berlin, in Bangkok for the Comintern South Seas Bureau, and in Hong Kong, where he was arrested and allegedly 'turned' by the British Secret Intelligence Service. (He had already been approached by French intelligence.) He disappeared to the Lenin School in Moscow and did not reappear – as Mr Vuong – until 1940 in Kunming, after about eight years in Moscow and Chinese gaols. At one point he is also said to have worked under Escoffier in the kitchens of the Carlton Hotel in the Haymarket.

Ho's permanent beliefs were twofold. Firstly, that only the workers, not the peasants, could be relied upon to lead the revolution, and, secondly, that the dictatorship of the proletariat must follow the path of the Soviet Revolution, a bourgeois stage preceding the full Communist structure. Only a Marxist-Leninist state organized through democratic centralism and proletarian internationalism was the correct form for independent Vietnam. Nationalism alone was inadequate for the acquisition or the holding of power and while he collaborated tactically with the non-Communists, he betrayed them when it suited. 'History knows no scruples and no hesitation . . . You and I can make a mistake. Not the Party. The Party is the embodiment of the revolutionary idea in history.'

In 1945 Ho received in Hanoi the GSOI to General Carton de Wiart, the British Cabinet Office's raffish, one-eyed representative in Chungking. The colonel found Ho very impressive, an 'ascetic and selfless visionary, impassive except for two huge dark eyes pulsating like a frightened hare'. Ho denied that he was a Communist or 'only as Sun Yat Sen had been on taking power'. He would ensure that his government would compensate the French over seven years for any lost investment, out of the vast sums which he was sure the United States would themselves invest in Indochina. In any case, he would give a predominant economic and cultural position to France, provided that Frenchmen in Indochina itself agreed to become paid employees of 'the country'.

Although he refused any negotiations with d'Argenlieu until the latter should 'stop firing on Annamites', he believed that unless the Viet Minh in the South could maintain their resistance, the French could ultimately bring superior forces to bear against his whole movement. Nevertheless, even if d'Argenlieu maintained his attacks, Ho and his supporters would move to the hinterland of Tonkin and resist from the mountains with the support of the whole of Indochina. Carton de Wiart's staff officer, with prescience, was confident that Ho would do what he said.

As minister of the interior, Giap had been in a position under Ho to direct and control his people's political course. As one of Ho's closest colleagues, he did not really lose this capability after 'dismissal'. As head of the Military Committee, he was able to ensure that the Viet Minh were powerful enough not to be ignored by the French in negotiation. As the actual commander of the Army, he also had a combined political and military role for which there have been few precedents since Napoleon, other than in the totalitarian world, to which the DRV was, admittedly, beginning to adhere. He was, in other words, both a military strategist with complete political authority, and the commander-in-chief. In neither capacity had he received significant theoretical or practical instruction.

Thierry d'Argenlieu, goaded on by calcified French settlers, businessmen and officials, objected totally to the 6 March Agreement or to any agreement between the French and Ho Chi Minh which permitted independence for a unified Vietnam. He rejected Ho's proposal for a conference in Paris which would expand and confirm the arrangements made in Hanoi. A substitute conference convened by him at Dalat came to no conclusions on matters of sovereignty, and divided on Cochinchina and on the definition of equal association. Giap was present as a delegate and spoke harshly and with great emotion – but mentioning only the death of his wife, not that of the rest of his family. His outburst met with a cool response from a French delegate, Monsieur Pierre Messmer, a distinguished minister who had been parachuted into Vietnam in 1945 and there grossly ill-treated, bound and kicked by the Viet Minh.

At about that time, another parachutist, a Prince de Bourbon Parme, was also captured by the Viet Minh, escaped, recaptured and sentenced to death. His life was saved by the British consul, Arthur Trevor-Wilson, who persuaded Ho that the 'Princes' Union would report the matter to the king of England', who would certainly turn his country against the revolutionaries. (It was Trevor-Wilson, incidentally, who persuaded Graham Greene to write the book already commissioned from Greene about Indochina, as an anti-American, not anti-French tract. *The Quiet American* resulted, from a cloud of girls and opium.)

In the cool hill-station of Dalat, the tensions and misunderstandings were as acute as in the plains. Since the French appeared to have reneged over various undertakings in the March agreement, the atmosphere was not conducive to calm, a phenomenon reflected in Hanoi, where several French families were poisoned by their Tonkinese cooks. It seems to have been at the Dalat Conference, after private conversations with Messmer, that Giap finally convinced himself of French intransigence and duplicity, an end to illusion.

Afterwards, back in Hanoi, Giap began to concentrate on the armed forces at his disposal. (He had been appointed Minister of Defence to coincide with the start of the Chinese departure.)

His Army now claimed a strength of over 50,000 men. He has said that he armed these soldiers by the purchase of 2,000 machine-guns and 30,000 rifles from the Chinese Communists under Mao, financed by the sale of gold. (A large bribe out of the sum realized was also handed to General Lu Han of the KMT.) He had also bought weapons through Bangkok and Hong Kong, paid for in rice and opium. Simpson-Jones, present when the first French troops with their modern equipment landed at Haiphong, said that Giap looked thoughtful, even crestfallen, afraid that his own men stood little chance.

Arms factories and workshops, sometimes supervised by Japanese, Chinese and even Germans – deserters from the Foreign Legion – were soon established all over the country. No member of his Army received pay until the late 1950s, but patriotism and terror were successful in accelerating recruitment. Meanwhile, his forces received an accretion from the South in the shape of 10,000 men under Tran Van Giau who had led the Viet Minh in Cochinchina; no doubt Tran's departure was one of the reasons why d'Argenlieu felt able to declare that the South had been 'pacified'.

Nevertheless, Giap realized that guerrilla warfare, widespread but small-scale, was initially the only method of conserving and building up his forces and, at the same time, of throwing off-balance an enemy equipped with much higher technology. Once again, through terror and patriotism, the Viet Minh could harness the people to this task, calling on the spirit of independence and the idea of liberty, which unfortunately they had no intention of providing. Giap lacked battle experience, compared with his Chinese contemporaries of the Route Armies and the Long March, and had absorbed the lessons of Maoist revolutionary military doctrine only from small-scale practical operations and theoretical study. (In 1944 he may also have attended an American guerrilla warfare course in Tsintsi.) Given his shortages of resources, he would have been a 'military illiterate' indeed to have concluded that main force action was yet an alternative.

In 1946, although regarded by the French as the most intransigent of the militants, he had said that he would do all that he could to prevent bloodshed when the colonials returned to Hanoi; 'But if Paris cannot accept our ultimate conditions, of independence and alliance, if the metropolis is so short-sighted as to unleash confrontation, then we shall fight to the death, without consideration for persons or destruction.' 'His smile was like a poisoned arrow.'

The French eventually agreed to a full conference in Paris in the summer and autumn of 1946. While Ho and Pham Van Dong were on the boat taking them to France, d'Argenlieu deliberately sabotaged the forthcoming talks by creating – albeit formally subject to referendum – a Cochinchina that was nominally autonomous, but was actually subject to French rule, which destroyed the integrity of a united Vietnam.

Before leaving Hanoi, Ho had said to a member of General Leclerc's staff that he sought the reunification of Tonkin, Anam and Cochinchina. Although he knew that the Cochinchinese, in any referendum, would vote against incorporation in Vietnam, he needed Cochinchina because, without it, Vietnam was not viable. He hoped to persuade the French, with or without a Cochinchinese vote, to agree. He failed, despite concessions on independence, to secure the unity he sought.

On arrival, France was between governments, and the president of the Democratic Republic of Vietnam (DRV) and his prime minister were left to kick their heels for five days in Biarritz. While the conference, which took place at Fontainebleau, was in formal session, Admiral d'Argenlieu – without reference either to Paris or to Hanoi – convened another Dalat conference, this time totally excluding the DRV and including representatives only from Cochinchina, Cambodia and Laos.

A *modus vivendi* signed in a minister's bedroom in the middle of the night, for which Ho had to apologize to his people on his return, was the only result of Fontainebleau other than the general conviction in Hanoi of French deceit and intransigence. The trust and confidence that Ho had placed in Jean Sainteny and Leclerc were dissipated; all he had been able to secure was an undertaking to hold a referendum in Cochinchina. Once again talks had foundered on the issue of the Viet Minh's demand for independence, albeit in association with France, rather than self-government in a sovereign French unit, Paris's preferred solution.

Ho said to General Salan in May 1946: 'Giap is totally devoted to me. He exists because I support him. He, like others, can do nothing without me. I am the father of the revolution.' Giap, for his part, commented on Ho Chi Minh: 'Uncle came to Leninism. Leninism is for him the sun which brings joy and happiness. And the flag of Leninism is the symbol of faith, the torch of hope, the only path of safety.'

On Ho's departure for Fontainebleau, he had appointed Giap as head of the government *ad interim*. The general decided that the first step in achieving a unified Vietnam was to smash the democratic parties and, to that end, he created a Populat Front (Lien Viet) as a ruse, mounting a nationwide movement for solidarity. The non-Communists, of course, opposed the front, since within it the Viet Minh held total power, and also because they regarded the Viet Minh as collaborators with the French and therefore enemies of independence.

Giap was able to present his opponents as opposed to unity and as socially resistant. To overcome, indeed destroy, the VNQDD, Trotskyists, Dai Viet, Constitutionalists and the Independent Party, with their relative absence of political ideas, was not difficult for him in the increasingly hysterical war fever of the time. Terrorists killed most of such leaders as existed; there were mass executions, death by harrow, some were buried alive, many after tortures of the vilest kind. The parties themselves were prorogued and their newspapers banned. Hundreds of supporters were arrested, imprisoned and murdered. All the local governments in the hands of the non-Communists were overthrown. 'Revamped' versions of the parties, wholly subservient to the Viet Minh, were later set up.

Giap said: 'The liquidation of the VNQDD was crowned with success and we were able to liberate all the areas that had fallen into their hands' – a Marxist statement of ineffable *froideur*. After this the government, one would have thought, had no further call for apprehension about internal security. But the French now began to believe that Giap was set on confrontation with them too, the Devil to Ho's Faust, leader of the militants.

In November the new assembly established the Democratic Republic of Vietnam, but did not meet again until 1953.

The general, once a natty figure in white or beige linen tropical suits with somewhat baggy trousers, like Oxford bags, and racy bow ties, found time during this period to escort a ravishing 'singer of sad songs', Thuong Huyen, in the nightclubs of Hanoi. There is no doubt that she was his mistress, a relationship not approved by Ho and his more prudish colleagues (although Ho himself had women – 'wives' – provided for him during his sojourns in Moscow and elsewhere.) Legend relates that in order to prevent scandal, Ho persuaded Giap to marry a well-born graduate, the daughter of Professor Dang Thai Mai, minister of education in 1946, by whom he was eventually to have two boys and two girls.

The French knew that the North Vietnamese Army was re-arming across land frontiers and through the port of Haiphong, where the Viet Minh controlled the customs and other regulatory bodies. A long list of incidents involved the loss of many French lives, not followed by retaliation. In August D'Argenlieu ordered the French commissioner to take over the Customs House from the legitimate authority, the Viet Minh, by 15 October. On 20 November a French warship seized a junk carrying smuggled petrol. Fire was exchanged, fighting took place in the town, barricades were erected and three French soldiers held. The cruiser *Suffren*, aided by artillery ashore and by aircraft, then bombarded the town, killing many thousands and wounding three times as many.

General Morlière, commanding in Tonkin, was then instructed by General Valluy, acting high commissioner, to demand complete control over Haiphong, Hanoi and the road between them. Clashes took place in Hanoi between soldiers and civilians. Reprisals followed. Viet Minh propaganda was torn from the walls. Civilians were assassinated. Some Vietnamese shops were looted. The French Army was confined to barracks but released by Morlière at General Giap's request, then returned to the *casernes* when the Army heard, via an informant within the Viet Minh, that the Vietnamese were planning a mass attack with their militia, the *Tu Vé*. The main body of the People's Army had already been sent away to the northern provinces after Ho had learned that Hanoi could not be held for longer than a month but that the countryside could be held indefinitely.

Sainteny returned. (Leclerc had left for good, succeeded by Valluy). He saw Ho but could change nothing. This time, unlike Haipong, responsibility for the explosion was the Viet Minh's, Giap's direct revenge.

Ho had said: 'Our people will not go back to another life of slavery. The resistance war will be long and hard, but it is bound to be victorious.' He himself, with his colleagues in the Politburo, left for the Bac Bo at the same time as the *Tu Vé* sabotaged the power plant and, at 8 p.m. on 19 December, attacked the Hanoi garrison, blocking the streets, blowing up buildings and trees, strengthening their own fortifications and overturning trams, railway wagons and vehicles. That evening, an hour later, Giap called for uprisings in the towns and villages. The president spoke to the nation on 20 December.

The fighting in Hanoi was severe and continued there until January 1947, by which time the French had at last secured the city. When the Viet Minh started this uprising, they had had an 'army' of 60,000 men with only 40,000 rifles, but in September 1946 Ho Chi Minh had said to an American: 'If the tiger ever stands still, the elephant will crush him with his mighty tusks. But the tiger does not stand still. He lurks in the jungle by day and emerges by night. He will leap upon the back of the elephant, tearing huge chunks from his hide and then he will leap back into the dark jungle. And slowly the elephant will bleed to death.'

Hanoi, with its lakes, bridges and pagodas, its cold, humid winter, was an Iron City, lacking frivolity, loving war, hard, unsmiling, narrow, cruel, implacable: nationalism incarnate.

V
Fast Forward: then and now

Ho Chi Minh said:

> In the beginning, it was patriotism and not Communism which induced me to believe in Lenin and the Third International. But little by little, progressing step by step in the course of the struggle, and combining theoretical studies of Marxism-Leninism with practical activities, I came to realize that socialism and Communism alone are capable of emancipating workers and downtrodden people all over the world . . . For the Vietnamese revolution and people, Marxism-Leninism is a real sun which lights the road to total victory of socialism and Communism.

His policy until 19 December 1946 was one of compromise in order that the Viet Minh could consolidate its military position and political alliances against the French. Ho always believed that he would beat them in the end, because of the conditions for battle in his country, because of the help that he could eventually expect from the socialist countries, because of the aura and image that his 'struggle for independence' would cast on him and his cause, because of terror, because of omnipresent internal controls. He was determined on a sovereign soviet state based on Marxism-Leninism, the dictatorship of the proletariat. The French, even the best of them, such as Jean Sainteny, sought a 'self-governing' Vietnam integrated into the French Union and the Indochinese Federation. (The worst, and there were too many of them, sought only to line their pockets.) As Sainteny himself said, 'Out of a turbulent state, the permanent generator of risings and other troubles, the agreements of 6 March 1946 would lay the first stone of that French Union of which many speak without grasping the precise meaning.'

But on 7 March after the announcement of those agreements, Radio Hanoi commented: 'The struggle is not over. Negotiation is only a form of battle.' Giap said: 'We are signing a peace treaty with France to gain time, preserve our forces and hold our position in order to move more rapidly to independence. One force drives us to long-term resistance, another to stop hostilities. In this agreement some features are satisfactory, some are not. France recognizes the Democratic Republic of Vietnam as a free country. Liberty is not autonomous, it is more than autonomous, but it still is not independence. When we achieve liberty, we will move toward complete independence. Sometimes one must be hard and sometimes soft.'

Viet Minh radio in August 1949 said: 'Ho Chi Minh will never give up the struggle, but he was obliged to "treat" in 1946 because 250,000 (*sic*) Chinese occupied our territory and our government was not strong enough to defeat both Chinese and French troops.' Ho Chi Minh elegantly commented that 'it is better to sniff France's *merde* for a while than to eat China's all our life'. That, of course, was the real reason why the Viet Minh signed a pact: it disposed of the Chinese Armies, no more and no less; it had little or nothing to do with durable Franco-Vietnamese relations.

It was difficult for France to be seen as capitulating to yet another totalitarian state after the humiliations of the Second World War; she needed to obliterate her defeat and to rebuild pride and glory in a world that *la nouvelle France* had not yet comprehended. And her tradition of colonialism, open-ended 'assimilation', of 'Français de couleur', was unlike Britain's, or at least lacked the doctrine of the return of power to native successors. It prompted her the more fiercely to resist the demands of the Viet Minh. For France, the 'option of India' really did not seem open.

But France did not have the means, as General Leclerc admitted, to break Vietnamese nationalism by force of arms. In July 1946 the general left his command in Indochina to take up another in the North African colonies where, during the Second World War, he had made his reputation. But if 'France could not herself provide the political appeal to accommodate Vietnamese nationalism, nor command the military means to dominate it', why should an atrocious political tyranny be the only framework – the Procrustean bed – to meet the requirements of that nationalism? As a Viet Minh commander said to Norman Lewis in 1951, 'Our enemies [the French] are slowly converting us to Communism. If it is only by becoming Communists that we shall achieve our liberty, then we shall become Communist.'

Yet after two failed bloody wars to install Communism, the Vietnamese economic reforms since 1986 to institutionalize free-market policies, end nationalization and permit private use of land resulted by 1993 in a growth rate of 8 per cent, a fall in inflation from 1,000 per cent to 18 per cent, a huge reduction in the trade deficit, and three quarters of GNP restored to the private sector. All this despite the ending of Soviet non-military aid worth US $1 billion and a US embargo and denial of multilateral economic aid which only came to an end in 1993.

Why did governments attuned to Vietnam's past, such as that of Emperor Bao Dai or, later, in the American era, of President Ngo Dinh Diem, not lead this wretched country without rivers of blood, to *today*'s juncture, where it is trying to join the human race? On what senseless wheel have so many lives been broken, only for the victor to seek to join the cause of the 'defeated'? Why did 'independence' have to exclude freedom for those Julian Pettifer called 'the thousands of ARVN soldiers, that wretched army damned by the victors, abandoned by its allies and screwed by its commanders'?

The graves of those million Vietnamese who fought for the democratic cause represented by France – and by the United States – should no longer remain dishonoured and forlorn, sneered at by smug diplomats and traders without memory or perspective. While not vociferous advocates of representative democracy, the French – unlike the Communists – never specifically excluded it: so long as lip-service is paid to virtue, virtue still has a chance.

Today in the tree-lined streets of Saigon and, more significantly, in Hanoi and in the dilapidated pink, green and cream villas and palaces of Third Republic provincial Indochinese towns, administrators are at last begininng to reconsider the positive contributions of France. They are starting to examine even more hopefully the potential advantages of co-operation with the United States, Japan, Britain and the EC. But without the old colonial foundation, any break out to the West would be even more difficult to initiate.

The mandarin or Confucian tradition was, unfortunately, maintained during the Protectorate by employing Frenchmen in even the humblest posts in the colonial system, down to tram conductors. Although this practice often brought the colonists into much closer contact with the colonized than their equivalents under the British raj, it deprived the Vietnamese of the opportunity to gain practical experience of almost any aspect of modern life. Or, more basically, to take advantage of the fruits of Westernization. The majority of Vietnamese, therefore, could hardly share the French illusion that colonial government was beneficial in liberating the people from mandarin rule.

The French, most importantly, supplied an infrastructure: electrification, major development of ports, dykes, roads and railways (Saigon to Hanoi and Hanoi to Yunnan), massive drainage and irrigation projects, sanitation, hospitals, scientific establishments. They began the exploitation of rubber, tea and coffee, coal, anthracite, apatite, tungsten, tin and zinc, hydroelectric power, cotton. But because they were determined on a largely colonial economy, one in which raw materials were exported to the metropolis for manufacture and export, the industrialization of the country, other than milling, glass and distilleries, was neglected. The most harmful consequences of their rule were brutal labour exploitation and a weak middle-class deprived of banking or commercial experience, restricted to the professions, and resentful, it not at first revolutionary.

Rice production, as a result of the considerable improvements initiated by the French, although heavily weighted towards Cochinchina, and leading to rice deficits in Tonkin and Annam, rose to an export total by 1937 of over 1.5 million tons. Vietnam was the third largest exporter of rice in the world. Ownership of paddi was, however, mostly in the hands of a tiny minority (2.5 per cent) of the population. Seventy per cent of small landlords held only 15 per cent of the land. Usury at cruel rates and terms by the larger landowners reduced the holdings of debt-ridden peasants yet further. There were over 350,000 landless peasants. A taxation system similar to a poll tax completed the usury. These injustices produced a rural class open to the seduction of a brilliant and ruthless Marxist campaign masquerading as *nationalisme pure et démocratique*.

This campaign was the more likely to succeed because of the expansion of the French educational system, which submerged traditional beliefs and cultures, in lycées, Hanoi University and in France itself. All too often the opportunities for employment after graduation among Vietnamese students were so slight that an intellectual vacuum was easily filled by Marxist arguments of surplus value, the Group, modes of production and class struggle, which also supported the false equation of independence with freedom.

As Marr said in *Vietnamese Anti-Colonialism*, 'By 1945, salvation from the foreigner was taken by the peasantry to include salvation from hunger, tenantry, and taxes, a message of activist and reformist ambitions that fuelled the deadly struggle that ended for the French in 1954 at Dien Bien Phu.'

The change, as Koestler said about the Soviet Union, was to be one 'from partial enslavement by landlords, tax collectors and money-lenders, to total enslavement by the State, which is landlord, tax collector and money-lender all in one'. General Giap, the political soldier, might not see it that way. During the war against the United States, he contended that 'the imperialists were being driven into an increasingly weakened defensive and defeated position opposed in increasingly strong measure by people in their own countries, and isolated in the world, their internal contradictions more and more fierce.' He was right in the 1960s but wrong in the long term – by the 1980s Vietnam had at least been forced to recognize the intellectual and material bankruptcy of its entire system.

It is difficult for Marxists – and for old soldiers – to understand that capitalism survives and flourishes precisely *because* it is in permanent crisis. Giap's hero, according to Stanley Karnow, was Robespierre. It must be particularly difficult for 'sea-green Incorruptibles', when the nightmares they have created are over, to accept that their revolutions, mounted by tiny minorities, are as dead as the dodo. Giap, unlike his model, physically survives, probably without remorse. He believes that only by the terrible ordeals through which he and Ho Chi Minh dragged his countrymen have the Vietnamese earned the civil rights that, in Jean Lacouture's phrase, may transform their country into a free society.

Or maybe Communism and colonialism were both red herrings. What may be happening is the latest act in a series of civil wars between North and South Vietnam, all of which the South has won. The South is rich – if hard to govern – richer than the North. Under-populated and now with an infrastructure left behind by the United States, it lacks only leaders and administrative ability. Economically the southerners are setting the pace – an entrepreneurial one – and the administrative skill acquired in Hanoi, shorn of reactionary Marxist ideology, may impose itself on the capitalist drive of Saigon.

The French in Indochina, despite the greed and grasping stupidity of some of their number, had great virtues. One must hope that, in the rush to enter the twenty-first century, neither the ancient qualities of the Vietnamese nor the benefits brought to their country by such as Doumer, Varenne, Sarraut, Leclerc or Sainteny will be discounted. Nor should the small but lovely cities – the tropical Aix's or Vichy's – planned for Indochina by French architects be obliterated or any longer submitted to continual degradation or neglect. In a despatch of 1985, Gavin Young concluded: 'Vietnam after ten years deserves more than just peace. Since the victory, too many people have died, are, or have been, in camps, or have left out of fear or the simple horror of living in a place incompetently ruled by privileged cadres, where there is no incentive, no chance to question authority, and above all no forgiveness.'

The two races have too much to offer one another for the matter to be concluded, in either quarter, by pride.

VI
The Formation of an Army

Giap had now, at last, to face the circumstances he had sought to avoid by supporting the 6 March Agreement with the French. Negotiation over Cochinchina and the unification of the three *Ky* (Annam, Tonkin and Cochinchina) no longer seemed possible. The time of 'peace' in which the Viet Minh could have strengthened the military, developed the economy, gradually raised the people's standard of living and organized their administration, had ended. The recognition by France of Vietnam as a free country with its own government, parliament and finances was a dead letter.

He had said in an interview with Jean Lacouture on 27 Februry 1946 that if 'independence and alliance are not accepted, if France is so shortsighted as to unleash a conflict, let it be known that we shall struggle unto death, without permitting ourselves to stop for any consideration of persons, or any destruction'.

On 19 December 1946 the struggle thus began. Giap moved the majority of his forces into the heights and jungles of the Viet Bac – North Tonkin – often only after losing to the French in the towns and populated areas.

By 1947 the United States, initially excluding Indochina from the projects which Washington was prepared to arm, was moving to support close association between Vietnam and France, not independence *tout court*. Horror of Communism prevented recognition of Ho Chi's Minh's pre-eminent position and inclined the Americans to accept Emperor Bao Dai as a figurehead. (The American ambassador in Paris, responsible for transmitting and effecting US policy on these issues was, curiously, Jefferson Caffery. In 1955 Caffery, then ambassador in Cairo, was to declare that he would not lay down his office until the last vestige of British influence had been expelled from the Arab world.)

In Paris Prime Minister Ramadier dismissed Admiral Thierry D'Argenlieu, replacing him by Emile Bollaert who, in May 1947, sent an emissary, Paul Mus, his advisor and an Asian scholar, to offer Ho a ceasefire on terms of virtual surrender unacceptable to the latter. ('There is no room for cowards in the French Union,' said Ho in a marvellously insincere statement, 'and a coward is what I should be if I accepted these conditions.') Ho's rejection of the proposal was one with which Mus privately sympathized.

Later in 1947, de Gaulle and his Rassemblement du Peuple Français (RPF) joined the demand for French intransigence. Even the French Communist Party supported a military solution. After the French defeat in 1954, of course, de Gaulle was to declare that just as the Javanese were the dominant power in the Indonesian archipelago, so the Tonkinese were the natural rulers of Vietnam and that intervention, particularly American intervention, was therefore a waste of effort.

Leclerc had said much the same earlier, and was ignored, when refusing the post of high commissioner: 'Circumstances demand a military effort which France cannot provide.' Nationalism, he continued, had to be satisfied before progress could be made and, until then, 'anti-Communism was a useless tool'. But then the main theme of Leclerc had always been 'Negotiate at all costs'. However, D'Argenlieu, qua admiral and priest, the two components of the violent French conquest of Indochina in the nineteenth century, had in 1946 won the battle for de Gaulle's mind and for war.

Giap had sagaciously observed the real weakness of France. It lay in the metropolis, in the French economy and its reluctance or inability to provide the sinews of war, in political division and unwillingness to reassume an Asian imperial mantle, in emphasis on Europe and Africa. Ho, nevertheless, claims to have made a number of attempts, all of which were rejected, to contact the French government in 1946 and 1947.

Although the Viet Minh were weak and the war would be long, Giap would try to conquer by following Maoist revolutionary strategy. He had to build large guerrilla zones, manned in the villages by local defence units, then regional mobile forces, all culminating in the main force or regular army. The latter grew in size and proficiency in direct proportion to the time gained by the Viet Minh for training and for the first guerrilla actions. Patience, remorseless patience Giap believed would transform initial impotence into victory, a concept not weakend by the eventual prospect of United States military and economic aid to the enemy.

Vo Nguyen Giap and Pham Van Dong, in another presentational manoeuvre by Ho, were removed from their ministerial positions in June 1947. Those 'democratic' politicians who had not been

murdered, were not were left bleeding to death in alleys or float-
ing in sacks down the Red River after Giap's purge during
Fontainebleau, were introduced temporarily into the cabinet.

Giap, nevertheless, retained his post as commander-in-chief. The
formation, training and political indoctrination of the three levels of
his armed forces proceeded. Ambushes of French patrols, sabotage,
intelligence collection, destruction of bridges and other infrastructure, and attacks on the outposts began. The Vietnamese, with
their superior tradecraft and local knowledge, evaded retribution by
melting away into caves and jungle.

French troops in Langson had broken the Viet Minh siege there
and made contact through Dinh Lap and the Nung country with the
Baie d'Along and the port of Tien Yen. Haiduong was relieved in an
amphibious operation mounted from Haiphong. Huë and Da Nang
were both recaptured. Legionaries, paratroopers and marines took
Nam Dinh by storm. Vinh Tuy, Son Tây, Gia Lam were reoccupied
by the French. The Haiphong–Hanoi 'beltway' was reopened to
motor traffic by January 1947, when Hanoi itself was in the hands of
General Jean Valluy. Saigon and the cities of the south had been
taken from the Viet Minh in 1946. Valluy had been one of de Lattre's
generals in the First French Army, 'Rhin et Danube', former
commander of the 9th Colonial Infantry Division, now commander-
in-chief of the Expeditionary Corps.

Giap's enemy thus held most of the towns nearly all the time. In
the countryside the Viet Minh were often in complete control in the
darkness, and exercised considerable freedom of action during
daylight. To stop this stagnation, sometimes referred to by the
French as 'the happy war', Valluy mounted Operation *Léa* to destroy
the Viet Minh leadership and thus the build-up.

Ho and his deputies, together with his Army, then thought to be
little more than 'a few thousand ill-equipped and malarial troops',
were believed to be ninety miles north of Hanoi in Bac Kan
province, karst limestone country. Ho Chi Minh was said in 1947 to
be living in a hut on piles in the jungle with a portable typewriter,
and a dog which was subsequently eaten by a tiger. In a later
dwelling, he had a garden where he grew vegetables and played
volley-ball; he built a pool at a bend in the river.

The terrain was extremely rough in these valleys and irregular
ridges, covered by mist half the year. Valluy realized that if his
troops were to reach Bac Kan as an effective force, they would have

to mount a pincer movement from Langson on Route 4 to Cao Bang, westward to Nguyen Banh, then south to Bac Kan on Route 3. The northern drive was composed of nine battalions, including artillery and armour. The southern leg of the pincer, three infantry battalions, would be taken by boat up the Clear River.

The operational plan was completed by the drop of a 'demi-brigade', an autonomous Foreign Legion unit of paratroops, on Back Kan just as the nine northern battalions were setting off for Cao Bang on Route 4. Giap has said that he and Ho only managed to elude the paras by scrambling into a camouflaged hide while the French searched the scrub around them. Another report claims 'the paras missed Ho by one hour only'. Both men escaped, and the war went on and on.

The landing craft suffered delays, because of pilotage problems, in getting up the river. Giap's demolitions on Routes 3 and 4 slowed down the northern pincer, but the paras were relieved on 16 October 1947 nine days after they had landed in the Bac Kan area, by North African troops who had got through after air and artillery bombardment. This relief was too late to enable the paratroops and the northern pincer together to destroy the Viet Minh, who escaped through a triple 'screen' of French troops much inferior in number to the 'ragged Viet Minh band' which French intelligence had incorrectly supposed at the planning of Operation *Léa*.

A further battle, in November, called Operation *Ceinture* (girdle or sash), was fought in a smaller area but, again, with twelve or fourteen battalions. It drove out two crack Viet Minh regiments from bases in which they threatened French positions in the Red River delta. Quantities of *matériel* were also captured, but the Vietnamese returned after the French had withdrawn in December, just as they did throughout the American war from 1965 onwards. Valluy had failed to establish a permanent Franco-Vietnamese presence in the Viet Bac, or to seal the Chinese border, which he feared might soon become menanced by the victory in China of Mao's PLA.

Leclerc had approved the incorporation of native Vietnamese tribes in the Corps Expeditionaire Francais de L'Extreme Orient (CEFEO). Some of the most effective replacements for white battalions – two yellow battalions replaced two white in the 43rd Colonial Regiment, for example, and groups of the 4th and 10th

Artillery Regiments were 'yellowed' – were drawn from the minorities.

The Airborne Commando Groups included Annamites, Cochinchinese, Tonkinese, Moroccans and French, as well as Xa, whose staple diet is dirt, Moi who wore French uniforms, Meo, of Samoyed stock, murderous red-toothed Huni, Nung with umbrella-handle emblems. Rhadés and Djarai were in the Darlac. In 1947 T'ai *montagnards* fought with enormous *éclat* in the north. The Viet Minh were unable to enter parts of the mountains of Tonkin for five years, hated and despised by the T'ai, in a relationship not dissimilar to that between the Senoi Praak (Sakai) and the Malays. By 1954 the French were aided by thousands of these native partisans, who surprisingly, were more effective as sappers and gunners than as infantrymen. (The Viet Minh later exploited these people with equal enthusiasm against the Americans and vice versa.) Using aggressive jungle craft, the T'ai in *Groupements de Commandos Mixtes Aeroportés* (GCMAs) tied down up to twelve Viet Minh battalions behind Viet Minh lines for long periods, as will be later seen.

The Sedang, in Annam, and their rivals the Katai, were particularly cunning, employing invisible traps, pits, spikes, poisoned darts, missiles concealed in the bushes, crossbows. The Rhé were horsemen, naked, covered in war paint, with long uncut black hair, bearing lances, who on at least one occasion speared all the inhabitants of a village, men, women and children, before being exterminated in their turn by Viet Minh units. Many of these 'tribals' accepted a degree of military discipline, under French NCOs or junior officers. (One of the bands survived in the jungle, the original of that in *Apocalypse Now*, years after the end of the French war.) In action, the men carried their rations – rice, salt, fish – and medicine (quinine) in a bamboo tube, in the forests in which everything, not least the humans, rotted, died of thirst or starved.

After *Léa* and *Ceinture* the Expeditionary Force concentrated on the Route 4 strong-points, Cao Bang, Dong Khe, That Khe and Langson, and on the Delta, both locations intended as protection against China. Giap continued to construct interzones and to strengthen local authorities in the Viet Bac. He sought to avoid the presentation of large targets by forming 'small pockets', or independent companies, which penetrated deeply into such French-controlled zones as the Delta. There they would conduct guerrilla warfare and establish bases in what became known as 'red zones', as opposed to the existing Viet Minh 'free zones' in the Viet Bac. From these bases Giap aimed to win over hearts and minds, or at least secure complicity by subtle indoctrination, reinforced by locally applied terror. And his troops behaved well. They did not steal, rape, bully, domineer or patronize.

The Expeditionary Corps was forced to disperse to 'thousands of posts' in order to maintain its many objectives, and was then spread too thinly for it to be able to handle the mobile attacks from all points of the compass that Giap mounted in increasing numbers. Giap although he made mistakes later, believed firmly at this time that protracted war, through relatively small guerrilla engagements, not main-force confrontation, was the correct strategy.

The Viet Minh established its 'red zones' with extreme caution. Their propagandists appeared first, to identify and convince potential cadres. Indoctrination would follow, and then recruitments, not unlike pyramid selling, but on a rigidly secure cell basis. Afterwards would come the sections and after them, the platoons. Everything proceeded very slowly, two steps forward, one back, *reculer pour mieux sauter*, but the advance was continual. One day the French outposts would find themselves alone in a hostile ocean trying to combat the arrival of formed Communist battalions, brigades, even, at the end, divisions.

In order to achieve unity among all sections of the population, Ho Chi Minh had disbanded the Indochinese Communist Party and established the Lien Viet or Vietnamese Alliance. Puppet organizations or 'parties', were set up, often based on professional groups (intellectuals, scholars, landlords, artists, lawyers, businessmen) to create the impression of a broad 'National Front'. The Front, however did no more than keep the bourgeois in check against the day when they could be ignored or, where suitable, eliminated. Nevertheless, during 'the anti-imperialist phase', the Viet Minh did take steps to develop technical skills in a neglected population, as well as greatly to reduce illiteracy, if not to produce a wide or deep body of cultured, educated men and women.

In the South, High Commissioner Bollaert offered no more than 'liberty within the French Union', without guarantee of three-*Ky* unity, and with the certainty of French interference. The offer was not subject to negotiation. Many Vietnamese, while detesting Communism, recognized that the failure of Emperor Bao Dai and his allies to present a plausible nationalist alternative, or to oblige the

French to agree to independence, could only mean acquiescence, however unwilling, in continued French rule. By attacking non-Communist nationalists who refused submission or collaboration, the French drove them into the arms of the Viet Minh, allowing it to monopolize resistance. The Revers report by the Chief of the general staff was discredited, but it did recognize this mistake, advocating instead rule by the French Army and the 'peace of the brave', one of Leclerc's ideas, to be negotiated direct with Giap and Ho Chi Minh.

As for the Viet Minh, their ambitions were clear. Giap was executing Ho Chi's Minh's concept of the tiger and the elephant. He would eventually bring under his personal influence Truong Chinh's 'candidates': Van Tien Dung, who became Giap's successor many years later, General Nguyen Son (a regimental commander during the Chinese Long March whom we shall see later and who was shot in the back during the Route 4 battles), Vong Truan Vu, later commanding 308 Division, all planted as commissars of the political bureau of the People's Army of Vietnam, or PAVN.

Truong Chinh, cold, doctrinaire, deliberate and meticulous, and the enthusiastic, romantic, dynamic and emotional Giap were incompatible. Giap, with his astonishing memory, appeared indifferent to detail; Truong Chinh watching his cards and struck at his opponent only when 'errors' had adequately accumulated. Giap resented criticism and loved praise. He 'spoke his mind', always, but was of an extensive culture, combining East and West, a product of the university, the only graduate in the Politburo. But both were 'men of blood', used to physical measures, and of the third and last Vietnamese revolutionary generations.

VII
The French Pacify Cochinchina and the Red River Delta

At the time of these battles, Giap was thirty-seven years old and, although lacking the 'girlish prettiness' that Ho ascribed to him in 1940, still had a smoother, more relaxed appearance than his Tonkinese colleagues. The widow's peak that one observed in his blue-black hair nearly twenty years later was not marked, but his round face was beginning to firm into the solid commander's face of the 1960s. In those later days, above the broad nose and nostrils shone eyes that could menace, assess harshly, seduce. They were authoritative, penetrating, cold, but capable of lighting up in pleasure, perhaps kindness. But the innocence and sweetness of the days of his marriage to Thi Minh Giang were quite gone: he was now nothing but a general.

Giap's strategy, as has been said, was that of protracted war, 'a stage of contention, a period of equilibrium, then a general counter-offensive' or uprising. Giap's shortage of resources meant he could not take literally Ho's comment to a French Socialist minister: 'You would kill ten of my men for every one I killed of yours. But even at that rate you would be unable to hold out and victory would go to me.' His objective was to maintain and strengthen his Army, taking no unnecessary risks, giving battle only when victory was sure, his aim to move from guerrilla, to mobile (allied to guerilla), to main-force actions, building from section, platoon, company, battalion, brigade and eventually, to division. In 1947 and 1948, however, Giap's largest units were deliberately of regimental size (2,000 men) only. He did not have the transport or the ammunition or the kit or the rations or the guns to build higher.

The country was divided in 1948, according to Robert O'Neill, presently Chichele Professor of History of War, by Viet Minh military interzones, one in Cochinchina, two in Annam, two in Tonkin, one in the Red River delta. 'Free zones were sub-divisions of the interzones, as were guerrilla zones in both the Red and Mekong river deltas, Annam, the central highlands. The main towns, North and South, were described as "occupied areas", as were the great rubber plantations of the South.' In the early stages, Giap lacked the communications and the control to be able satisfactorily to command the South in the way that he could the North.

An American estimate of the PAVN in 1963, when it was far larger than in 1948, gave a strength of 223,000 men, a figure which had been greatly increased by conscription – a concept that Viet Minh propaganda did not acknowledge, preferring always to refer to a volunteer army – and by recruitment in areas 'freed' from French control. (On the other hand, it had not yet been significantly reduced by combat losses.) For 1949, O'Neill recorded thirty-two regular and 137 regional battalions; some battalions later became regiments, but presumably not all at 2,000 men.

The French Expeditionary Force of Moroccan, Algerian, Sene-galese, Foreign Legion and metropolitan troops had then reached 150,000. They were mostly in fixed posts and confined by the roads to motor transport, rather than travelling on foot in the jungles, the method used to conquer Indochina in the nineteenth century. Native Vietnamese soldiers under French officers numbered 250,000.

Apart from the 'back yard' factories in the Viet Bac already referred to, arms and equipment stolen from captured French posts and units, and supplies bought from the Chinese nationalists or via Hong Kong and Bangkok, the main – perhaps only – hope for acquisition of *matériel* by the Viet Minh was through a Chinese victory in the Civil War. We must suppose that Vo Nguyen Giap and his government had the intelligence and contacts to tell them that such a victory was inevitable. They probably did not know *when* it would happen, still less what it would mean in logistical terms, categories and tonnage, but Giap did begin to recruit porters on a massive scale and plan new roads for the trucks that would then come.

Giap knew that until he had cleared the French out, first from the Sino-Vietnamese border area and then out of the Viet Bac, his capacity to receive Chinese arms and armour would be restricted wholly to porterage on narrow paths over the treacherous northern mountains of Tonkin. O'Neill has shown that Giap's initial calcu-lations for this involved 40,000 porters per infantry division, and one million for an army of 300,000, until the railway and roads had been cleared of the French.

Valluy's operations in 1947, *Lea* and *Ceinture*, using about 15,000 men against 55,000 Vietnamese, had resulted in 10,000 Viet Minh dead, a magnificent return on operations which, otherwise, did little more than demonstrate that French forces were too small by a factor of thirty to contain an enemy operating on interior lines in mountains and dense jungle. (The United States Army would have regarded the force as ludicrously inadequate). General Valluy's only operations the following year, other than defence against harrassment by Giap at Backan, were the destruction of relatively large Viet Minh depots at Viet Tri and Son Tay. Giap had plenty of time to think ahead, and in the spring of 1949 he mounted a main-force operation against Lao Kay on the north-west sector of the Sino-Viet border. It failed, although only just.

By the end of 1950, however, Viet Minh forces in the South were in general retreat. The Nam Bo (Southern Committee) under Nguyen Binh had almost taken over Saigon for two months that year through a terrifying campaign of assassinations, riots and massacre in the streets of the city, which the French, after Emperor Bao Dai declared 'independence', were powerless to counter. The Central Market was burned to the ground. The city was blockaded. Execution teams moved freely through the town. Europeans and Chinese 'piastre' kings locked themselves in their homes. Minister of the Interior Tran Van Huu was stoned by schoolchildren. Nguyen Binh then launched a full-scale military offensive across the length and breadth of Cochinchina.

So far as Saigon was concerned, the stoning of Huu was the last straw. The millionaires and the establishment, in the summer of 1950, then found the courage to appoint as head of the Vietnamese Sûreté the 'Executioner', Nguyen Van Tam, two of whose sons had been murdered by the Viet Minh. (Tam was also known as the 'Tiger of Cai Lay' for having faced down *alone* thousands of Communist peasants (*nha-qués*) armed with machetes in 1940. He himself photographed clandestinely the ring leaders, bringing them to book.) Tam found his own Sûreté heavily penetrated by the Viet Minh, cleaned it up, conducted in his turn an assassination campaign against the Red assassination squads and, finally, captured in bed the leader of the whole Viet Minh organization in Saigon, Le Van Linh. Soon the informers against the Whites became again the informers against the Reds.

Bay Vien, leader of the Binh Xuyen, which is sometimes described as a 'sect', but was in fact a highly organized gang of murderous pirates, controlled Cholon, the casinos and brothels of the

Grand Monde, and the whole network of Sino-Vietnamese crime and power. He kept two crocodiles in a pool between his flat and his office, with a full-grown leopard on a chain outside his bedroom near the Arroyo Chinois. He also kept a tigress, a python and some monkeys, all about a hundred yards away from the Binh Xuyen cocaine factory. His whores ranged from twelve-year-old Cambodians to fine Hainanese, Thais and Cochinchinese. Bay Vien had once been a Viet Minh cadre but, in 1949, he had become General Le Van Vien and, in 1950 ran – on Bao Dai's behalf – the security forces of the entire government. As head of those services, his first act was to build 'a palace of prostitution in which an army of 3,000 whores was guarded by an army of Binh Xuyen', the Hall of Mirrors in Cholon.

The police and Sûreté, after Huu became prime minister, with Tam as his minister of the interior, were shared between Bay Vien and a pupil of Bazin, the head of the French Sûreté who had been murdered in April 1950 by Annamite killers from Viet Minh Battalion 905, Le Van Linh's suicide assassination squad. The terrorists were now mostly identified, arrested and shot; those few who escaped got away to the North via the Plain of Reeds.

A former gunner colonel called Chanson, Commissioner of Cochinchina (which had the status of a French territory), against the opposition of High Commissioner Pignon, the new commander-in-chief, General Carpentier, and the businessmen, in late 1950 forbade the export, without permits, of rice from Cochinchina's 'granary' west of the Bassac. Supplies of food, not only to the Viet Minh in Cochinchina, but also, via the long pedestrian convoys, to Giap's armies training in the Tonkin quadrilateral, faltered and ran dry.

At the same time, from Hanoi General Alessandri – the Corsican who had led 6,000 of his men to China after the Japanese coup on 9 March 1945 – occupied almost the whole of the Red River delta, cutting rice supplies to the Viet Minh even further. (The Viet Minh slogan now was 'a grain of rice is worth a drop of blood'.) Only Giap's leading cadres had enough to eat; the rest – the party officials, the ordinary soldiers, above all the peasants – suffered and starved; moreover because rice was also a currency, they had nothing with which to buy salt, clothes or medicine. Unless the Viet Minh were to mount an early uprising or an offensive, it was now difficult for the French to imagine that their Expeditionary Force was not on the way to victory.

The French Pacify Cochinchina and the Red River Delta

It was at this moment that Nguyen Binh chose to mount his own mistaken general offensive on three fronts, the largest of which was against Can Tho on the Mekong, the 'rice capital'. The next most important was at the large town of Soc Trang, south-east of Can Tho, with a feint at Tra Vinh. Although Giap was perhaps not yet in detailed day-to-day command of the Southern Committee, it is hard to believe that Nguyen Binh in his Plain of Reeds base was deliberately disobeying Giap's orders or even acting against his counsel. Binh had been appointed in 1945 by Ho Chi Minh himself.

His troops were well-trained, vicious and dashing, numbering six regiments. Their initial attacks, at diverse points in the Bassac between the Gulf of Siam and the South China Sea were for the most part in regimental or battalion strength. Binh's plan achieved complete surprise. The Viet Minh seized the guard towers and some defended posts, commanded – at least temporarily – the roads, destroyed bridges. In some areas the first indications of a strike were huge balls of dried grass inside which were Nguyen Binh's soldiers rolling into their objectives. Elsewhere, they forced the villagers into buildings covered with the Viet Minh flag, while they themselves lay up in the paddi, as the *na-qué* drew the French fire.

Hand-to-hand fighting was general, but after ten days the offensive was crushed by a combination of fighter aircraft, parachute drops, and amphibious French cavalry vehicles ('crabs') operating in the paddi, rivers and canals. The Viet Minh dead in their black pyjamas lay piled in hundreds, one on top of another, slaughtered by the cavalry's machine-guns, the survivors fleeing into the jungles to be killed or betrayed by the Moi. There were very few French dead.

Thereafter, throughout 1950, under the analytic command of Chanson, now promoted to general, who divided Cochinchina in half along the Mekong, the economy revived, the schools reopened, trade flourished, administration was effective and the land was developed. The soldiers of the Expeditionary Force behaved properly and spent their money to their own and the people's benefit. Information started to come in to the commands. Military activity was negligible. Cochinchina was pacified, and the credit was due to little, kind, self-effacing, systematic Chanson.

Giap despatched Le Duan to reconstitute the Nam Bo Committee and to purge it. He sent for Nguyen Binh on the pretext of offering him the task of establishing communications between Cambodia and Tonkin. Nguyen Binh knew that he would be executed on the way

71

but, as he said in a pathetic diary found after his death, had he defected to Bao Dai he could never have persuaded himself that he was not a traitor. He was very ill on the journey, escorted by thirty men selected by Le Duan. They pushed on through the jungle, subsisting on a little rice, berries, bamboo shoots, impure water, their wounds putrescent, covered in leeches, stumbling through the pouring rain, sick and feverish. A real ideologue in the group forbade the purchase from the Moi of a calf, on the grounds of economic sabotage: a calf unkilled could become a bullock 'for the people'.

Giap, perhaps, knowing Nguyen Binh to be at the end of his tether, obviously meant him to die *en route* without the trouble of assassination. But in the end the group was betrayed by some Moi to a Cambodian Army post. When the Cambodian platoon arrived, Binh had been unable to escape into the forest with the others; two of Le Duan's killers shot him dead before the enemy could get him. Or perhaps Giap did betray him directly or indirectly to the Cambodians.

Chanson himself was murdered at a ceremony at Sadek while the band played the *Marseillaise* and the crowd shouted with true feeling, '*Vive la France*'. His killer was no Viet Minh but a member of the 'revived' Buddhist-cum-Catholic sect, the Cao Dai, which the general had refused to arm. (The assassin blew up himself and Vietnamese bystanders, as well as Chanson, with a grenade secreted in his trousers.) Chanson's death did not disturb the peace of Cochinchina but, had he lived, he might have controlled the increasing confusion and corruption of that little world.

In Tonkin, Alessandri, now high commissioner and commander of the armed forces in Tonkin, had hoped to become commander-in-chief of the whole Expeditionary Force. (That post was taken in fact in 1950 by General Carpentier, a stranger to Asia.) On arrival in Tonkin, he understood the senselessness of the situation, the CEFEO tied down helplessly on Routes 4 and 7. Within months, in a chain of operations which took place almost without bloody confrontation with the enemy, he and his few battalions with their worn-out equipment covered Hanoi from the enemy, and then by the end of 1950 had methodically occupied the entire delta, in dykes, villages, rivers, hamlets, paddi, canals.

The nationalists now worked with him against the Viet Minh. Nguyen Huu Tri, once Bao Dai's governor of Tonkin, armed his people as militia forces and self-defence units, and also organized the identification and elimination of the hated Viet Minh who, in 1946, had massacred their leaders and persecuted or tricked the survivors ever since. Alessandri, after difficult negotiations with the ferocious and obscurantist Catholic Church in Tonkin, also persuaded the Christians to form their own militias, even armies. There were over one million of them, fanatics in a feudal world, priest-ridden, disciplinarian, arrogant, under severe medieval Vietnamese bishops. (Catholicism was brought to Vietnam by ultramontane Spaniards in the sixteenth century.)

In Tonkin, therefore, pacification reigned, as it did in Cochinchina. The government in Paris and its servants in Saigon were also entranced by prospects of United States aid – money, arms and equipment – in response to the defeat of Chiang Kai Shek by Mao Tse-tung, and to the need for an anti-Communist bastion in Indochina. American distaste for French colonialism remained but was suppressed in the interests of the new crusade in which, paradoxically, the French experts on China did not believe, regarding the Chinese as immune to both efficiency and militant Communism.

The end of the Indochina wars seemed in sight at last.

VIII
The Chinese Draw Near . . .

The French 'China experts' were wrong in both respects. Chinese Communism assumed a Marxist-Leninist character of unmatched rigour, while the training given to the PAVN by the PLA totally reversed the balance of forces in Indochina.

The Chinese border was originally guarded by a series of French posts in the deep jungle of Tonkin or in the even more inaccessible remote mountains beyond Cao Bang. These little, distant posts were evacuated first. Others lay to the west towards Laos, Lao Kay being the largest, Phongtho, Lai Chau and Son La in the country of the White and Black T'ai to the east of Dien Bien Phu. Here Meo *montagnards*, believed to be of Samoyed origin, cultivated the opium which on Asian markets could provide the Viet Minh with the money to fight their war. These garrisons, invisible in fog, storm and mist, or in the monsoon, were mainly supplied by parachute drops from ancient Junkers. Before the Viet Minh became ubiquitous, inter-post traffic was possible by horse and jeep. An amazing French railway ran all the way across the border to Kunming.

In 1949 Giap mounted his first attack in regimental strength on one of the posts, Lao Kay on the Red River, the main entry point to Yunnan in China. Lao Kay held on that occasion, but the Chinese armies (and Chinese Communist victory) were coming closer to those mountains like the crests of continuous breaking waves, impenetrable jungle in the troughs below.

The eastern defences towards Kwangsi and Kwangtung, in the Viet Minh quadrilateral where Giap's soldiers were at home along the jungle paths, consisted of posts on the straight line of Route 4, permanently vulnerable to Viet Minh ambush from the jungle, in 1949 in regimental strength, by mid-1950 in divisions. French access to the posts of Cao Bang, Dong Khe, That Khe, Langson, Tien Yen and Monkay was limited to armoured convoys along limestone ravines amongst hundreds of huge peaks pitted by caves. To site the path along Route 4, which was bordered by dense jungle and subject to Viet Minh intervention at almost every metre, was a strange, if not ludicrous, strategic concept, as the report in 1950 by General Revers,

74

chief of the general staff, pointed out. (The political scandal which resulted after a copy of the report had been found in the hands of a Vietnamese in Paris caused the postponement of most of the recommendations.) At all events, the error was certainly one which Giap had spotted and, by continually breaking the road, he eventually brought it to its disastrous defeat.

Giap knew that the enormous length of these convoys – jeeps, Chinese-owned private lorries, armoured cars, fighting vehicles of most sorts, trucks – made complete protection impossible. Nothing – French road patrols, jungle sweeps, air observation, armed reconnaissance into the mountains on either side of the road – could prevent him from placing his ambush parties on the commanding heights or, in their hundreds in the bush. Thence they leapt out at the halted convoys, leaving them burning and slewed across the road. Mines placed in advance would blow up the leading vehicles, grenades and machine-gun fire from the slopes showered the stopped trucks in the middle. Then the Viet Minh infantry would move in to loot the lorries and, in manifold single combat, engage the French and Vietnamese troops disembarked from the flaming trucks.

On one such attack, Giap had ordered that Colonel Simon, commanding officer of the 3rd Battalion of the Foreign Legion should be taken alive. But that hero, an old bullet in his head, together with a hundred Legionnaires held the Viet Minh for hours until he was relieved by tanks and heavy AFVs (Armoured Fighting Vehicles) from Langson.

Once safely in the posts, the soldiers would find a little barrack, a go-down, some Annamite whores in frayed *ao dais*, Chinese shops stocking anything from dried squid to condensed milk and Tiger Balm, the administrator's house and office, perhaps a grass air-strip cut out of the looming jungle, a Chinese coffee house . . .

Cao Bang, the northern post on Route 4, had been an ancient kingdom under the Mac for six hundred years. The population was Tho and, as late as the beginning of the twentieth century, had been administered by Chinese mandarins. The French organized the whole region on Tho models, although the commands were 'military territories, circles, sectors, cantons and communes', led at various levels by colonels, majors and captains. From their slender budgets the administrators built their quarters out of local wood, brick and stone, importing iron-work, locks, nails, padlocks, corrugated iron, screws and tools for carpenters, masons, sawyers – trades at which the Tonkinese became adept. The French planted maize, wheat and sweet potatoes and cleaned out the streams so that the water could be drunk. Fish and game abounded.

At night lightning furrowed the sky and set the mountains ablaze, while stars blazed in the tropic firmament. Fireflies glowed. Isolated peaks rose like pyramids, surging up from the depths of valleys in circles of ravaged hills ploughed by deep grottoes. At Lanchau, the 'Chinese' village lay between two rocks crowned by pagodas; the town, with its streams, rocks and pagodas among their wooded mountains, formed, under the setting sun, a classic scene. Elephants roamed the jungle, their tracks mingling on the damp path with those of tiger and tiger-cat. At Tuyen Quang an annual sacrifice of an orphan was made to the tiger-god.

The various tribes, including six sub-groups of Man subservient to the Tho, wore slightly different variations on a theme of blue with red ornaments, copper and silver jewellery, white shells. Heads of families, but no one else, might wear a skimpy beard. The Meo lived higher up, and defended themselves competently with French arms against the local Nung and Chinese pirates. The women of the Nung, a race disliked by the Tho, wore Chinese dress, little silver chains in their hair.

All the *montagnards* loathed and despised their Chinese neighbours to the north, the ancient conquerors.

By the autumn of 1949, however, it was not only the tribes who feared the coming of the Chinese, nationalists as well as Communists. A broken Kuo Min Tang seeking asylum in Indochina, or the Army of Kwangsi under its warlord, neither party willing to give up its arms and both seeking to re-establish their resistance to Mao in French Indochina, presented the immediate threat for the Saigon government. Their presence in Tonkin would then offer an intolerable provocation to the Chinese Communists. Even if Mao were not determined on conquering the whole of South-east Asia, 'wiping out colonialism everywhere', he would be obliged to destroy his enemies, not just in China, but across the Sino-Vietnamese frontiers. Lin Piao, commander-in-chief of the PLA, directly threatened as much. In 1950, when MacArthur sought to cross the Yalu and the Americans were brandishing the nuclear weapon, the French feared mass Chinese retaliation in Tonkin, the nearest and weakest 'enemy' territory. Before then, however, if Mao had decided to concentrate on massacre and re-education within his own borders there could at least be a breathing spell for Indochina.

On 9 December 1949 a forward French garrison east of Langson on Route 4 reported the arrival across the Chinese border of a massive unidentified KMT Army, under attack by Communist troops from the rear. Both sides included thousands of men. They were observed by only a few hundred Moroccans and Foreign Legionnaires, posted with personal weapons, machine-guns, some armoured cars and artillery, on the hills above Kwangtung.

A delegation of Kuo Min Tang senior officers then raged, wept and shouted at their French counterparts for the right to retain their weapons on entering Indochina. The French refused absolutely, grossly exaggerating – as a deterrent to violence – their own strength in the mountains. In the end the Chinese submitted, handing over the guns while bitterly accusing the French of dishonourable conduct. Soon their retreat became a flood, first of organized troops, then irregulars, bandits, women with yoke and basket, wounded, dying hideously, pushed at bayonet point to the rear beyond Tien Yen. And, on the way, at least one French garrison robbed and looted the prisoners of every one of their possessions.

The Legion opened fire on the first Communist detachment following up the nationalist rout. The PLA drew back. In the morning another unit appeared, whose leader attempted to kidnap the Legion commander, a battle-scarred colonel named Charton. Charton drew the PLA commander, a giant northerner, step by step back to the border, until the Chinese could see that he was right in the line of fire of the French guns. The PLA detachment withdrew again, protesting, and eventually disappeared from the village in which it had first confronted the CEFEO.

In the jungles and mountains of Giap's Tonkin quadrilateral, between Cao Bang and Langson, serious clashes then took place between a KMT Vietnamese called Vo Hong Khan commanding 6,000 Chinese nationalists and Charton's Legionnaires back from the frontier. The unfortunate Chinese, attacked not only by the Legion and the Moroccans, were also viciously harassed by the Viet Minh. Giap, in a brilliant stroke, killed plenty of nationalists but refrained from attacking the Expeditionary Force on to whose guns he drove them. 'First things first.' After a fortnight Vo Hong Khan and his Chinese surrendered to the French.

More refugees arrived in Tonkin, mostly from Yunnan, and up to

30,000 were sent under French guard to Phu Quoc, an island in the Gulf of Siam, before being despatched in 1954 to Taiwan. As for the Communists, there had been no further trouble after the encounter with Carton. Mao had decided that there was no need for open PLA intervention. The Viet Minh, after instruction, could do it on their own.

Across the border in Yunnan, the nationalist commander who had occupied Hanoi and North Vietnam in 1945, General Lu Han, defected to Mao. The defection enabled the PLA to eliminate the two remaining KMT divisions in Yunnan and to allow the embryo People's Army of Vietnam (PAVN) to enter China for training by the People's Liberation Army.

In January 1950, after walking for seventeen days, Ho Chi Minh had arrived in China, where he was received by Liu Shaoqi, who reported the visit to Mao, then in Moscow. Ho joined him there. Because of European and other commitments, Stalin was reluctant to devote Soviet resources to the Viet Minh, so the Chinese Communist Party, with Stalin's agreement, assumed the duty of support for the Vietnamese, using Lo Gui Bo as their representative at Giap's headquarters.

Chinese bases were built in which Giap's troops learned to become part of a professional revolutionary army, with formations up to division. The arms with which they were supplied by the PLA were mostly American, seized from the KMT. Cross-frontier roads were begun, and hidden underground depots constructed. The roads, capable of carrying artillery and heavy vehicles, led to Lao Kay, Cao Bang, Langson and Monkay. Five élite divisions were formed, 304, 308, 312, 316 and 320, with political commissars under Nguyen Chi Thanh, Giap's deputy, in charge of the Political Department.

Manpower was no problem for Giap. Supply, because of the chain of *matériel* from the Chinese, the Viet Minh jungle factories, and food transports (except rice) from China, was not a problem either. Ammunition, machine-guns and mortars poured in by Chinese Russian-made trucks. Whole armies of coolie labour were in preparation. Rice remained a problem and given French control of the Red River and Mekong deltas, it led Giap to believe that the war of movement must now pass to the offensive to pre-empt re-equipment and reorganization of the relatively weak French forces. The staff in Saigon, convinced that the nationalists were a greater threat to Indochina than a Communist China 'bent on peace and reconstruction', understood none of this. Nor did they grasp that the recent conquest of Hainan Island by the People's Liberation Army locked the French escape hatches from the outside.

In the spring of 1950 Giap's 308 Division which delivered the *coup de grâce* four years later at Dien Bien Phu – took a post called Pholu on the Red River near Lao Kay. Pholu, made out of logs, lay by a lake in the forest. They took it as they took Dien Bien Phu four years later, by hiding the guns in mountain caves camouflaged against the French Air Force, and then by bombarding non-stop the garrison below with light and heavy artillery. Weapons and ammunition came in by coolie supply trains. The battle lasted over a week. The local paras could not help the garrison, which numbered only a hundred. Faced with fifteen Viet Minh battalions, they disengaged and were saved only by bombing attacks on Giap's soldiers by French fighter-bombers. Pholu fell; Nhado fell, or, rather, was abandoned; Banlao fell . . . The upper Red River posts were almost all evacuated and the Expeditionary Corps – including the best part of two parachute battalions – withdrew to tribal partisan country, still surrounded by 308 Division until it moved east.

On the Black River, too, even at Hoa Binh, the smaller posts were being taken by powerful units conversant with the terrain, mobile on ridges, valleys and rivers, ruthless, savage, moving from blockade to breakthrough to massacre. North-east of Hoa Binh the 308 Division re-emerged on Route 4 to take the vast fort of Dong Khe by the same tactics as they had used at Phulo. An artillery and mortar barrage destroyed the French guns and the fortress. Next day the Viet Minh took the garrison by storm, the clouds so low that the French Air Force could not penetrate them in the driving rain.

Nearly the whole small garrison, in fact, escaped. Next day, the sky was clear and a parachute battalion retook Dong Khe, in spite of accurate and damaging anti-aircraft fire from its Viet defenders. Infantry came in from That Khe. The Viet Minh left a lot of weapons behind when they ran off into the jungle. But a diary entry found on a Vietnamese corpse promised that 308 would return in September, 'with two or three other divisions, to take Dong Khe, That Khe, Cao Bang and Langson'. The French staff drew no conclusions, preferring to maintain the 'hedgehogs', while admitting that the linear system of the Route 4 was now impossible. Perhaps 'face' was the explanation . . . But it would soon be too late to implement Revers' recommendation that Cao Bang be abandoned and the

Expeditionary Force allocated in defensible positions, not manacled to a road across which Vo Nguyen Giap could attack whenever he chose.

The morale of men confined to their trucks on an open, empty road, dominated from above by guns concealed in the hills and at ground level by the presence of remorseless foes in the jungle, was rapidly deteriorating. The French and the mercenaries fought with valour, but the Viet Minh had height, surprise, concealment and a murderous ambition. Given French strength in the Red River Delta, and the miraculous improvement in Annam and Cochinchina, they should have surely evacuated Route 4, indeed the frontier itself, before Giap's army became too powerful for evacuation to be possible.

Seventy-nine PLA officers under General Wei Guo Quing had arrived in Vietnam from Peking by August 1950 as the Chinese Military Advisors' Group (CMAG). In July General Chen Geng, a Chinese nominee of Ho's, also arrived and, after consulting Ho and Giap, received Peking's authority for a campaign on the Sino-Vietnamese border, 'to concentrate forces and destroy the enemy troops by separating them'. Chinese advisers were sent to Vietnamese units at division, regiment and battalion level with Ho's approval. By September the Vietnamese had also received from China 14,800 guns, 1,700 machine-guns, ammunition, grain, communications equipment and 150 cannon.

The French in Tonkin, occupying untenable positions, without hope of reinforcement, opposed by superior forces, were trapped. Against the intellect of considerable political and military commanders, they could only offer, until de Lattre's arrival, incompetence, a lack of will in Paris, and intrigue among generals.

IX
The French Lose the Frontier: Hanoi Threatened . . .

General Alessandri did not believe that the Expeditionary Force was doomed to be trapped. Instead of the folly of the single-road strategy, the little Corsican planned to exploit his firm rear base in the Delta by attacking the Viet Minh on their own ground and terms. He would lead fifty battalions into the Tonkin jungle and forest to destroy Giap's Army before its training was complete and before it could acquire enough rice to survive. The drive, from six starting points, would involve infantry, paratroops, air power and the tribes. It would not include artillery. The troops would march light, as had Jean Dupuis, Francis Garnier and Henri Rivière in the nineteenth century.

His objective was to keep the Viet Minh out of the Delta. Thus there was no alternative to retaking northern Tonkin, nor of meeting a rejuvenated Viet Minh Army 'at the edge of the Delta'. No one will ever know whether Giap was already strong enough to defeat Alessandri. The French commander-in-chief turned down the plan out of hand in favour of a continued defence of Route 4, with the 'decisive battle' to be precisely 'at the edge of the Red River delta'. Carpentier and Alessandri hated one another. They fought their mutual battle before ministers in Paris, as well as in the colony. A scenario that might have worked in the central European plain was preferred to concepts attuned to Asia.

Little at first happened during the summer, time of rains. Carpentier decided to evacuate Cao Bang, but planned a cover operation to take the 'Viet Minh capital' of Thainguyen, the only effect of which was, in the event, to deprive the Route 4 troops of 10,000 men uselessly engaged in a Thainguyen empty of enemy. By September the PAVN's training was complete, the roads from China to Vietnam had been built and the airfields in China were operational, whereas in Indochina the Expeditionary Force had been reduced by six battalions sent to help King Sisavang Vong and Prince Sihanouk in Laos and Cambodia.

Giap did not wait for the end of the monsoon. On 18 September, after a battle lasting less than three days, the Viet Minh, again after an artillery bombardment took and destroyed Dong Khe, this time completely. All the fortifications were obliterated, the guns knocked out and – except for an officer and section who escaped – the soldiers killed or taken prisoner. Dong Khe was a ruin and, this time, French paratroops were not employed to recover it. Once again, the Route 4 system and the 'hedgehogs' had show themselves to be defenceless against Giap's new army.

Cao Bang could have been evacuated by air, which the French rejected on grounds of face, or by Route 3 to Thainguyen, or – the accepted plan – in retreat down Route 4. The original plan was that the Cao Bang column would be met at Dong Khe by another column from That Khe, returning south together to that post. After Dong Khe had been captured by Giap, it was arranged that the two columns would instead meet nearer Cao Bang.

Carpentier devised another deception operation. He appointed the famous Legionnaire, Colonel Charton, whom we saw earlier on the frontier near Monkay, to command at Cao Bang, and ordered troops up from Langson* (under an inexperienced gunner colonel called Lepage), as if to strengthen the That Khe garrison. The overall intention was to present a picture not of evacuation, but of aggressive defence. An airlift took troops into Cao Bang, and brought civilians out.

Giap, however, whether from better intelligence or from military skill, was not deceived. He waited in Dong Khe, knowing that his enemy's mass was far away in Thainguyen. He knew also that on Route 4 the divisions, the guns, the tactical superiority were with the Viet Minh. Even French air superiority could not be employed. Charton and Lepage, in conditions with which Giap was familiar but they were not, lay in the palm of his hand.

Four North African units under Lepage set off from Langson on 18

---

* According to William Colby, director of the Phoenix *épuration* Programme and, later, of the CIA, Langson was attacked in 1945 by a famous CIA officer, Lou Conein, working with Gaullist French officers and Franco-Vietnamese troops. Their target was a Japanese divisional headquarters and the guerrillas claimed to have massacred the staff, after an unfortunate start in which the Vietnamese in the team accidentally killed one another. Conein returned to Indochina in 1954 on Colonel Lansdale's staff and was one of the models for Graham Greene's *The Quiet American*. He also helped to set up the Green Beret Special Forces team. His principal stupidity was to act as US liaison officer with the plotters in the grieviously mistaken coup against Ngo Dinh Diem.

September, clashing with the Viet Minh (and losing Moroccans) almost from the start on a badly damaged road, until they reached That Khe, where a crack unit of Foreign Legion paratroops joined them, sending back one of the Moroccan battalions. The Legionnaires did not trust the Moroccans and had no confidence in Lepage. Langson then ordered this little force – code-name *Bayard* – of four battalions to take Dong Khe, held by thirty Viet Minh battalions in prime condition.

Bayard met no resistance until reaching the heights above the deserted Dong Khe, when troops met a patrol and lost surprise. The Legion was ahead, down into the 'bowl'. Half a mile from the burned-out shell of the fortress, the paratroops ran into machine-gun fire. Lepage, instead of launching the whole of his 2,000 men, with a good prospect of success, to be reinforced in time by the Thainguyen force, decided to wait on the ridges until guns could be flown in and aircraft take off from Langson.

The thirty Viet Minh battalions, the main force of Giap's Tonkin Army, were also sitting on their own peaks. In the morning Lepage mounted an unsuccessful pincer attack on Dong Khe while aircraft from Langson reported very large Viet Minh contingents advancing fast from the direction of the Chinese border. Dong Khe could not now be seized by the French, at least with the units present in the area. And without Dong Khe, Cao Bang could not be evacuated.

Despite intervention by Alessandri, Carpentier refused to cancel the plan. Lepage, who until then had had no idea of the real purpose of *Bayard*, was ordered on 2 October to drive westward into the jungle along an almost indistinguishable track that was supposed to emerge on Route 4 twenty miles south of Cao Bang. At that point, he was required *by the next day* to meet Charton's troops coming south, his journey among great crags and green jungle, with no water, no knowledge of the uninhabitable country through which he moved, no supplies, no reserve ammunition.

Giap knew that Lepage had moved into the jungle. He knew that Charton was about to leave Cao Bang on Route 4. He had to harass and eliminate *Bayard* in the mountains so that when Charton arrived at the Namnang rendez-vous, the Viet Minh divisions could then destroy the Cao Bang force. Charton appealed to showy Colonel Constans at Langson for a day's delay and for more aircraft to evacuate invalids and pregnant women. Both requests were turned down. So Charton blew up Cao Bang, marched out with the sick and wounded, and the suicide began on Route 4.

The great horde of civilians, Legionnaires, whores, cooks, tribesmen, shopkeepers and Moroccans, in a column initially only one mile long, also containing trucks and two guns brought against Constans' orders, moved deliberately down Route 4. They had a peaceful day and a good sleep that night.

Next morning, at the rendez-vous with Lepage, nobody was there. Constans then wired Charton, saying that Lepage had been caught by the Viet Minh as he had moved along the Quangliet track northbound in order to bypass Dong Khe. *Bayard* was surrounded in a hollow dominated by Viet Minh artillery and was in the process of being liquidated. Charton was to take the Quangliet track from the northern end of Route 4 and, among the rocks, weird creepers and gigantic trees, fight his way through to Lepage within twenty-four hours, and save him.

The Cao Bang column shed its transport and artillery, taking a long time to find a track. When one was found, the column moved, strung out in a single file of over three miles, in jungle and mountain. It lost men but maintained patrols against an invisible enemy on valley and ridge, making no more than six miles in one day. (Once a light French aircraft spotted them but did nothing except drop English cigarettes, before the trees closed over again.) Every yard had to be cleared by machete. The civilians began to collapse. Much of the march, when not in endless patrol on the peaks or the flat, was in water up to the waist. The wounded had to be carried, tormented by leeches and mosquitoes, their sores open and suppurating.

To avoid the evident dangers of ambush on the trail, Charton led his men up to and along the mountain ranges. Some partisans were jumped by the enemy and had to be extricated. Some of the civilians could go no further. The commander of the Legion's infantry would not advance on Thatkhe until he had collected all his dispersed men. The Viet Minh then attacked in strength, with guns, machine-guns and mortars. The Legionnaires held and killed them.

Charton's lines were not breached but, next morning, his Moroccans, 'Goums', broke and ran. (The French revered Moroccan or, rather, Goum courage; but, when it was gone, it seemed quite gone.) The following day, Lepage's Moroccans, who had escaped from the Cocxa ravine thanks to his Legionnaires' courage, arrived in the general chaos and, in the now 'merged' columns, spread further panic. He and his men had been brutalized by physical and psychological attack from overwhelming, silent and superior Viet Minh forces, alien and merciless. Their spirit had endured until they could see that even the arrival of Charton's relief column on the ridge, the event for which they had longed, could not save them. Then they could take no more.

Both columns moved off towards That Khe, only twenty miles away, but they were attacked again by 'tens of thousands of Viets', and destroyed. Charton himself was taken. Some survivors reached That Khe, but many staggered in to find the base in Viet Minh hands. That Khe had been abandoned on 10 October. (Interrogation, re-education and brain-washing followed.) The final Viet Minh assault, beginning on 6 October, was directed, if not commanded, by General Chen Geng, operating on Mao Tse-tung's detailed telegraphic instructions. The French had lost the priceless blockade line.

A column from That Khe took out the helpless mob of civilians, wounded and beaten men to a post called Dongdang, where trucks and aircraft waited to evacuate them. This march had lasted two days, a hideous climb in the limestone cages without food or water, the Viet Minh all around on the road and hills. Only five men of the only fighting unit left, the Third BCCP, cut to pieces in the mountains, under a bridge, on the river, in the jungle, trapped by flash floods, reached Langson.

Then Langson was abandoned on Carpentier's orders, complete with all its food, medicine, ammunition, automatic weapons, gasoline and bomb-proof store rooms. (Technical reasons were alleged for Colonel Constans' failure to blow up this *matériel* before evacuation.)

Marshal Juin recognized both the shame and the strategic errors. 'More mobile groups must be established,' he said. Many more aircraft had to be provided. A National Vietnamese Army should be created. But unless these measures were taken – and France would have to approve them – with American aid and support, the French might just as well negotiate with Ho Chi Minh.

Nothing whatsoever was done. Alessandri and Carpenter remained, Carpentier apparently planning a campaign of withdrawals to a front just north of Cochinchina. Thainguyen, Hoa Binh, the vital post on the Black River, finally Lao Kay, key to the Red River, were all abandoned, the last evacuation clearing the routes to Yunnan, as the loss of Langson and Cao Bang had opened

Kwangtung and Kwangsi, betraying loyal tribes as well. The abandonment of friends is a customary feature of the end of colonial rule. In this case, it was the Man who were destroyed, the Chinese – not the Vietnamese – their probable assassins.

Thirteen hundred tons of ammunition, food, equipment and artillery passed into Viet Minh hands at Langson. The French had lost 6,000 men, thirteen field guns, 125 mortars, three squadrons of armoured vehicles, hundreds of lorries, 8,000 rifles, over 2,000 machine guns, 'enough to equip a Viet Minh division'. On exactly the same date, similar losses were inflicted on US forces by the North Koreans and the Chinese in Korea.

Giap had described his Indochina strategy in three stages: initial retreat of the Viet Minh, training and re-formation; Viet Minh re-equipment with Chinese help and destruction of French posts in the Tonkin quadrilateral; the destruction of the entire French army. As he said, both about the French and the Americans:

The enemy will pass slowly from the offensive to the defensive. The blitzkrieg will transform itself into a war of long duration. Thus, the enemy will be caught in a dilemma: he has to drag out the war in order to win it, yet he does not possess the psychological and political means to fight a long-drawn-out war.

Giap knew that he had to eliminate the French before they could be restored in military strength by US aid. With the benefit of Chinese, Soviet and East European aid to the Viet Minh, 'mobile warfare will become the principal activity, positional warfare and guerrilla warfare will become secondary'.

By the end of 1950 the Viet Minh battalions were ready to attack Hanoi, from the junction of the Cao Bang and Langson roads (the 'Route 4 divisions') and from the confluences of the Red, Black and Clear Rivers, both positions about twenty miles from Hanoi. The third *point d'appui* was in the Delta, where pacification had been disturbed as the rule of the Viet Minh challenged the massive weight of the Expeditionary Force. Thousands of peasants had been killed and, thus, thousands of recruits gained for the Viet Minh. But the French mobile groups had still not been instituted, and the Air Force was still inadequate.

General Boyer de la Tour ordered the evacuation of women and children from Hanoi, and advocated withdrawal of the

Expeditionary Force to Cochinchina, with the Tonkin war to be fought by the 'Vietnamese National Army'. Giap's forces had won a victory near Tien Yen. Binhlu fell. The Viet Minh started to attack the posts around Hanoi itself. Giap was ready to move against the city. Despair and terror reigned: defeatism was in the air.

On 6 December 1950, however, the government of France appointed General de Lattre de Tassigny as commander-in-chief. Among other attributes, de Lattre was the equal, if not the military superior of General Vo Nguyen Giap. He was a worthy opponent. Unlike Giap he lacked the support of a totalitarian government indifferent to public opinion at home and, for that reason, accepted his post on condition that it also carried that of High Commissioner.

X
General Jean De Lattre De Tassigny: Giap Goes Too Far

General Jean de Lattre de Tassigny was born in 1889 at Mouilleron in the Vendée, also the birthplace of Clemenceau, and was the only soldier whose presence the 'Tiger' requested for his obsequies. After an education at a Jesuit college at Poitiers, later attended by General Leclerc, typhoid prevented him from sitting the oral examination for the Navy. He entered Saint-Cyr where according to one of his instructors 'the violence of his character, his aggression and the trenchancy of his opinions' debarred him from the highest honours.

He fought in the First World War, originally as an officer of the 12th Dragoons when, wounded in single combat, he received the Legion d'Honneur, transferring to the Vendéen Regiment of 93rd Infantry where, at the age of twenty-seven, he commanded a battalion and was awarded the Military Cross. In peacetime, he fought in the (Moroccan) Rif Wars, together with Giraud and Juin, both also to become marshals, and served under the great Lyautey.

In the Second World War, as commander of the 14th Infantry Division, de Lattre was congratulated after the surrender by General Weygand who, addressing the division, said: 'You, at least, have the right to hold your heads high.' After commanding troops in Tunisia, he was recalled to France because he had refused to consider opening the frontier to supply Rommel's Armies. In France, as head of the 16th Military Region at Montpellier, he was imprisoned by the Vichy régime for disobeying an order grossly aiding the German occupying forces. He was the only senior officer to oppose the take-over of the Unoccupied Zones.

He landed in England in October 1943 after a daring escape from gaol, forced to leave behind his beloved wife and his son Bernard. In Algiers, on the orders of General de Gaulle ('You have not grown old,' said de Gaulle; 'You, General, on the other hand have grown'), he formed the First French Army, the famous 'Rhin et Danube' which, landing in the South of France with the US 7th Army, crossed the Rhine on 1 April 1944 and the Danube later that month, victories which 'returned youth, strength and hope to France'.

General Jean De Lattre De Tassigny: Giap Goes Too Far

After the Armistice, de Lattre served as French commander-in-chief in Germany, then as inspector-general and chief of the general staff, finally as commander of land forces, Western Union, under Field Marshal Montgomery. It was then, when all of French Indochina seemed about to founder, that France sought a saviour. De Lattre's son, Bernard, a platoon commander of the 1st Chasseurs in the Delta, had written to his father: 'Our morale is perfect . . . but we need to know why we are here, and we *need to be led*.' De Lattre, unlike all his colleagues, accepted the challenge, offering no excuses to avoid a duty which he had every reason to doubt would lead to success.

The General arrived with Madame de Lattre, not in Saigon but in Hanoi which Ho Chi Minh had promised to attack on 19 December, the anniversary of the 1946 uprising. He immediately addressed the junior officers: 'The era of hesitations is over. You are no longer on shifting soil. I undertake that you will be led.' So far as some generals and colonels were concerned, de Lattre showed that he would tolerate neither weakness nor indecision, nor the appalling corruption of the military. His anger and his demands rose in direct ratio to the rank of his audience. Despite the elegance of his address, his language was often brutal.

General Boyer de la Tour's evacuation orders were immediately revoked. 'As long as the women and children are here, the men won't *dare* to let go.' He mobilized the civilians. Confidence, including that of the many soldiers in Hanoi who had served in the First Army with de Lattre, somewhat revived. This confidence was reciprocated by de Lattre, now in Saigon, when he heard that the Viet Minh might unleash on Christmas Day the promised offensive against Hanoi: in fact, it did not begin until January 1951.

He learned also from General Salan of Boyer de la Tour's proposal to abandon all the remaining northern Tonkinese posts, yielding the whole Tonkin and Hanoi zone of operations. De Lattre instantly annulled the proposed instruction, replaced de la Tour by Salan, consulted Emperor Bao Dai at Dalat, and flew back to Hanoi. From January onwards he had a line of bunkers built to the north of Hanoi which barred access to the Viet Minh from the seaward and *de tous azimuths*. On that line, in April, Giap's offensive would break, at Dong Trieu and Mao Khe.

On 10 January, Giap had decided, despite the doctrines of Sun Tzu and Mao Tse-tung, to achieve control of the vast populations of the

Red River delta through direct confrontation. He commanded *sur place* eighty-one battalions, including twelve heavy-weapon and eight engineer battalions, but his opponents were still superior in mobility and in fire-power, possessed complete air superiority and were operating on interior lines. As Field Marshal Slim had drawn Mutaguchi and his Japanese divisions into the Imphal plain in April 1944, so Giap might have triumphed – and thus ended his isolation in the Tonkin jungles – by luring de Lattre out of the Delta on to Viet Minh territory on his own terms. A French defeat could, by the use of his guerrillas, have turned into rout. 'A clever military leader,' said Moltke, 'will succeed in choosing defensive positions of such an offensive nature that the enemy is compelled to attack them.' Giap did not follow this dictum nor, perhaps, did he give proper consideration to the French military quality of dash or *élan*, particularly under the new commander. It is possible, also, that his own judgement in the battles which followed may have been distorted by the opinions of his Chinese advisors under Lo Gui Bo.

French intelligence knew that 308 and 312 Divisions were massing in the Tam-Dao mountains, the ideal point from which to strike Hanoi, with roads linking the hills to Vinh Yen and thence to Hanoi, ten and twenty miles away respectively. The French were thus able, with some confidence, to identify Vinh Yen as the first likely target. As the Viet Minh themselves had now deferred to Tet (February) their intention of taking Hanoi, even the date of the offensive could be approximately determined. Strategic surprise was therefore lost to Giap.

The initial French defence consisted of two mobile groups, each consisting of one artillery and three infantry battalions and 3,000 men, with sappers and armour positioned in the hills above the plain north of Vinh Yen. Division 308 mounted a feint against an outpost manned by about one hundred Vietnamese and Senegalese, wiping them out to a man, and then ambushed the Mobile Group under the dedicated, obsessional Colonel Vanuxem, who had taken 308's bait.

Vanuxem, before retiring, lost one (Senegalese) battalion and part of another, Spahis. He found himself with his back to the lake of Dam Vac, and was saved only by the French Air Force and by the big guns of Vinh Yen. The Viet Minh commanded the hills. There was a gap in the French defences three miles wide.

De Lattre now flew into Vinh Yen in a Morane, landing blind at night in fog and mist, descending from the light aircraft in full

uniform, the stars blazing on his kepi, just 400 metres from the battle
field. 'The psychological shock of such an arrival in the middle of the
night at the low point of the battle was worth a division's
reinforcement.'

On returning to Hanoi, he told Colonel Allard, head of the Fourth
Bureau, to send in three battalions. Mobile Group 1, a crack North
African unit of three battalions shifted out of their tropical uniform
in Saigon, and were in winter kit to Hanoi by Air France Sky-
Masters, the Saigon–Paris Consellations and the Aéropostale
aircraft. Four thousand men were carried in seventy-two hours by
fifteen aircraft. We do not know whether de Lattre knew of Slim's
airlift in 1944 of 5th and 7th Indian Divisions from the Arakan to
Dimapur, which won the battles of Imphal and Kohima.

The group came to Vanuxem's aid by 15 January. On 16 January
the Viet Minh seemed to have melted away but, that evening, 308
Division reappeared in a human wave attack against the French
positions in the hills to the north of Vinh Yen. De Lattre, who came
back a second time, as he had promised the men, now ordered
massive napalm attacks from fighter bombers and any other available aircraft, literally grilling the enemy where they stood.

But the Viet Minh fought on until only two hills were left in
French hands. De Lattre sent in yet another mobile group, number 2,
this time of one paratroop and two Moroccan battalions, while
Mobile Group 3 counter-attacked hill 210, taking casualties from a
suicide attack by Division 312. Napalm bombing intensified – 'huge
egg-shaped containers, spreading immense sheets of flame . . . a
torrent of fire in all directions burning everything in its passage' –
while ground artillery and mortars completed the destruction.

The Viet Minh fled to the Tam Dao massif, despite the efforts of
their officers, pistols in hand, to hold them. Behind them they could
hear the yells of the pursuing enemy. Many of them believed
themselves to be the victims of an atomic attack, and it was unfair of
Giap in his subsequent apologia to have accused his men of
cowardice. The Viet Minh lost 6,000 dead and 500 prisoners, against
only 700 French killed.

The French had won the battle. Giap, however, despite his
obvious unreadiness for a stage-three offensive, believed that the
principle of direct confrontation had not been vitiated by this single
defeat. He therefore sought another target. No doubt he was also
conscious of the need for an early victory, both to ease his men's

disappointment at continued residence in the awful quadrilateral, and to match the creation of the overtly Communist Lao Dong or Workers Party.

He accordingly selected, because of its proximity to coal mines and its access to France's main colonial port of Haiphong, the lightly defended post of Mao Khe, whose surroundings permitted both unobserved approach and good lines of communication for the attacker from the shelter of hills at Dong-Son. The Viet Minh rapidly took the covering posts, but 316 Division was prevented from exploiting this success by fire from the French destroyers and two landing craft operating from the Song Da Bach. Giap had discounted this waterborne feature, known as *Dinassaut*.

De Lattre could not be sure whether the initial attack represented a feint or the main attack. He therefore strengthened his naval forces by one parachute battalion. The principal defenders against 316 Division, which with 308 and 312 at Dong Trieu made up a total Viet Minh force of 30,000, were 400 men. One hundred of these, 96 Tho guerrillas and three French NCOs commanded by Vietnamese Lieutenant Toan, garrisoned the mine itself. With the aid of airborne napalm and other missiles, and despite the death of their NCOs, the Tho held until evacuation that night under the wounded Toan.

A Moroccan armoured-car platoon held Mao Khe village itself. Senegalese and Tho manned the post at the church against very heavy artillery barrages which opened the way to screaming hordes of Vietnamese, destroying watch towers, houses, bunkers and the church itself after a holocaust of shell fire. Probably for fear of other napalm raids or, at least, further devastating fighter-bomber attacks next day, Giap withdrew. Of 2,000 Viet Minh casualties, 400 were killed at Mao Khe. The three little garrisons, plus the parachute battalion and the Navy, had given Giap his second major defeat.

His position as Commander-in-Chief, given the collective nature of Communist decision-making, need not have come under serious threat despite the known disapproval of Le Duan, secretary of the Lao Dong Party and of Truong Chinh. His dismissal, as Robert O'Neill remarked in *General Giap*, would have been seen by the general public as a grave attack on the entire revolutionary movement.

In an intriguing analogy O'Neill compared Giap's position with that of 'an imaginary leader holding the offices of both Defence Secretary McNamara and General Westmoreland in 1968, who had occupied these positions since 1956, played a leading role in restoring American government after the expulsion of a foreign occupying power in 1962, organized for the Democratic Party the suppression of all Republicans, and in 1963 occupied the presidency while President Kennedy spent four months negotiating in Moscow'.

Meanwhile de Lattre returned to Saigon, and handed out tickets for Paris to 300 'useless' (i.e. corrupt) civil and military employees. ('The boat for France, Monsieur.') He then had 180 broken-down vehicles repaired and sent to the front, restored the appearance and bearing of his troops, terrified the profiteers and defeatists alike, laid down the constitution of the Vietnamese National Army, and restored confidence in France among the Americans as well as such Vietnamese leaders as were close to Bao Dai.

Around Hanoi he strengthened his northern bunkers for an operation, *Méduse*, to the south of Haiphong, which increased the pacified area of paddi, permitting an increased harvest and further closing the rice fields to the Viet Minh. To the south of Hanoi he built over 2,000 concrete pillboxes in the fortified de Lattre line, while at the same time organizing more and more mobile groups. Each consisted of an armoured regiment, one or two infantry battalions and an artillery unit.

On 29 May Giap mounted a third attack against the Delta, which combined two regular infantry regiments (42 and 64) clandestinely infiltrated *à la Russe* behind the French line, with major attacks by 304, 308 and 320 Divisions against Phu Ly, Ninh Binh and the Catholic diocese of Phat Diem. 312 Division was allocated a diversionary role towards Yen Bay and Nghia Lo, which deceived neither de Lattre nor his commanders, nor caused them to divert resources.

The main attacks were mounted from the karst, the limestone mountains which we have seen before, packed with inaccessible bomb-proof caves, running almost alongside the Day River, the whole way from Phu Ly via Ninh Binh to Phat Diem. Although less favourable to the French than the Delta near Mao Khe, the Day River did at least support the flat-bottomed vessels of their Navy which, in part, composed the *Dinassaut*.

Giap achieved surprise. Division 308 overran Ninh Binh and eliminated a number of posts across the Day River on the east bank. It was here, on rocks above the river, that Bernard de Lattre, commanding troops of the newly formed Vietnamese Army, was killed by Viet Minh artillery. His death broke his father's heart. The general organized a magnificently theatrical mass in the Cathedral at Hanoi and, in a cable to Madame de Lattre said: 'Forgive me for having failed to guard our child.'

The other divisions had less success and the infiltrated regiments failed to interfere with the movement of French reserves. The Catholic militias fought obstinately, and the peasants did not help the Viet Minh at all.

De Lattre reinforced the French Army on the spot, after the initial reverses at Ninh Binh, with a paratroop battalion and no less than eight groups, artillery, armoured and mobile, sent in by the *Dinassaut* up river. The Viet Minh water-borne supply line of junks was devastated by the *Dinassaut* and, on 18 June 1951, Giap withdrew his troops to the mountains, losing hundreds of prisoners en route.

In all these operations, the Viet Minh had suffered over 20,000 killed and wounded. Giap retired into the Viet Bac to revitalize his army and, then, to discover a strategy which would beat down the new expeditionary Force and its Vietnamese ally before the tide of his countrymen's opinion turned against him and the Viet Minh.

Reflection, nevertheless, did not deter him from sending 312 Division to Nghia Lo in the north-west highlands via Yen Bay at the end of the rainy season in September. His objective, to break the French hold on the T'ai country, was defeated by the use of three parachute battalions. De Lattre was out of Indochina on this occasion, persuading the US administration in Washington that the wars in Korea and Indochina were the same war fought to defend the liberty and economies of Asia. Because of his enthusiasm and his victories, he received assurances of American aid. He knew that he needed yet more victories both in Vietnam and in terms of the French budget.

After returning to Saigon on 15 October, now mortally ill and aware of it, de Lattre took Cho Ben, south of Hanoi. On 14 November he attacked and seized with three battalions the 'capital' of his Muong allies at Hoa Binh, thus further insuring Muong loyalty and depriving the Viet Minh of the important supply link between that city and the ancient porcelain-making town of Thanh Hoa. A very large French force, perhaps thirty battalions of all arms, then proceeded to move up the Black River, taking all their objectives in an initial Viet Minh military vacuum.

Giap characteristically refused contact with this mass offensive, even though success for the French would have cut a corridor from Haiphong through Hanoi and Hoa Binh to Son La, dividing the Viet Minh in the North from the Viet Minh in the South.

On 19 December, Général d'Armée de Lattre de Tassigny underwent an operation in a Paris clinic to remove a cancerous growth, and a second operation on 5 January 1952. On 11 January France learned from the radio that 'his condition had worsened and must be considered serious'.

That evening, in the presence of Madame de Lattre, the general took the last rites. Although apparently unconscious, he struck his breast three times at the words '*Domine non sum dignus*'. His own last word was 'Bernard'. At 5.53 pm he died, promoted by the National Assembly to Marshal of France, the last since the war. In the church at Mouilleron, after a night vigil by the cadets of Saumur, his father Roger de Tassigny, ninety-seven years old, nearly blind and the last of his line, touched the coffin and its stars, and sought to touch again his grandson's lance pennon.

De Lattre, 'le roi Jean', was a vain, ambitious man, his charm edged with total offensiveness to those he considered his inferiors in competence and courage. He was, however, despite rumours in 1945 of Communist connections, loyal, devoted and sincere. He restored French morale and extended French control, holding and improving a critical positon. Although a 'European' general, he perceived that Tonkin was the key to the defence of Indochina and, hence, in those days, of South-east Asia itself. In December 1950, indeed, before assuming his appointment, he told Ernest Bevin, the British Foreign Secretary, that he saw his role as helping to buy time in Asia to build up non-Communist strength in Europe: he would, without antagonizing or otherwise drawing-in the Chinese, hold out as long as he could.

He saw clearly that unless Vietnam and the associated states of Laos and Cambodia could be brought to independence within the French Union, his task would be very difficult. His strategic aim, therefore, included the early creation of an indigenous Vietnamese Army to handle pacification, while the French Army occupied the offensive role in the northwest and elsewhere under a system of mobile groups, available throughout Indochina and providing steadily growing security. (This idea was revived by US General Gavin in 1965–6, proposing highly mobile forces patrolling out of enclaves in Cam Ranh Bay, Da Nang and Nha Trang, developing

General Maxwell Taylor's 'enclave' theories.) De Lattre believed that he could accomplish this, despite disappointment at Vietnamese apathy, within eight to twelve months. He was not given the time.

Had he lived, 'victory' might have been beyond even 'le roi Jean', despite his military skill and command authority. But only de Lattre could have persuaded his government to grant Indochina an independence that would have made the Viet Minh an irrelevance. If he had failed in *that*, only he could have obliged Paris to understand that Leclerc's peace with honour was the sole alternative to battle with inadequate resources.

It is significant that, outside the Army, in the slothful atmosphere of Saigon, there was little reaction to his death other than relief at the end of a martinet whose lash had frequently cut deep wounds. During his period in office, he had encouraged Bao Dai, rallied Vietnamese youth, organized the training of 60,000 Vietnamese reservists. Forty of his battalions were fully mobile and the French numbered 150,000 men. But Giap, although soundly beaten in the field, had now achieved a general implantation in the Red River Delta as widespread as before the first large French clearing operations, especially in the bishoprics of Phat Diem and Bui Chu.

As High Commissioner, de Lattre had presided over the first year of Vietnam's independence as an Associated State, with Laos and Cambodia, within the French Union. At the end of 1950, the Pau Agreements had been signed, transforming those services hitherto run by the French on a federal basis. Justice, education and security were already within the states' competence. The French, nevertheless, partly because of the character of General de Lattre, retained large powers, not just in defence and foreign policy.

When taking over from him on 16 January, General Salan said, 'One does not succeed General de Lattre . . .' The latter's plan of campaign was to establish a fortified base and mount large operations from there. In practice, after he died the French merely occupied key posts but failed to mount offensive operations: the Viet Minh were able to take the initiative as the French chose not to emerge from their strong points. Salan, the 'mandarin', avoided gross error by doing very little.

The Viet Minh consistently avoided confrontation with superior forces. In any case, as most of the French reserves were tied up in the north-west or, after the Laos operation, back in the Delta, they found themselves unable to undertake a major offensive until Dien

Bien Phu, the wrong choice. Few French officers, after de Lattre, believed the war could be won, because of inadequate numbers, poor leadership at the top, a static, even deteriorating, political scene, and an incompetent national Vietnamese Army, albeit of 250,000 men.

In 1950, Truong Chinh in Tonkin had ordered the execution of Giap's chief of logistics, Tran Chi Chan, which further widened his differences with Giap. After Giap's failures in 1951 against de Lattre, Truong Chinh accused him of 'responsibility for useless massacres, which had no other purpose than to promote personal interest'. He denounced him for failures of judgement about his commanders, forced him to sack his staff, to submit an auto-criticism, and to reorganize his command, giving priority to political commissars over the military, also inserting Chinese military advisors at all levels, sharing power and authority. Direct military confrontations were precluded; a return to a people's war, ambush and so forth, was demanded. 'The countryside was to encircle the towns, the mountains to dominate the paddi.' The pro-Chinese clan, Truong Chinh and Hoang Quoc Viet, became stronger.

XI
De Lattre Dead, Giap Retakes Hoa Binh

By 14 November 1951, when de Lattre's paratroops seized Hoa Binh, Giap was aware not only of his own recent defeats but of the fact that the United States was becoming armourer to the forces of the French Union, whose confidence and spirit had been raised by their new commander. But he knew too that reinforcements were still lacking, that a rival Vietnamese Army was barely in embryo form and, above all, that the attack on Hoa Binh had caused the Expeditionary Force severely to disperse its resources, weakening the Delta and the north-west. He also understood the French Metropolitan political scene – the domestic situation could deteriorate appreciably as a result of reverses overseas.

It was therefore essential for Giap to destroy the base at Hoa Binh, not in order to regain territory (always a secondary concept), but to stop it being used as a centre for offensive operations by de Lattre's new mobile units. Enemy occupation of the Muong minority capital represented loss of face, also, he could not afford to lose control over his land link with the strong point at Thanh Hoa. Another factor was the brilliant opportunity offered him to exploit the dispersion of French forces and consequent weakness in the Delta.

The general did not intend to expose his troops to air bombardment through frontal assault. He decided instead to concentrate his attacks along the French lines of supply to Hoa Binh. These were the Black River, from its confluence thirty miles to the north with the Red River, and the old, almost disused Route 6 via Xom-Pheo and Xuan Mai to Hanoi.

French sappers fought unremittingly to improve Route 6's condition. The Black River was the main avenue of supply to the garrison at Hoa Binh. In the steep river valley to the north, the French were obliged to establish a multitude of small posts and forts on the steep hills of the canyon in order to protect the unarmoured landing craft with their heavy cargoes against the Viet Minh artillery. Behind them, in the large territories to the east and west of the Black River, Giap had considerable freedom of manoeuvre in which to pick off the smaller posts at leisure.

Giap placed his 312 Division to the west of the Black River, all the way up to the Red River junction. 304 Division lay in wait to the south of Route 6, between Xom-Pheo and Xuan Mai. 316 was just north of Route 2 and the de Lattre line to the north-north-east of Vinh Yen, where de Lattre had defeated Giap's attack on Hanoi in January. 88 Regiment and 308 Division were positioned north-west and south-west of Hoa Binh itself. The role of 320 Division was to damage French lines of communication and divert operational units in the Day River area, a somewhat similar task to 316's further north.

The area to the north-east of Hoa Binh, dominated by the mountains Ba Vi Tan Vien and Hui Vien Nam, was the fiefdom of Viet Minh regional and guerrilla forces, which harassed the enemy and restored guerrilla bases.

The first French post to fall on the Black River was Tu-Vu, on the west bank, held by two companies of Moroccan infantry and half-a-dozen tanks. The post was physically split in the middle by a tributary and could only be relieved by a party from the other side of the river. A heavy mortar bombardment preceded the main night assault, when 'human waves' broke against the French mines and wire, attack upon attack, with the infantrymen screaming '*Tien-lên*' ('Forward') as they drove on through the darkness.

French guns from the east bank added to the garrison's artillery, covering the wire with Tonkinese bodies. Four hundred corpses were found after the battle when the Moroccans reoccupied Tu-Vu. But then five Minh battalions came in against the tiny garrison of two hundred in their contracting square. The tank 'platoon', with guns depressed, fired point blank into the howling infantrymen of 308 and 312 Divisions, hundreds going down, crushed to death under the tracks of the armoured vehicles slowly and awkwardly rotating, in the hellish light of early morning. All around them Moroccans and Vietnamese slashed, tore and stabbed at one another in a rapidly declining space. Then the Viet Minh fired bazookas directly at the hulls of the tanks, fired machine-guns into the driving slits and crammed incendiary hand grenades into turret hatches where they could, or into the very cannons when the hatches had not burst open. Without exception, the tank crews burned to horrible death. In

Bernard Fall's phrase, 'the sweetish smell of searing flesh rose into the air.'

French airborne and mobile groups were thereafter unable to get at the enemy, who slipped away into the limestone caves until they emerged, silently and suddenly, to eliminate the west-bank posts. The battle was now more than a battle to hold Hoa Binh and to exploit it as a spring-board into Tonkin and Laos; it had become a battle to supply, maintain and keep those forts ancillary to Hoa Binh. Having no sound choice, General Raoul Salan, de Lattre's successor, later famous as commander in Algeria, and as the putschist leader of the OAS (Organisation Armée Secrète), ordered evacuation of the west bank and of positions around Ba Vi Tan Vien.

Thenceforward, the effort to keep open the Black River was maritime, conducted by the *Dinassauts* in an extraordinary variety of landing craft and ships, with ramshackle mortars and *ad hoc* artillery. Sometimes they carried armour and marine landing parties, as well as escorting river gun-boats. One final ambush, however, caused such losses to the French Navy that this means of supply was abandoned by the second week of January 1952.

The Hoa Binh airstrip was already under the Viet Minh guns. The town itself was lightly defended by five battalions. Route 6, to which the battle was moved, was held by only five more battalions in posts spread along the twenty-five mile stretch to Hanoi. Against them Giap put Regiment 88 (308 Division) and the entire 304 Division. Both carried new Chinese equipment as well as fresh US material captured in Korea by the PLA.

In a gallant and magnificently impertinent night operation, troops of 304 Division followed two Foreign Legion patrols right into 13 Half-Brigade's position at Xom-Phéo, straight through the Legion's own mine-field. The Viet Minh action which followed, against two Legion companies, 5 and 7, in the post's four-man bunkers and against two other companies (4 and 6) on either side of Route 6, employed mortars, artillery, recoilless rifles, 'Bangalore torpedoes' and explosives. 7 Company, pinned down under fire, could not get to the support of 5 Company, the latter under concentrated attack, nearly overrun, most of its NCOs and officers out of action, wounded or killed.

That night the sky was a great bowl of blue, its infinity pointed with a million stars over the black distorted trees and the purple distance. The flash of high explosive hideously illuminated the darkness. In the early morning of the next day, the Legionnaires could still counter-attack with grenades, followed by ferocious use of the bayonet in bloody hand-to-hand combat. By dawn, two platoons of 5 Company had been almost wiped out, the other two platoons losing men. But 700 Viet Minh were dead around Xom-Phéo.

304 Division pursued its assault on Route 6, first cutting up a French mobile battalion. The division then so effectively ambushed the road that over fifteen French battalions, artillery and infantry, and the whole French Indochina Air Force had to be deployed in order just to resupply the five battalions occupying the useless base at Hoa Binh. Even this huge task force under Jean Gilles, commanding Airborne Forces, took eleven days to fight the twenty-five mile leg from the Delta to Hoa Binh, leaving the Delta drained of those mobile forces needed to suppress the Viet Minh guerrilla and regional forces now pouring into the vacated plains.

In Giap's words:

The enemy occupied Hoa Binh. We replied by immediately launching the Hoa Binh campaign. On the one hand we contained and overwhelmed the adversary's forces on the 'opposite' front; on the other hand we took advantage of their exposed disposition of troops to get our divisions to strike direct blows at their rear in the Red River delta. Our large guerrilla bases were extending further still, freeing nearly two million inhabitants. Hoa Binh was released. De Lattre's plan was checked.

Elsewhere Giap said:

De Lattre was aware of the too great dispersal of French forces and of the danger arising from our guerrilla warfare. So he energetically regrouped his forces and launched extremely fierce and barbarous mopping-up operations to 'pacify' the areas behind the enemy's lines in the Red River delta. [Vinh Yen, Mao Khe, etc.] But he found himself very soon face to face with the same insoluble contradiction. By concentrating his forces he found it impossible to extend occupied territory. De Lattre had, in the end, to resign himself to scattering his forces to launch the famous offensive on Hoa Binh. The results, after his death, were not long in coming. While his crack troops suffered very heavy losses at

Hoa Binh, our guerrilla bases in the Delta were restored and extended very considerably.

It is not clear whether de Lattre would have agreed. The Viet Minh had taken severe casualties, particularly during the human-wave assaults. Giap once said, 'Every minute, tens of thousands of men die. Even if they are Vietnamese, that doesn't mean much,' but it did delay preparations for phase three of protracted war – the counter-offensive – even though Giap was no slave to the Maoist interpretation of that concept. But a French officer observed at the time that 'de Lattre had died just in time not to be associated with retreat'.

Retreat there was. Salan, 'le Chinois', the subtle, equivocal, colonial soldier, seeing evident French weakness in the north-west and the Delta – zones in which further action by Giap was predictable – gave the order in January 1952 for the complete evacuation of Hoa Binh. The operation took two days in late February and was initially not spotted by the Viet Minh. Water-borne withdrawals of equipment and men from the Black River, including the Muong, took place under fairly massive air and artillery cover. A leap-frogging withdrawal was then executed down Route 6, remorselessly harassed by 304 Division and the crack 88 Regiment.

French losses were heavy, 'several thousand from the whole battle,' according to Robert O'Neill. The High Command's claim that the more severe casualties among the Viet Minh forces were of greater significance cannot now be justified in the light of France's reduced capacity to fight effectively in Tonkin north of the Delta. But the claim by Monsieur Letourneau, Minister for the Associated States, that the withdrawal had freed twenty battalions was true, and more important.

Giap, with Chinese military advice from General Lo Gui Bo of the Chinese Military Advisors' Group (CMAG), had devised a superb strategic and tactical engagement, admittedly from advant-ageous topographic positions, following his own and Mao's precepts with skill and flexibility, in surprising contrast to his errors prompted by the rice shortage in 1951. (More than one observer has repeated the charge that the 1951 failures were also due to the advice of Lo Gui Bo.) It was now his intention to bring about a further dispersal of the French Expeditionary Force into regions where it could be further damaged, even fatally weakened, while filling the vacuum in north-west Vietnam and in the Delta caused by that dispersal.

After the diversion of French troops to Hoa Binh, the 'Delta vacuum' had become extremely grave, under pressure from 316 and 320 Divisions placed by Giap north of the de Lattre line and on the Day River for that very purpose. Alessandri's triumphs had been swept away. When 304 Division left Route 6, it too joined its comrades behind French lines, together with other Viet Minh regiments. To keep those lines open behind them, the French employed mobile groups under various leaders who displayed gallantry, skill and panache. These included intellectuals such as the enormous General René Cogny, crippled in a concentration camp by the Germans, later northern theatre commander; and Colonel Vanuxem, huge, the tribal leader, red-bearded, an *agrégé* in philosophy; ex-sergeant Marcel Bigeard, escaped from a German prison, made colonel at Dien Bien Phu; the flamboyant Christian de Castries, cavalryman and philanderer, fortress commandant at Dien Bien Phu; de Kergavarat, English in mode and dress. All of them, in the end, were driven to exhaustion and worse by those hostile and imponderable forces subsumed in General Mihailovic's phrase, before Tito killed him, 'the gale of the world'.

It is little remembered that at this very time, the US Joint Chiefs of staff were seriously considering helping the French in the Red River delta, or even replacing them by eight US divisions, who would free the Expeditionary Force for combat elsewhere in Indochina. The plan was never carried out because of its potential effect on US military resources worldwide.

In the South, the Bao Dai régime with its preponderance of corrupt and despotic mandarins represented no magnetic alternative to the apparent purity of Ho Chi Minh's example. Nor was great progress under way in the belated creation, under the son of Nguyen Van Xuan, Bao Dai's former Prime Minister, of a native Vietnamese Army. Xuan was a French citizen. His son, Hinh, believed that, in spite of de Lattre's optimistic estimate, he needed seven years to get his men trained to a point when they could take over even pacification, let alone offensive actions, from the forces of the French Union.

Nevertheless, in the South, in Cochinchina and Saigon especially, but also in southern Annam, security remained as satisfactory as it had been under the reign of Brigadier Chanson. It continued in that fashion almost to the end of the first Indochina War.

Further north, shortages of rice, ruthless tax collection by the Viet Minh and the use of impressed labour, resulted in a peasant uprising in Thanh Hoa proviince and disturbances in Ho Chi Minh's native province of Nghe An. Ho promised agrarian reform, which in the end, produced far worse consequences, and offered rent reductions in return for total peasant loyalty.

XII
The Shape of Things to Come

Giap, planning his next strategic move towards victory, had observed the weakness of the French military position in Laos. Since he knew the importance of that country to France as the most amenable component of a potential Indochinese Federal Union, he judged that a Viet Minh drive through the mountains of the northwest, Son La, Lai Chau and Nghia Lo, would further divert French troops from other regions. The Chinese agreed to this plan but refused Genral Gui Bo's request that they send native Chinese troops into Vietnam itself.

This diversion would be to a terrain where the enemy Air Force would be least effective: the jungle and hills would also be the least appropriate terrain for a mechanized Army, except, of course, for the extraordinary French Airborne Commando Groups (GCMA) operating behind Viet Minh lines. For the Viet Minh, on the other hand, conditions were ideal: trained jungle fighters operating under impenetrable tree cover, disposing of surprise, initiative, speed, and a degree of self-supply, at least compared with Salan's long lines of communication.

Most of Giap's tactical requirements, therefore – enemy weakness, shock, enemy dispersal – were more satisfactorily met by battle in north-west Tonkin and Laos than anywhere else in Indochina, with the possible exception of the Central Highlands. But the Central Highlands did not present the 'exercise and training area' for the Dien Bien Phu battle which Giap may at this early stage have had in his mind's eye.

At all events, he was near 'the third stage, that of a general counter-offensive':

We shall attack without cease until final victory, until we have swept the enemy forces from Indochina. During the first and second stage, we have gnawed away at the enemy forces; now we must destroy them. All military activities of the third stage must tend to the same simple aim – the total destruction of French forces . . . The enemy will be caught in a dilemma: he has to drag out the war in order to win it and yet he does not possess the psychological and political means to fight a long-drawn-out war.

This statement, made to the staff of 316 Infantry Division at the end of 1950, may have been premature, but in October 1952 it was more realistic. Certainly the second stage – destruction of the French presence in the Viet Bac – had been nearly accomplished.

In April 1951 Giap had sent 312 Division on a reconnaissance into the T'ai mountains. In September of the same year, the division attacked Nghia Lo and, as described earlier, was defeated by the French despatch of three parachute battalions. The Viet Minh had withdrawn.

In October 1952, 308 Division crossed the Red River and, after six days' march, had eliminated the French posts – many, admittedly, tiny – in its path to Nghia Lo. There, camouflage and tradecraft had defeated both rigorous French patrolling and overhead reconn-aissance by the Air Force. The first mortar attack on the post achieved complete surprise, destroying French artillery and fixed positions. It was followed by a charge of thousands of Viet Minh infantry shouting 'Tien-Lên' on to the parapets, covered with leaves and other foliage beneath camouflage netting, using the grenade and bayonet with customary enjoyment. Under their brusque and professional assault, Nghia Lo resisted for no more than a day. Air support on 18 October arrived in time only to watch the garrison limping to captivity with their hands up, dead and wounded on the ground.

312 Division, which had splashed across the Red River with 308 on 11 October, reached the post of Tu-Lê, to the north-west of Nghia Lo, on 17 October. In a plain four miles long, surrounded by hills, Tu-Lê was only a lightly fortified spire and bell-tower on a low eminence, defended by the Sixth Colonial Parachute Battalion under Major Bigeard. His battalion had been flown in under instructions to hold Tu-Lê until the other posts in the T'ai country had withdrawn to greater security south of the Black River, before 308, 312 and 316 Divisions reached and destroyed them. General Salan's staff at Hanoi did not imagine that these three Viet Minh divisions could be successfully opposed *sur place* by the remaining French posts, and assumed that Bigeard's paratroops had no role other than to draw the enemy's strength from the departing French units. The 6th Parachute Battalion was to be a chopping block. One T'ai

Montagnard and two Moroccan battalions got away in time to Lai Chau and to Na San, where they were reorganized by the French in quasi-divisional strength.

Bigeard and his men at Tu-Lê could hear the battle at Nghia Lo. They defended their position for three days, and for twenty-four hours after the high command told them to evacuate, holding out partly in an attempt to save a nearby rifle company struggling to reach them. On 20 October they left for the Black River, leaving their dead and over 100 wounded, of whom only four lived through the horror of Viet Minh prisoner-of-war camps and those four had twenty-two months to wait for liberation. The battalion could do no other. Either Giap would bypass Tu-Lê, or he would destroy the 6 Parachute. In the heat and humidity, carrying their weapons, equipment and the wounded in loads weighing 200 pounds, they moved up and over the steep Meo hills and down again, hearts beating, covered in sweat. Just when they thought that they were safe, their rear companies were caught and eliminated in a massive ambush mounted by 312 Division with automatic weapons of every kind. The Viet Minh had balanced French vulnerability on the march against relative French strength. Guns in fixed positions won the day.

Bigeard, in order to safeguard his own and the other battalions, had to order another unit at the little post of Muong Chen to hold for three hours until reinforcements could arrive to save the garrisons moving westward to the Black River. The log bunkers here were protected only by sharpened bamboo. The compound contained eighty T'ai troops and four French NCOs. When the paras left that evening, the sergeants and their men did what little they could by digging deeper to prepare for the overwhelming attack they knew would follow. By ten o'clock that night, the blockhouse had been taken by Viet Minh grenadiers, many of whom had been killed, but Muong-Chen still endured, almost submerged under the weight of enemy bodies on top of the automatic rifle emplacements and communication trenches. The wire and the bamboo had gone. The ammunition was exhausted.

Sergeant-Major Peyrol led a break-out (the 'three hours' had long elapsed) with his three NCOs and the forty T'ais left. Pursued by the Viet Minh, they ate roots when they could find them, travelling for twelve days, over 200 kilometres of jungle and high mountains, avoiding patrols, traps and ambush. Sixteen of the eighty-four men originally at Muong Chen reached the Black River alive.

The GCMAs also helped to save the garrisons. The Viet Minh impaled their severed heads, with those of Bigeard's men, on bamboo staves along the paths followed by the paratroops. When the T'ai saw the heads, they burned down Vietnamese villages as often as they could find them. The GCMAs were mainly but not exclusively T'ai tribesmen, a race living on both sides of the Laos Vietnam border. The French had organized them and other tribes as stay-behind volunteers operating in absolute clandestinity, sometimes for years at a time, under French NCOs and junior officers. Their bases, usually with a minute 'grass' landing-strip for helicopters and light aircraft, lay in the Tonkin mountains, and the commandos' role was to attack stores, roads, supply dumps and small Viet Minh units. They were lightly rewarded in money and honours. They were too few and too late, although 15,000 of them were enough of a threat for Giap to allocate ten battalions in defence against them.

Two years after the 1954 Agreements, some T'ai, Nung and Muong were still fighting in Tonkin and, five years after Geneva a French Army captain escaped from the Democratic Republic to the South, the Republic of Vietnam.

Salan believed that Giap's divisions, now mostly across the Black River, were not totally self-supporting. Having strengthened the defences of Lai Chau and Na San by airlift, he mounted an attack against the lines of communication running from Yen Bay and other Viet Minh bases on the Red River to the mountains of the northwest. This operation, known as *Lorraine*, was designed to force Giap to withdraw substantive elements of 308, 312 and 316 Divisions from the Black River in order to defend his beleaguered supply points. Giap, in fact, very rarely drew on 'reserves' to support units in difficulty and nearly always left isolated units to defend themselves on their own.

Two armoured land columns, an airborne group, and a *Dinassaut* force on the Red River were to meet at Phu-Doan where a major Viet Minh arms dump had been located. The total French strength for *Lorraine*, including the airborne group, infantry battalions, mobile groups, artillery and so forth, amounted to 30,000 men. Despite the vast weight of the armoured and other vehicles operating on roads and bridges extensively mined and flooded by the Viet Minh, the force took Viet-Tri, Hung Hoa and moved on to Phu To, Ngoc Thap and Route 2. Beach-heads had been secured on the Red River.

Giap, of course, was aware of *Lorraine* or, at least, of its direction and strength. He miscalculated, however, the one element of an advance which could never be precisely measured, its speed. He thought that two regiments (36 and 176) of 308 and 316 Divisions would be enough to hold Salan, if not before Phu-Doan, then at Yen Bay and Thai Nguyen, which held the largest quantities of equipment: he took no action to reduce his operations across the Black River, probably assuming that *Lorraine* would soon lose momentum, and withdrew no troops at all from the mountain zone.

The French planning for Phu-Doan was a complete success, land, air and riverine units meeting at the given time. Only one relatively minor engagement took place, against a road block set by 36 Regiment at the opening to the gorges of Chan-Muong, a valley some three miles long south of Phu-Doan. When Salan's troops arrived at Phu-Doan itself, it was clear that they had indeed gone fast enough to achieve some surprise. The town was full of unguarded weaponry, while further up the road, towards Yen Bay, the crew of a tank in one of the mobile groups came upon abandoned trucks of an unusual design and lettering. *Lorraine* had found the first examples of Soviet equipment, which flowed in immense quantities into the Viet Minh armoury and eventually gave the Viet Minh superiority in land fire-power over the forces of the French Union.

The advance continued almost unopposed for some forty miles in the spitting rain of the *crachin*, through deserted villages and an empty countryside, bypassing Yen Bay. Only the occasional sniper slowed its victorious progress. But the objective of *Lorraine* – to oblige Giap to withdraw his troops from the T'ai hills to the west – had not been achieved and was plainly not going to be. Meanwhile the ground forces and the vital air power needed to stop Giap in the north-west and to maintain French strength in the Delta were being dissipated in an uncontested area of Tonkin.

Giap had resisted the temptation to fight a confrontational main-force battle. Once again he had obliged the French to disperse their effort in vulnerable, secondary engagements. Salan understood that *Lorraine* had not succeeded in its main objective. He knew with hindsight that the operation – so well-planned and executed – was doomed to failure. Yet it is hard to see why the French did not at least take the depots at Thai Nguyen and Yen Bay. Perhaps Salan feared that the casualties that might arise in a collision between his forces and 36 and 176 Regiments would add another negative to unrequited hopes.

On 14 November, Salan ordered a general withdrawal behind the de Lattre line. As Bernard Fall remarked 'The last deep French penetration into Communist territory had ended'. In the approaches to the Chan-Muong gorges, the first Viet Minh ambush was mounted, against an Algerian battalion which instantly called for support from Kergaravat's Mobile Group 4 and from the Foreign Legion Regiment. Between the towering limestone hills, in the wet heat of the valley, the first units reached Thai Binh village in safety.

The verges of the road, however, planted with manioc, had not been cleared. Now from these verges, on both sides, Viet Minh mortars and artillery fired at point-blank range into the mass of armoured and unarmoured vehicles in the middle of the convoy, a concentration covering almost half a mile. A tank blew up and blocked the mobile group behind it. All but the north and south sections of the convoy were caught in the trap.

The yelling infantry of 36 Regiment charged out of the manioc with grenades, knives and machine-guns, killing drivers and passengers; the Viet Minh climbed and swarmed over the vehicles in a repetition of the attacks on the five tanks at Tu-Vu, blowing up as many of the trucks and half-tracks as they could. Hand-to-hand struggles erupted in the roar and glare of the exploding lorries, the assault ending in a massacre, with no mercy accorded the wounded French.

The French Air Force answered Kergaravat's call for support, adding to what was left of his own artillery against the guns and command post at Hill 222. At the same time Colonel Bastiani, commanding Mobile Group 1, directed the *Battalion de Marche Indochinois*, or BMI, a brilliant Cambodian, Vietnamese and French unit, in a counter-attack against the eastern guns. The Legion moved against Hill 222 and other hills near the Chinese fort further to the south-east. The Algerians, under Bastiani's control, and part of Kergaravat's Mobile Group 4 – later to link up with the BMI – took care of the convoy.

None of the Viet Minh artillery, sunk deep in the hills, had been silenced by Kergaravat or the Air Force. It was not until Bastiani's infantry stormed the guns, after a final bayonet charge to the bugle by the BMI that 36 Regiment broke off the action. The French force of 500 men was badly mauled, but it held the hills. Later that evening, however, 36 Regiment got through again with mortars before coming under artillery fire.

The French had lost seven armoured and five other vehicles at Chan-Muong. Fifty soldiers were killed and the Viet Minh murdered a large proportion of the 250 wounded and missing. Further action by 36 Regiment, against a Muong battalion at Phu-Duc, and elsewhere, cost the French another ninety casualties, dead and wounded.

Whilst all this was going on, the reinforced French garrison at Na San to the north-west defeated two major assaults by the full strength of 308 Division and 148 Regiment, which not only failed to breach the inner defences but suffered 1,000 dead and many more wounded. The remainder of that division then withdrew, although leaving behind sufficient force to prevent the Na San garrison in its unknown range of mountains from interfering with Giap's westward drive.

As Robert O'Neill commented, the French drew the conclusion from Na San 'that they could challenge Giap with impunity from a divisional-sized fortress anywhere in Tonkin'. At Dien Bien Phu in April 1954 this doctrine was to have terminal consequences for France's rule in Indochina.

148 Regiment and 316 Division took a T'ai village called Muong Thanh or, in Vietnamese, Dien Bien Phu, 'Seat of the Border Court Prefecture', after it had been evacuated by a Lao infantry battalion. The valley was a centre for the sale of opium grown by Meo in the hills, but French rule had been established there by the great nineteenth-century Consul and explorer, Auguste Pavie, the 'Raffles' of Indochina, who had negotiated a peace with Ho pirates from China.

General Salan, who recognized its importance, ordered a counter-attack for January 1953 to regain the T'ai hills and expel Giap from north-west Tonkin and Laos. Due to the forces tied up by Na San, *Lorraine* and operations in the Delta, the assault did not take place, but the reconquest of Dien Bien Phu continued as a factor in French military thinking under Navarre. Meanwhile, the yellow star and not the tricolor flew over the post. The early part of 1953 saw a stalemate in Indochina. This, coupled with a relative and temporary easing of the Cold War, led to so great an emphasis on the security of the forces of the French Union that any territorial gains were abjured. No one thought about that, however, when Navarre was planning Operation *Castor* and Dien Bien Phu, after Salan's departure.

The short-term lessons of all these operations should have been that France might no longer be able to handle Giap's new strategic grasp and his Army's tactical ability. His north-west campaign had been an undoubted success whereas *Lorraine* had not secured a single stated objective and had, indeed, diverted, with little effect, land and aerial forces more sensibly deployed in the hard-pressed T'ai hills. It had certainly killed a lot of Viet Minh and deprived them of supplies, but the major fire-power battle, longed for by the French Army, had not come about. And 80,000 French troops were now 'locked in' to 2,200 pillboxes in 900 forts behind the de Lattre line: that, certainly, was not what the Marshal had intended.

The time when Armageddon would be fought on Giap's terms was coming closer.

XIII
Back to Laos

Giap had set his face from the beginnning against the kind of confrontation inherent in the Korean War, still more against the positional battles of the First World War, with their emphasis on mass fire-power and enforced absence of mobility. It was unfortunate for the French that these were exactly the battles at which they could excel and which they were fruitlessly to seek until the end. And when they found what they were looking for, they found defeat as well.

Intelligent French soldiers knew, of course, that the war would be lost or won as much off the battlefield as in the field. The nationalist or Bao Dai alternative to Ho Chi Minh had to present a believable programme of independence for Vietnam, the abolition or substantial reduction of the mandarin system, 'land to the tiller', and/or substantial reductions in agricultural rents. Little of that was attempted. The lack of enthusiasm, therefore, for a 'national' Vietnamese Army, political uncertainty in the metropolis, shortage of men and resources in Indochina, the absence – after de Lattre – of a 'great captain', combined with social stagnation to make military victory improbable.

After the Black River campaign of 1952, Giap withdrew to regroup, replace losses of men and equipment, and to plan the assault on Laos. French defences were still weaker in that country and more accessible to Viet Minh attack than in Cambodia or the Bassac. Laos, because it was politically 'favourable' to France, could not be neglected by the high command, still less after the Matignon Treaty or Mutual Defence in 1953. The opportunities for dividing the forces of the French Union once again and concentrating the Viet Minh against a weakened and dispersed enemy in the Red River delta, Laos, Tonkin or the Central Highlands, were strategically evident to Giap. In April 1953 his troops advanced in multi-divisional strength into Laos, through the cruel, empty, inhospitable uplands. The eastern column moved first down the Nam Hou River on Muong Khoua, half the force driving on to meet their central column north of the royal capital, Luang Prabang.

The latter was much like an Austrian mountain village, 'with palms instead of conifers'. It had a post office, closed from twelve to two, a football field, main street and French school, a little palace, several temples with gilded pagodas, and a tiny airfield across a river with no permanent bridge. When one dined with the crown prince, the car could drive up to the door of his village palace in forward gear, but had to reverse out. The women were of a heart-rending beauty; the men wore heavy, highly coloured silk round their waists, above silk stockings; everyone smiled . . .

At this point, the proper strategic course for the French might have been to abandon not only the royal capital at Luang Prabang (allegedy warned of the Viet Minh advance by a sooth sayer 'the Blind Bonze') but also the whole of northern Laos. Giap would have been left to flounder with his armies in huge areas of useless mountain jungle. But the old King insisted on remaining, so politics prevailed, and the French were condemned to further military handcuffs.

International attention was drawn to Laos. Messages were exchanged between world leaders and the beautiful, gay and dignified royal village. The French ordered their northern outposts to hold out, either for specified periods, like Bigeard at Tu-Lê and Peyrol at Muong-Chen in 1952, or to fight to the last man to delay Giap as long as possible.

Muong-Khoua was bound by Colonel Boucher de Crèvecoeur, Commander Laos, to endure *à tout prix* for fourteen days. The position resembled Kohima nine years before in that it had a tiny outlying post, at Sop-Nao, which for six days fought an entire Viet Minh battalion. However, Sop-Nao's commander, Lieutenant Grézy, unlike the equally gallant Young of the Assam Regiment at Kharasom, would lead his little garrison by jungle path and river canoe to 'safety' at Muong-Khoua. Captain Teullier commanding, Grézy, a few French sergeants, and three hundred *Chasseurs Laotiens* were there left to face a Viet Minh infantry battalion, a mortar company and other parts of 316 Division.

Fourteen days later – the period Teuiller had been asked to hold – a Legion of Honour for himself and several Croix de Guerre for his men were dropped by parachute on the pretty little fortified village among its green trees and little hillocks. His only armament, other than rifles, were five mortars and two machine-guns. Under continual mortar fire and infantry rushes ('*Tiên-Lên, Tiên-Lên*'), 910

Battalion crouching forward in the charge, bayonets fixed and horizontal, the Lao held the wire, trenches, bunkers and fort *for thirty-six days*, losing men but inflicting heavy casualties on the Viet Minh. Only then did cannon and heavier mortars, followed by no less than seven human-wave assaults in the foul white fog of the *crachin* finish off – in rubble and hand-to-hand battles – the brave Lao recruits and their French leaders. Two sergeants and two Lao infantrymen were the only survivors, struggling into the larger post at Phong Saly a week later, having travelled without food, compass or machete across fifty miles of montainous jungle, one of them on a pony. Muong-Khoua had fought, literally, to the last round.

Before and during these assaults, the other half of Giap's eastern column – six Battalions – had moved toward Luang Prabang, manned by one French and three Lao battalions. After meeting the central column, the latter then altered course for the south-east, heading towards Sam Neua, where one Lao battalion originally stood. The western or left column had recently passed through Xieng Khouang, where another Lao battalion had been based, *en route* for the Plain of Jars – with its prehistoric urns, its surroundings somewhat resembling Salisbury Plain. This had been chosen by Boucher de Crèvecoeur as the barrier to Vientiane, the small administrative capital defended from the Luang Prabang and Xieng Khouang roads by up to four battalions. Giap's centre force then moved on from Sam Neua and, united with the western battalions, began to invest and encircle with fifteen battalions the Plain of Jars and its camp of some seven battalions. The Viet Minh in north-west Vietnam were now almost linked to their troops in Sam Neua and Phong Saly in Laos.

The French in Saigon had always expressed confidence to the few Western embassies there that Giap would not take Laos, at least on this occasion. Few believed them. But while the garrison of Muong-Khoua was dying under shell, mortar and bayonet attacks, the Viet Minh had already begun to withdraw, leaving Sam Neua on 13 May. On 17 May, the day the heroic fortress of Muong-Khoua fell, the French were only fifty miles away.

Giap had brought elements of three, even four, divisions 130 miles from Vietnam into Laos. His communications were stretched beyond the needs of his present purposes, which included armed reconnaissance rather than immediate conquest. The monsoon, although late, was imminent. It may also be, as the French believed, that various operations of theirs – a raid on Hoa Binh, sorties from Na San, an attack on the Hautes Alpes in the southern part of the Delta, and a 'feint' amphibious operation – contributed to his 'retreat'.

But his withdrawal was no defeat. His advance had coincided with the Viet Minh establishing the Pathet Lao, the 'Free Laos' government-in-exile under Vietnamese control. Giap had shown the French and the Lao that his reach was as long as his grasp. He had left the high command in ignorance of his future intentions, obliging them to spread their efforts throughout Tonkin, if not most of Vietnam and Laos. He had radically impressed the city-dwellers. He now had time to plan, organize and prepare for the next assaults. By depriving the Red River delta of French troops, he had made solid military progress there with regional and independent regiments, keeping his main force intact. At all events, by November 1953 the Vietnamese accepted the advice of their Chinese adviser, General Wei Guo Quing, to revert to concentrating on Lai Chau in the north-west and, then, on Laos.

Above all, Giap had deprived the French of a little more confidence. No one, except General Alessandri, now thought of recapturing the central redoubt in the Viet Bac, that area of administration, command and military build-up between the northern borders of the Delta and the Chinese frontier. Here were the head and the body of the octopus: attacks on the Viet Minh in the Delta were attacks on the tentacles only. In order to defeat the Viet Minh, the French needed back Langson, Cao Bay, Viet Trui, Yen Bay, Lao Kay, Viet Tri, Tuyen Quang, Clear River. They also needed fifty-six Vietnamese battalions by 1953 and sixty more by 1954. Eight 'local' divisions were not enough to launch the Expeditionary Corps at the octopus's head, let alone to meet Minister Letourneau's assurance of a French withdrawal by 1955.

Giap remembered the words of Marshal Tran Hung Dao, alone in defeating the Mongol commanders almost 700 years before: 'The enemy must fight his battle far from his home base for a long time . . . We must further weaken him by drawing him into protracted campaigns. Once his initial dash is broken, it will be easier to destroy him.' Because circumstances compelled it, Giap was a master of flexibility.

This flexibility may have been shaken by the airborne landing in 1953 of a three-battalion French paratroop group and a mobile group at Langson, the site of France's 'shame' during the battles under General Carpentier and Colonel Constans for the China gate in 1950. Here, in belated revenge, 5,000 tons of priceless petrol, oil and lubricants (POL), arms and ammunition were destroyed, with few casualties to the attackers, most of whom got back safely to Hanoi after a difficult escape.

In August 1953, furthermore, the French conducted a successful deception operation which cleared Na San – where so many Viet Minh had been killed and wounded during Operation *Lorraine* – of 10,000 French troops under imminent dry-season threat. (The post had immobilized French fighting men without diverting Viet Minh strength.) The garrison commander sent an *en clair* signal, intercepted by Giap's wireless services, urgently appealing for reinforcements. When French aircraft landed at Na San, they indeed brought extra paratroopers, but departed carrying far more, including, at the end, the 'extra' paratroopers. Na San was thus evacuated as the French had planned, without Viet Minh interference.

Giap commented falsely that 'there were not many troops stationed at Na San and the time did not coincide with that of our major operations. We considered that if Navarre evacuated the garrison, well, that suited us fine.' In another statement, he claimed that the losses at Langson were insignificant, and denigrated the withdrawal from Na San as French military flight.

Both of these operations were a consequence of the plan devised by Salan's successor, General Henri Navarre, who arrived in Indochina as commander-in-chief in May 1953. Also on Navarre's early watch, the French mounted a large amphibious land airborne operation against a damaging position on the coast of Annam between Huë and Quang Tri. The target was the 'Street without Joy' where beneath groups of villages underground facilities, including trenches, tunnels and supply dumps, only thirty yards deep were strung out for twenty miles along Route 1. The 'street', in its horrid setting of bamboo, swamp, paddi, quicksand and bog, had been the base for a long series of murderous ambushes against military convoys mounted by 95 Regiment from this refuge behind French lines.

The expedition mustered thirty battalions, including infantry, armour, artillery, paratroops and sappers, sixty aircraft, landing ships (Crabs and Alligators inshore) – a force comparable to those seen in opposed landings in Europe, and even MacArthur's Pacific operations. Although its strength was much greater than the Viet Minh, it took, as well as gave, casualties. The Moroccans, in particular, were killed or wounded by machine-gun fire. The Vietnamese parachutists were so light that they were literally blown sideways in the strong winds: some fell in the sea, some into Viet Minh lines, some were dragged at speed over rough territory.

Viet Minh intelligence was, as usual, better than French. The terrain slowed the vehicles, bogging them down in swamp and sand dunes, to an advance of no more than one mile an hour. The ratio in favour of the attackers was not great enough, so battalions were asked to cover a front of 3,000 yards each instead of 1,500. The defenders were often able to slip through the cordon which, because of the slow advance, did not constrict fast enough.

Nevertheless, 95 Regiment was driven out after two days, they and their local helpers losing some 200 dead and 300 prisoners. The French and Vietnamese took over, repairing the infrastructure – roads, bridges and so on – and destroying the underground fortifications.

But 95 Regiment came back again a year later, in 1954, just in time for an ambush or two before Geneva, on the Street without Joy.

The French, in 1953, probably had about ninety battalions on entirely static duties, keeping communications open in the controlled areas. Thirty had been locked up in Lai Chau, Na-San, the Plain of Jars, with another twenty-five as local reserves. Even the mobile groups were stretched. The high command had just enough troops to preserve the status quo in the Delta, Annam, Cochinchina and Cambodia. They had almost nothing with which to bring the regular Viet Minh Army to battle.

Alessandri's proposal for the recapture of the Viet Bac was the only long-term hope, but lack of will in Paris and Salan's Maginot mentality – perimeter defence and 'strong points' – devoted to the preservation of French lives and forces, had not been encouraging. Anyway, Alessandri needed over 110 battalions, or sixteen divisions – not an enticing requirement in the political atmosphere of the day.

XIV
The Navarre Plan

Giap's new adversary, Henri Eugène Navarre, had no Far-Eastern experience. He had served in French army intelligence from 1937 to 1944, but his career included service in the trenches from 1917 onwards and against rebels in Syria and Morocco thereafter. He commanded the 5th Spahi in Germany, later holding a command in Algeria, a staff job in Germany, command of 5th Armoured Division. He had been most recently chief of staff to the commander of Central Land Forces, NATO. His new appointment had not been sought by him.

He had been widely discussed in the press and elsewhere as 'cold, feline, simultaneously cordial and distant, debonair and icy, clever and ruthless'. Major-General René Cogny, commander of the Tonkin theatre, described him as 'air-conditioned, the man who served in intelligence and whose reasoning finally (becomes) crooked because he must deal with so many crooked people', a romantic picture of the intelligence community. There was no doubt, however, of his ambition.

Although Viet Minh intelligence operated brilliantly at a tactical level, it is unlikely that Giap would have secured from his enemy the actual Navarre plan. This was presented by the general in July 1953 to his superiors in Paris, after some weeks touring his command, often under anti-aircraft fire, visiting dangerous and distant posts not hitherto reached by any commander-in-chief. His audiences in Paris were the Joint Chiefs of Staff under Marshal Juin, and then the National Defence Committee, which included the Joint Chiefs, the President, Prime Minister, Foreign, Finance, Interior, Defence, Indochina and Overseas Ministers of France.

The plan did not apparently refer to Dien Bien Phu or other detailed projects, except in glancing terms. It involved the accelerated creation of an indigenous national Vietnamese Army, a reserve in the Delta, more mobile groups for the Expeditionary Corps, a major action to expel the Viet Minh from the Southern Highlands, the prevention of major Viet Minh offensives, presumably in the north-west towards Laos, and preparation for a major

French offensive and main-force battle to destroy Giap's rice supplies and his reserves. Navarre sought ten more battalions from the metropolis. Juin warned him that not all his demands could be met.

After Dien Bien Phu, Navarre insisted that he had not, as Prime Minister Laniel claimed, been instructed in Paris that Laos should be abandoned if necessary. (He was rightly convinced that the Viet Minh, through their reversion to a major movement against Lai Chau, were building up in Tonkin in order to thrust into that country.) The transcript of the meeting, which Navarre believed could have been falsified, shows that he had. General Catroux, whose commission investigated the loss of Dien Bien Phu, confirmed, however, that the formal instruction did not reach the commander-in-chief until fourteen days after French paratroops had actually taken the post.

The point is, of course, that if the defence of Laos had not been a requirement, the occupation of Dien Bien Phu by the French would not have been necessary either. Navarre's conviction that no decision had been taken to abandon Laos was further strengthened by the Matignon Agreement in October 1953, which reaffirmed the independence of Laos and inferred a French obligation to defend it. And Navarre believed that only direct intervention, not an attack on Giap's supply lines and bases, would save Laos.

At all events, on 25 July, Navarre's staff issued a directive for the reoccupation of Dien Bien Phu, a move already suggested on 16 June by Brigadier, later Major-General, René Cogny, the new commander of the northern region, formerly commanding the *2me Division de Marche de Tonkin*. Cogny was a huge man, educated at the Ecole Polytechnique, a graduate in political science and holder of a doctorate in Law – qualifications 'moonlighted' while ostensibly studying extra engineering on army time and money; like his former superior, de Lattre, he was explosive, vengeful and 'sensitive' to rebuke or slight.

Navarre, to whom unnamed officers after the defeat sent a loaded pistol in an enamelled box, quarrelled violently with Cogny over the subsequent years. Ultimately, they went to court.

Cogny saw Dien Bien Phu only as a *môle d'ammarrage* ('mooring point') for T'ai and other general service GCMAs and guerrillas operating against Viet Minh columns. He insisted in a letter to Navarre that it was *not* a major rice supply area. He added that Giap could bypass it as easily as he had bypassed other strong points. ('In this kind of country, you can't interdict a road. This is a European notion without value here.') The proposed operation would immobilize three French regimental combat teams needed to resist the grave threat in the Red River delta. Navarre, persuaded by Colonel Louis Berteil – now his chief of staff but formerly commander of the Na-San base which had 'defeated' the Viet Minh – of the virtues of the *base aero-terrestre*, believed differently.

The commander-in-chief's view of the usefulness of Dien Bien Phu was as an air-supplied 'hedgehog' from which the enemy could be attacked on a scale sufficient to cause him substantially to disperse his forces, and thus delay if not halt the drive for Laos. He saw the base, therefore, as a 'fortified airhead' which, supported by the Air Force, could also endure a siege by the two light divisions with minimal artillery considered to be the most that Giap could bring to bear. His general view superseded that of Cogny's 'mooring point'.

Cogny certainly agreed, nevertheless, with the evacuation of Na-San, the daring raid on Langson and the amphibious operation against the Street without Joy, all described in the preceding chapter, and all envisaged under the Navarre plan. (Unfortunately, a key action in the Delta against 320 Division under Van Tien Dung showed the PAVN to be the equal, if not the superior, of the Franco-Vietnamese force.) What Cogny feared was that Dien Bien Phu, under siege by forces he thought likely to be superior, would be unsuitable for the safe and unhampered launch of substantial or even guerrilla attacks against the Viet Minh.

The overriding argument for Navarre lay in his belief that the location and armament of the base would prevent Giap from seizing his main targets in Laos before the monsoon and the inevitable Viet Minh withdrawal during the rainy season.

Colonel Jean-Louis Nicot and Brigadier Jean Dechaux, commanding Air Transport and the Northern Indochina Air Force respectively, raised their own objections on various grounds: distance, weather, anti-aircraft and the condition of the air fleet. In his second letter to the commander-in-chief – a more conciliatory communication – Cogny asked for more troops and aircraft to compensate for units which would have to leave the Delta to reinforce the five or six battalions planned for Dien Bien Phu. On 11 and 12 November, however, he gave his orders to the commanders, emphasizing the 'mooring point' concept to Brigadier Jean Gilles commanding the paras, 'excluding any system designed to provide a belt of strong-points for the airfield'. He also warned Lieutenant-Colonel Trancart at Lai Chau of the evacuation of that base and the transfer of the capital of the T'ai Federation from Lai Chau to Dien Bien Phu.

On 14 November, General Navarre issued his main orders to Cogny, and to Boucher de Crèvecoeur still commanding in Laos. Dien Bien Phu was described therein as an 'air-land base' covering T'ai territory in Tonkin, linked to the French Army in Laos and supporting Lai Chau until the latter's evacuation. Two commanders, not one, were thus to direct the battle, a matter for subsequent complaint by General Cogny.

When Monsieur Marc Jacquet, the secretary of state for Associated States (Indochina) Affairs, arrived in Saigon next day, he had not even heard of the directive recommending that 'no obligation be put upon Navarre to defend Laos', which, as we have seen, did not in fact reach the commander-in-chief until 4th December. Jacquet therefore saw no reason to report a purely military decision to his government. That day the French received intelligence that Dien Bien Phu was held by 148 Regiment and that 316 Division, with its T'ai regiments, was moving westward, but Navarre did not recognize its importance.

Lieutenant-General Pierre Bodet had said that, if the weather were unfavourable, 'Dien Bien Phu would never take place'. Unfortunately, on the morning of the landing, 20 November, the weather was relatively fine, which prompted Marcel Bigeard to say much later, on his release from a Viet Minh prison, 'Oh, why did it not rain that day?'

The 6th Colonial Parachute Battalion (6 BPC) under Bigeard and the 2nd Battalion of the 1st Parachute Light Infantry (II/I RCP) under Major Jean Bréchignac were the first to load, with sappers and an artillery battery. (6 BPC, it will be remembered, had fought at Tu-Lê, and II 1 RCP at the Street without Joy). Six hundred out of 1,487 men were Vietnamese, and BPC, the next battalion in, had 411.

The landings were supported by B-26s and, although opposed by Viet Minh regulars with mortars in house-to-house fighting, resulted in only fourteen French dead against 110 Viet Minh. Brigadier Jean Gilles, commander of Airborne Forces, who looked like a less self-questioning Norman Wisdom, landed next day, with 8 BPC, two bulldozers, one of which buried itself in the paddi, and the first air freight. Colonel Dominique Bastiani – last seen in *Lorraine* – then flew in to take over from Gilles, accompanied by the 5th Vietnamese Parachute Battalion and a woman called Brigitte Friang, a reporter and trained parachutist of skill and gallantry. Operation *Castor* had brought a total of six infantry/paratroop battalions, two artillery batteries, sappers and mortars.

Seven hundred men of the 1st T'ai Partisan Mobile Group had evacuated Lai Chau on 13 November, moving through the jungle on mountain ponies in the direction of Dien Bien Phu. They were ambushed frequently by 148 Regiment, but fought them off ably and insistently, with rifle, machine-gun and mortar fire. The Group, wearing slouch hats and bearing the tricolor and T'ai federation banner, rode on their ponies into Dien Bien Phu between a guard of honour from the II/1 RCP, which had escorted them from an earlier rendez-vous.

On 22 November, Major-General Cogny, with his blue eyes and great height, limping from old wounds, inflicted by the Gestapo, visited Dien Bien Phu. He was the first of many: Navarre; French ministers and senior officers; American generals: Malcolm McDonald, Commissioner-General for South-east Asia and son of a prime minister; British soldiers; Graham Greene – all came to see the raree-show. General Blanc, Chief of Staff of the French Army, told René Pleven and Pierre de Chevigné in private that the monsoon could render the base useless as a site for the destruction of Giap's main force. None of the others, including Greene, expressed anything other than admiration.

Cogny's orders of 30 November reflected the news about 316 Division and the possibility of a major assault. (Navarre did not question the viability of the base in these new circumstances, nor thought of reinforcing it to a practical fifty-battalion strength, still less of abandoning it). His directive demanded the withdrawal of the rest of the Lai Chau garrison; 'free usage of the airfield'; and strike operations to the north-east, to be conducted by a garrison of only 5,000 men who also had to spend more than half their time digging defences.

The French now learned that elements of Divisions 308, 312 and 351, the heavy (artillery) division, were moving to the north-west. Cogny immediately proposed, and the commander-in-chief instantly rejected, strikes into the Viet Bac from the Delta to stop a potential move against Dien Bien Phu, a sort of emergency version of the

Alessandri plan. (Navarre's staff thought that the Viet Minh's drive in force was against Laos not Dien Bien Phu.) Cogny's concrete suggestion was a raid into the limestone like Valluy's Operation *Lea* in 1947, which so nearly caught Ho and Giap. Alternatives advocated were another Langson-type raid, or a repetition of *Lorraine*. However, the troops required for repeats of *Léa* and *Lorraine* would have been so numerous, and the results so unpredictable, that Navarre's refusal was understandable, if depressing.

In a directive of 3 December, Navarre commented on the news of Giap's divisional moves that they would need six weeks' 'movement', a recce phase of six to ten days, and a battle lasting 'several' days, ending in Viet Minh failure. In fact, the reccee phase lasted a hundred days, and the Battle fifty-five, ending in total success for Giap.

It was certainly true that Cogny's proposals would have involved an enormous diversion, perhaps of thirty thousand men, from the defence of Dien Bien Phu and elsewhere. Yet it is astonishing that Navarre should have persisted in that defence with his (recently increased) strength of only nine battalions against twenty-seven and more Viet Minh battalions, while also implementing Operation *Atlante*, a semi-amphibious *fifty-battalion* operation designed to counter a threat to the Central Highlands. In addition the French had again been provoked into defending Thakkek, Seno, Luang Prabang, Attopeu and the Bolovens in Laos, and a number of objectives in the Red River delta. All these operations drew reserves away from Tonkin and, in particular, from Dien Bien Phu, in far greater number than those urged towards the Viet Bac by Major-General Cogny.

Navarre underestimated the fighting and logistic capabilities of Asian troops, just as Wavell had underestimated the Japanese in 1942. Both their armies suffered in pain and humiliation for their generals' ignorance, but unlike Wavell, Navarre did have intelligence telling him that his resources were wholly insufficient to resist the enemy forces about to overwhelm his regiments.

He also knew that to defend the garrison against its precisely identified assailants would take an airlift of equipment lasting five months. The engineers decided to concentrate, therefore, on barbed wire and on underground materials to protect part of the hospital, the signals room, and the command post: the wire was surmounted in the end by the Viet Minh over their own dead. No sound fortifications remotely defensible against artillery or monsoon were ever constructed.

But even Giap was not completely certain that his staff and soldiers could do everything that would be asked of them, whether in terms of supply or attack against fortified positions.

While he hesitated, the evacuation of Lai Chau, its garrison and attached tribal *maquis* groups, proceeded further, the majority in successful airlifts. Two thousand T'ais and thirty-six of their French leaders, however, had to make their way on foot through sixty miles of jungle. Many T'ai, unable to abandon their homes and families, deserted in whole companies. Others, including women and children, were dogged and massacred by an enemy snapping at their heels, died of thirst and hunger, or simply disappeared into the undergrowth never to be seen again. Under 200 walking T'ai, and only a few of their officers, reached Dien Bien Phu.

Commando missions (Parachute Commando Groups) had little more success in cutting the jungle tracks in the ravines and mountains. The Lao *Chasseurs* and a Moroccan battalion from Laos at least reversed the heroic defeat of May 1953 by taking Muong-Khoua, where they then met a Foreign Legion battalion, sick, starving, and subsisting on opium leaves to quench their thirst. (Brigitte Friang was with the Laos contingent.) Colonel de Castries, the garrison commander of Dien Bien Phu, flew into the jungle in order to be photographed by the world's press shaking hands with the survivors. Many were suffering from typhus, most had lost much weight. Recoilless-rifle and mortar ambushes by the Viet Minh made nonsense of the 'mooring point' theory of raiding forces, which, nevertheless, continued in an unbroken string of failures into March, although with particular courage shown by the Goums.

French tactical intelligence was inadequate. Viet Minh codes were never broken. March discipline, scattering of personal possessions, failure to obliterate traces, etc, were also bad. The Viet Minh adopted absolute clandestinity under Air Force monitoring. For example, if trucks had to bring equipment to an exposed jungle clearing, they would unload just before it and carry the weaponry to fresh lorries, also clear of exposure.

The Viet Minh equalled the Second World War Japanese in their mastery of concealment and underground bunkers. They excelled the Japanese in their use of informants (reporting the commandos' whereabouts), as they gradually tightened the ring round the valley.

In one ambush, a large-scale map of Dien Bien Phu was found on the body of a French officer. The Communist artillery then began to range accurately on the airfield and strong points. Every time the reconnaissance teams broke out, they were caught by entrenched Viet Minh parties in cross-fire. One ambush was mounted by a Viet Minh team wearing captured French uniforms. By 15 February, the garrison had lost 840 private soldiers and over 120 officers and NCOs.

Little or nothing was done to fortify the position as a base of resistance to the coming Communist assault. Even ammunition supplies were not renewed for a whole week 'because of other priorities', at a time when the Viet Minh were at the most vulnerable stage of installing their own guns in the limestone caves. By 13 March Dien Bien Phu was completely overlooked from its surrounding hills by a force of four Viet Minh divisions with full artillery support. Even a break-out by the garrison, had one ever been contemplated, would have resulted in useless sacrifice.

Elsewhere, Marshal Juin commented bitterly, 'the French have had a remarkable success. They have infiltrated the Delta,' referring to the 50–80,0000 Viet Minh operating there. Only three to four main roads were open by day, none at night. For every loyal or even neutral village, three were controlled by the Viet Minh.

The government in Saigon was at odds with itself, not over issues but over privilege, graft, personal jealousies. Bao Dai and his prime minister quarrelled uselessly. Although Ho Chi Minh's overtures for peace were really effective only in Paris, especially with Jacquet, an astute and sympathetic observer asked: 'How can a healthy united Vietnam grow on this bed of corruption, intrigue and dissipation?'

René Pleven said that the questions, in the light of an apparent peace 'initiative' which Ho channelled through the Swedish newspaper *Expressen*, were 'whether the French people were willing to wait for Navarre to succeed', and 'when would the Vietnamese Army be ready to take over responsibility for the war?' The second question was odd, since no one in Saigon contemplated a role other than static defence duties for the national Army over the next five to seven years. The Vietnamese Army (not the French Army of Indochina, which included 50,000 Vietnamese), stood at sixty-two fairly good and fifty-four fairly bad battalions, with nineteen guard battalions. There was a desperate shortage of competent officers, yet Navarre spoke of French military withdrawal by 1955.

The Viet Minh main-force strength included 110 regiments in six divisions plus one heavy division. Giap's forces as a whole totalled 300,000 men, regulars, regional forces and guerrillas.

For their part, the powers sought a negotiated settlement. The Chinese wished to prevent a military succession to France in Indochina by the United States; the Russians probably wanted, by conciliation over Indochina, to scuttle French participation in the European Defence Community. On 25 January 1954 the USA, USSR, Britain and France at Berlin agreed on a five-power conference (including China) to be held in Geneva in April to settle the Indochina and Korea questions. Its result would be conditional on the battle of Dien Bien Phu.

XV
Dien Bien Phu:
20 November 1953 – 26 April 1954

The Australian 'journalist', Wilfred Burchett, said to have brain-washed allied prisoners held by the North Koreans, has described a conversation with Ho Chi Minh in 1954. (It was Burchett who advised the DRV to nominate Harrison Salisbury for the infamous visit of 1967). Ho, Burchett said, turned his khaki solar topi upside-down. The rim of the helmet represented the mountains concealing the Viet Minh divisions. The bowl of the hat held the valley of Dien Bien Phu and the French Expeditionary Corps. 'Like the Germans at Stalingrad, they will never escape,' said Uncle Ho.

With customary imprecision, Burchett claimed that the French had taken Dien Bien Phu in order to attack the Viet Minh from the rear and destroy their headquarters. In fact, the valley was almost as far forward as the Viet Minh could get in Vietnam, while their base and headquarters were in the Viet Bac, hundreds of miles to the east, seldom attacked except by the Air Force. Navarre's main objectives, on the contrary, were the protection of Laos and a pitched battle on his own terms.

Only poor General Alessandri and, later, Cogny advocated ground attack in the far north of Vietnam, between the Delta and the Chinese border, the head of the Viet Minh octopus. As we have seen, Alessandri had admitted that fifty-six Vietnamese battalions would be required for the purpose in 1953, more in 1954, and that 'eight divisions would not be enough to take the essential posts of Langson, Cao Bang, Viet Tri, Yen Bay and Tuyen Guang', lost by Carpentier in 1950. But without those posts, action in the north-west or the Delta would be against the tentacles only.

Vo Nguyen Giap believed that the French reoccupation of the valley on 20 November 1953, with the presumed reseizure of Na-San, Lai Chau and Tuan Giao, was intended to threaten his armies in Laos, to mount an offensive against the Delta, and to oblige the Viet Minh to scatter their forces.

Giap's dilemma had been between concentrating on the Delta, where the French were fairly strong and could reduce his formations, and attacking where the French were most vulnerable, in Laos and the north-west, thus risking Viet Minh defeats in the Delta. In following the Central Committee slogan of 'dynamism and initiative', he chose to risk the Delta to gain the 'vulnerable points'. His aim was to threaten Navarre in so many places that the French would divide and disperse their units to the detriment of the main offensive at Dien Bien Phu. His analysis was that

> The (French) war had no other aim than to occupy our country. The object of the war forced the enemy to scatter his forces . . . a continuous process of dispersal of forces . . . The enemy found himself face to face with a contradiction: without scattering, it was impossible for him to occupy the invaded territories; in scattering his forces, he put himself in difficulties. His scattered forces would fall easy prey to our troops: his mobile forces would be more and more reduced; and the shortage of troops would be all the more acute. On the other hand, if he concentrated in order to move from the defensive position and cope with us with more initiative, the occupation forces would be weakened and it would be difficult for him to hold the invaded territory . . . if the enemy gives up occupied territory, the aim of the war is defeated.

Giap saw Dien Bien Phu as the battlefield where the French, not the Viet Minh, could be defeated in that pitched battle which the French so insistently sought. With Chinese aid and Tonkinese manpower, he would overwhelm with fire-power as well as numbers an enemy that relied on fire-power and assumed the Viet Minh could not match it. By now Giap had created the roads and transport to bring both the supplies and the artillery which would prevail, a fact of which Navarre was not fully aware until too late.

This time, therefore, Giap could bring about the third phase, 'the final offensive', which in 1951 against de Lattre had led to disaster. But this time in 1953, French battalions had been diverted to Operation *Atlante* on the south coast of Annam, from which the Viet Minh simply withdrew; more had to be deployed in the western highlands after Kontum had fallen; Giap also attacked against Phong Saly and Luang Prabang, drawing French troops from support positions for Dien Bien Phu; many smaller attacks were launched in the Delta and, as earlier described, southern and central Laos came under assault.

Navarre's reserves for Dien Bien Phu were thus brilliantly diminished at a time when Giap, as both commander-in-chief and a leader of the Democratic Republic, knew that he must achieve victory by the date of the Geneva Conference, May 1954 at the latest.

'Strongly fortified entrenched camps,' of which Hoa Binh, Na-San and Pleiku were examples, and Dien Bien Phu the strongest, were a new concept for the Viet Minh, developed by the French, according to Giap, to match the new, more conventional deployment of the People's Army. Hitherto Giap had preferred not to attack the camps directly, but to pin down their garrisons. But Dien Bien Phu was the foundation of the Navarre plan. The Viet Minh held the surrounding mountains of this lonely, isolated valley, to which the French had access only by air. Supply for the Viet Minh, on the other hand, could be maintained by land from a support base which had vastly increased. First-class regular troops could be deployed and concentrated.

Giap decided on a battle of annihilation of the whole enemy force by direct assault coupled with diversions elsewhere, including those referred to above, in the North, in central and South Vietnam, and in Laos.

Because of the PAVN's experiences against defended targets, the commander-in-chief decided not to 'strike swiftly and win swiftly' by mounting a major offensive with fresh troops, cutting Dien Bien Phu into segments, and wiping out the enemy. The advantage of speed, and the avoidance of supply and reinforcement problems were outweighed by uncertainty of victory. Instead, Giap followed the principle of 'striking and advancing surely – the fundamental principle of revolutionary war: strike to win, strike only when success is certain; if it is not, then don't strike'.

On 26 December, with most of his troops in place, Giap made 'the most important military decision' of his life: he changed the method from a mass attack against the whole position to piecemeal attacks, segment by segment. The main onslaught was to begin on 13 March.

Not all his officers or men, either then or during the battle, were convinced. On 23 April, Giap admitted there had been 'negative rightist tendencies, the fear of having many killed, the fear of suffering casualties, of facing fatigue, difficulties, privation'. By 27 April many unit commanders were known to have been 'doubtful' – about US air intervention, French ability to reorganize the Delta, the stubborn gallantry of the Army of Indochina. They feared a long campaign, supply difficulties, the effects of the monsoon, consolidation of the French defence, exhaustion. Indeed, in the end, 5 per cent or less of the Expeditionary Force held 60 per cent of the Viet Minh main battle force, five divisions, for nearly six months.

Colonel Christian Marie Ferdinand de la Croix de Castries, an aristocrat whose forebears included a marshal, nine generals, an admiral and four lieutenant-governors, had joined the Army from the ranks as a cavalryman, and later served under General Navarre as a sergeant and as an officer in the Spahis. He was a horseman, pilot, gambler and insatiable *coureur de femmes*, whose notorious glamour is not reflected in such pictures as exist. It was his record in the Delta in command of mobile armour that led Navarre to name him commander of the Dien Bien Phu garrison.

Commanding the Airborne Forces was Lieutenant-Colonel Pierre Langlais, a hard drinking Celt who had served in the Camel Corps before several tours in Indochina, where he qualified as a paratrooper. The two men, incorrigible *flâneur* and serious professional, never lost their mutual professional regard even in the worst of times.

Despite endless reverses in mobile operations outside the perimeter, de Castries asked Cogny on 13 December for 'a minimum of twelve battalions to control a battlefield of forty square miles, and to launch raids and reconnaissances with effectives of three battalions'. He was refused.

In January, the French first came upon the extraordinary Viet Minh bunkers, with their tiny firing slits, sunk into the ground. It was at that time also that the French map was found which 'gave' the Viet Minh all existing French positions in the valley; thereafter they were open to Giap's well-positioned 105 and 75mm guns. In late January Viet Minh Division 308 left for Laos, leaving 'only' 304 and 316 Divisions to hold the ring around Dien Bien Phu. Navarre made the incorrect assumption that the garrison was about to be bypassed, and proposed reducing it to six battalions. Cogny rejected this suggestion, but his subordinates had already failed in their offensives outside the garrison area, and would not succeed in driving the Viet Minh off the northern hills from which the French battalions and airfield were overlooked.

As noted earlier, French artillery fire had to be curtailed because of consumption in Laos, thereby ensuring that Giap could install his

guns unhindered in almost invunerable ports, redoubts and revetments in the mountain jungle commanding the flimsy strong-points
below. The French had already lost thirty-two officers, ninety-six
NCOs and 830 men, 10 per cent of all units, losses too great for the
small gains accomplished, while Dien Bien Phu was now encircled
by 304, 308, 312 and 316 Divisions and much of 351 Heavy Division.
The garrison had lost all purpose in its declared aim of stopping
Giap's progress to Laos, but the staff at Hanoi believed that a
withdrawal, however desirable, could now turn into hopeless
retreat.

The fortress, nevertheless, could have been evacuated, as could
the other strong-points in the earlier Viet Minh offensives against
Laos. The French with their superior mobility could have moved in
accordance with Alessandri's and Cogny's proposals against the
'strong rear' of Giap's Army in its Viet Bac bases, leaving the best
Viet Minh divisions stranded in the military vacuum of the Lao and
Tonkinese mountains.

Dates suitable for such a contingency might have been mid-
December, before 316 Division had actually arrived, or in late
January 1954 before 308 Division returned from Laos and before all
of 304 Division joined the siege. The position should certainly have
been abandoned before the siting of thirty-six 75 mm, forty-eight
100 mm, forty-eight 120 mm, forty-eight 75 mm recoilless guns and
thirty-six anti-aircraft guns, nearly all inaccessible to counter-fire
from air or ground. Against them, the French only mounted sixty
guns above 57 mm, largely unprotected. French air power could not
cut this deficit, particularly after Giap's artillery had destroyed Dien
Bien Phu airfield; from then on his flak rendered air drops pitifully
inefficient.

The high command had not foreseen their enemy's ability to bring
in guns and ammunition along primitive jungle tracks, through the
rains, in Russian trucks, on thousands of bicycles, in innumerable
sampans and bamboo rafts, with convoys of pack horses and
hundreds of thousands of porters. Giap claimed that in order to
bring one kilo of supplies to the troops at Dien Bien Phu, each
porter required twenty-one kilos to sustain him. They were attacked
by B-52s, beset by malarial mosquitoes and the monsoon as they
built shelters and bridges, cutting their way through mountain
and forest. When the French did understand what a dedicated
fierce, indomitable race they were fighting, their Air Force

had an interdiction strength of only seventy-five aircraft.

In 1966, the USAF could put 200 aircraft into one single raid on the Democratic Republic of Vietnam (DRV).

On 13 March the Viet Minh had a total of nearly 50,000 fighting men at Dien Bien Phu and 31,000 support troops, with 23,000 more further back. The French garrison numbered only 13,000 of whom less than 7,000 were combatant. Even these troops varied in capability from the Foreign Legion, through uneven Algerian and Moroccan battalions, to the T'ai battalions, their stamina often quite dissipated.

That day the airfield came under fire from 75 mm and 105 mm Viet Minh artillery. Fighter bomber and reconnaissance aircraft were destroyed on the ground, and it was clear that enemy artillery could not now be matched by locally based air power. In the evening the last Dakota landed. In December the garrison's artillery commander, Colonel Piroth, had told Navarre, '*Mon général*, no Viet Minh cannon will be able to fire three rounds before being destroyed by my artillery.' On 15 March professional shame drove this one-armed officer to pull the pin from a grenade with his teeth and hold it until death against his chest.

De Castries' battle plan was based on a connected group of five 'centres of resistance', on the concentration at every point of four fifths of available fire power, and on counter-attacks led by 2nd Airborne Battle Group (2 GAP) under Langlais. Within these 'centres' were his strongpoints, most of which bore the names of women, allegedly his mistresses, including the wives of brother officers: Gabrielle, Béatrice, Françoise, Claudine, Dominique, Eliane Lily, Juno, Huguette and, far to the south, Isabelle. One of his comrades commented, however, that 'even de Castries wasn't *that* strong'!

Béatrice was manned by Colonel Gaucher's Mobile Group 9, which included part of the legendary and unbeaten 13th Foreign Legion Half-Brigade of Bir-Hakeim, with Algerian and Moroccan riflemen. Béatrice and Gabrielle had been shelled for over a week and, on 13 March, Viet Minh approach trenches were within yards of both positions, while artillery continued to bombard Béatrice. By 9 p.m. Mobile Group 9 reported that the Viet Minh in human wave assaults had broken through the wire. 'The Viet are all over the place.' At 2 a.m. the strong-point had fallen, albeit with severe losses to three battalions of Viet Minh. De Castries did not counter-attack, preferring to have troops available for Gabrielle. At Béatrice all officers, including Colonel Gaucher had been killed or severely wounded, with 300 Legionnaires dead.

On 14 March the 5th Vietnamese Parachute Battalion (BPVN) was successfully dropped. The battalion regrouped on Eliane. At Gabrielle, the bombardment continued: the Viet Minh infantry of 308 Division held an eight to one superiority over the French and Algerian riflemen. Algerian prisoners were marched out over the corpses of Communist soldiers hanging on the barbed wire. Over one such, still living, with his bloody guts hanging out, a Viet Minh officer waved on the prisoners: 'Step on him. He has done his duty for the People's Army.' Counter-attack by a company of the Legion, with tanks and the Vietnamese of the 5th BPVN, failed. The latter were severely punished, including degradation to coolie labour, for alleged cowardice. Five hundred Algerians, of whom seventy were killed, were missing when Gabrielle fell, taking about 2,500 Viet Minh dead with them. At Anne-Marie a company of T'ai riflemen deserted, disappearing to their tribal homes or joining the many other 'rats of the Nam Yun', *embusqués* hiding in the banks of that river.

On 27 March Bigeard led 6 and 8 BPC in an extremely effective strike against Viet Minh anti-aircraft positions, which greatly, if temporarily, helped the air supply crews.

Cogny chose this moment to tell Navarre that disaster at Dien Bien Phu might be inevitable. (He had already referred to Navarre's choice of the valley as 'a mouse-trap'.) Were this to be so, he would need three mobile groups within eight days to defend the Delta. Cogny proposed that Navarre should forthwith cancel *Atlante*, the southern Annam operation, in order to provide reinforcements for the North. After fifteen days without responding, the commander-in-chief rejected his subordinate's suggestion. But Cogny did not then land at Dien Bien Phu as he had considered doing, like de Lattre at Vinh Yen, and direct the battle himself.

Viet Minh entrenching, so successful at Béatrice and Gabrielle and Giap's main method of approach, could now be heard at the Eliane, Dominique and Claudine posts, and was also beginning to cut off Isabelle in the south. Giap had started to throttle Dien Bien Phu. The airfield remained unusable and the daily air drops of supplies and arms were inadequate, too high a proportion falling behind Viet Minh lines. De Castries unsuccessfully sought General Cogny's permission for Lieutenant-Colonel Lalande to break out to Laos from Isabelle in Operation *Albatross*, presuming the 'early fall of Dien Bien Phu itself'.

The battle for the Five Hills (strongpoints Dominique 1 and 2, Eliane 1, 2 and 4) then started. 316 Division was assaulting Algerians, Moroccans and T'ai in bloody hand-to-hand combat; counter-attacks were led by the great Major Bigeard, deploying his own 6 Colonial Parachute (BEP) and Tourret's 8 Parachute Assault, with the Vietnamese parachutists of 5 BPVN bravely redeeming their failure of 14 March.

Giap's tactics, as described in his field manual, had now moved from human wave to penetration in concentrated assault waves at the point of effort, 'holding that penetration to the bitter end', a means he pursued with maximum thrust throughout the battle. There was a relative lull between 14 and 26 March, and on 29 March the French were astonished to see thousands of torches, held by porters or soldiers, moving 'like glow-worms' eastward out of the valley under the red glare of napalm flares in the forest. Major Vadot, one of Langlais' officers, believed that the enemy were leaving the field: 'They are stealing our battle from us.'

On 31 March, because Cogny had not yet reinforced the garrison with the balance of Bréchignac's 2nd Battalion of the 1st Parachute Light Infantry Regiment (II 1 RCP), or the 2nd BEP, or the 1st Colonial Parachute Battalion (1 BPC) under Bazin de Bezon, no reserves of men and only one day's ammunition existed at Dien Bien Phu. Langlais and his paratroop 'mafia' had now taken effective command from de Castries, who had not collapsed but could not, it seemed, handle a defensive role and was, in his mind, seeking an honourable defeat. 'It was as if a spring had broken inside him.' The paratroopers rejected such notions. But their relations with him then, in the Viet Minh prisons, and afterwards, remained correct and courteous, while all communications during the battle continued to be signed by de Castries himself.

That evening, the garrison learned that General Giap had arrived in the valley to take direct command from General Hoang Van Thai. His command post was beneath a waterfall, among huge rocks, Wagnerian. He was allegedly accompanied by a Chinese military adviser, General Li Cheng Hu. In 1993 the *Chinese People's Daily* in Peking claimed that it was the Chinese General Wei Guo Quing, commander of the Chinese military advisory group, who had masterminded the defeat of the French Army 'through the use of human wave tactics'. Giap's field manual belies this, so the press release was probably provoked by bad Sino-Vietnamese relations. In January 1954 the Chinese instructed Wei Guo Quing: 'While attacking Dien Bien Phu, you should avoid making assaults of equal strength from all directions; rather you need to adopt the strategy of separating and encircling the enemy forces and annihilate them bit by bit' – a strategy accepted and adopted by the Viet Minh high command. Chinese engineers of the Volunteers in Korea had been imported to teach the digging of trenches and tunnels. Chinese experience in Korea of using hidden sites for artillery had been exploited by the Viet Minh. Large quantities of ammunition and equipment were sent from China to the battle, including two Vietnamese battalions trained in China and equipped with 75mm guns and rocket launchers. Much tactical advice was given by Peking via General Wei but it was not always accepted by resentful Vietnamese.

At dawn on 1 April, Bigeard and the 6 BEP held Elaine 7. Lieutenant Lucciani of 1 BEP and assorted troops were on Elaine 2, Tourret on Dominique 3. Huguette 7 was retaken by the 5th Vietnamese Paratroops. Air supply was in dribs and drabs. A Viet Minh deserter told the French, possibly as deception, that the Viet Minh would give up the struggle if they had failed to defeat the French by 15 April. Langlais had to abandon Huguette 7. The last reserves were committed on Eliane 2. On 3 April, twelve Legionnaires deserted, something hitherto unheard of among those heroes.

The battle continued to see-saw throughout April. Viet Minh trenches came yet closer in. Some French reinforcements landed but more dropped equipment had to be retrieved, in hideous danger from the enemy. Colonel de Crèvecoeur, still commanding in Laos, was ordered to mount Operation *Condor* as a diversion, moving three battalions from Laos to Dien Bien Phu.

On Eliane 1 on 10 April the Legionnaires marched into battle singing German and French paratroop songs, while the Vietnamese paratroopers sang the only fighting song they knew, the 'Marseillaise', in counter-attacks of astonishing gallantry. The 1st BEP and the Vietnamese held the post for twenty days, almost to the end. Bernard Fall called it the 'French St Crispin's Day'.

Since the start of the siege the French had killed or wounded

10,000 Viet Minh, against Giap's reserve of 25,000. On 11 April Giap gave up frontal attacks in favour of attrition, in particular through trenches, mine galleries and shafts. (Some Viet Minh units had 'mutinied', advancing only under the threat of their own guns from the rear.) These tactics worked, encircling the Huguettes, Lily and Eliane 1, followed by a major attack on Eliane 1 and continued artillery on the hill of Huguette 6. Thirst now became a serious menace for the French.

On 15 April, a French Navy aircraft accidentally dropped maps of all the French positions on to the Viet Minh, together with details of Viet Minh targets. All codes throughout Indochina had to be changed. French decorations for the garrison, including de Castries' stars – Cogny had promoted him to brigadier – fell into the Viet Minh lines. So did more weapons, ammunition and other supplies.

Huguette 6 was evacuated on 17 April, thus helping to bring the Viet Minh's anti-aircraft closer in and to endanger further the path of the French air transports. (Even Bigeard had found Huguette 6 beyond rescue, and the breakout involved heavy losses.) The fight for Huguette 1 then began under Giap's trench strangulation. It was lost by 22 April. The battle for the northern Huguettes ended next day, despite another counter-attack under Bigeard's overall command. The assault had cost the Viet Minh three regiments and the French 500 men. It was now that Giap made his comment, quoted earlier, about rightist tendencies and 'the fear of having many killed, of suffering casualties, of facing fatigue, casualties and privations'.

Far from giving up on April 15, as the deserter had claimed, the Viet Minh then numbered 35,000 infantrymen and 12,000 others, including sappers and gunners, against no more than 5,000 French effectives. Food stocks had been destroyed by Viet Minh artillery. The garrison went on half rations. And despite the efforts of the marvellous Dr Grauwin, the garrison medical officer, gangrene had begun among the hundreds of wounded in his tiny underground hospitals.

The supply position to Dien Bien Phu worsened further on 24 April when US civilian air crews refused to continue flying the C-119 box-cars. Only sixty tons a day were flown in on the next three days, none at all on 28 April. The garrison itself was now reduced to 3,250 infantrymen, many wounded, some of them missing a limb or an eye. Isabelle was reduced to 1,400.

Cogny, while telling Navarre that Dien Bien Phu could last another two or three weeks if reinforced, recommended that, for the time being, only individual volunteers be flown in, battalions to be dropped later. At the same time, he drew attention again to the deterioration in the Delta and to the uselessness of major reinforcement in the context of Dien Bien Phu. In Paris and Geneva, however, Dien Bien Phu was the most important thing of all. But, without the C119s, the valley was 'starving and bleeding to death'. Fifty aircraft were hit and three downed on 26 April. The bomber strength was now only forty-five aircraft. Viet Minh flak had proved more deadly than even German or Korean and Chinese. And all this happened as sixty B29s stood ready in the Philippines, and more than four hundred fighters and bombers waited in US aircraft carriers for a presidential order which never came; only Richard Nixon, then vice-president, recommended bombing.*

---

* Appendix B gives a remarkable description of Giap in his command post at Dien Bien Phu from Huu Mai's *La Dernière Hauteur*. Foreign Languages Publishing House, Hanoi, 1964.

XVI
Dien Bien Phu: 27 April - 8 May 1954

The French appeal for United States air support was greatly discussed in Washington, but did not meet congressional conditions of early independence for Indochina, nor was there allied agreement to USAF deployment. Eden and Churchill refused on the grounds of probable Chinese retaliation, the inevitable requirement for American and allied ground troops, and the certain failure in these circumstances of the Geneva Conference. (The political climate, in particular the recent end of the Korean War, should be recalled.) Precision radar, essential to prevent French as well as Viet Minh obliteration under US bombing, could not be installed in time. The proposal was never put to Congress by President Eisenhower.

It had become evident to General Giap that the dissension, now amounting to hatred, between Navarre and Cogny aided his purposes. Navarre's conviction that Cogny was betraying his own commander-in-chief, Cogny's belief that Navarre was sacrificing good soldiers at Dien Bien Phu and the security of the Delta as well, Navarre's rejection of Cogny's planned offensive against Giap's rear base, all worked for the Viet Minh. So did Cogny's opposition to *Condor*, the relief operation from Laos, and to *Albatross*, the break-out plan from Isabelle: he was always concerned primarily for the Delta and Dien Bien Phu's role in its protection.

From now until the very end, the disparity grew between Viet Minh reinforcements and the pitiful quantities of men and *matériel* dropped to the garrison of which up to a third fell behind enemy lines as the French perimeter shrank. Seven hundred brave volunteer parachutists had come, in 'penny-packets'; all Cogny sent on 3 May was one company of the 1st Colonial Parachute Battalion (BPC), 107 men.

It is therefore extraordinary that, as late as 27 April, Viet Minh morale was so low that Giap was forced to 'launch a campaign for moral mobilization' to correct 'erroneous tendencies affecting Viet Minh tasks'. His casualties had certainly been heavy, and there was the new threat of US intervention. No doubt Giap also took *Condor* seriously, believing furthermore that the continued struggle at Dien

Bien Phu provided time for the French to re-organize the defence of the Delta.

At all events, the garrison not only continued to defend the Huguette, Eliane, Lily, Dominique and Claudine posts, but actually mounted successful aggressive patrols, in which casualties were inflicted, bunkers blown, prisoners captured and positions retaken against odds. The men were still on half rations of rice, and *nuoc-mam*, the Vietnamese fish sauce of pungent odour. The mud in the trenches was one metre deep, soldiers were up to their knees in water for days at a time. The monsoon and the artillery barrage were beginning to collapse the flimsily built fortifications. The noise of the guns and the horror of the cirumstances were reaching the intolerable. After fifty days of fighting, the French combatants numbered no more than 2,900 against over 30,000 under Giap, who had begun the battle with 49,000 combatants and 55,000 'support' troops. The Viet Minh suffered 23,000 casualties by the end.

On 1 May, the doctors in the French aircraft-carrier *Arromanches* grounded that vessel's magnificent squadron because of its total exhaustion. There were now only twenty-eight fighters, twenty-eight B-26 light bombers and five Navy privateer bombers available. Only eight air crew existed for nineteen Cricket reconnaissance aircraft. That day, in Dien Bien Phu, the great Viet Minh artillery barrage began followed by the main infantry assault in two-division strength against the Dominiques and Elianes. The whole of 308 Division assaulted Huguette 5, *manned by only twenty-nine men*. 'Death volunteers', covered like ghosts in white parachutes which concealed heavy explosive, ambulant human bombs, in-filtrated the positions. Throughout the garrison, twenty-eight French were killed on 2 May, 168 wounded and 303 missing, not remotely compensated by the BPC Company dropped early next morning.

The monsoon grew more torrential, affecting the shaky electricity and telephone systems, disintegrating fixed sites, crumbling the dug-outs, flooding the trenches. More and more posts, despite Foreign Legion counter-attacks of the utmost gallantry, were lost. Severely wounded men, swaddled in bandages, returned to their units from Dr Grauwin's trench hospital: 'If we've got to go, we'd rather go with our mates.' Huguette 4 was commanded by an officer who had already been wounded three times, one of his eyes covered by a thick bandage. Isabelle provided good news by the retaking of strong-point Wieme, named after the officer responsible for the epic T'ai march from Lai Chau. Over Dien Bien Phu, 50 per cent of the C-119 drops now reinstituted were irretrievable.

The garrison commander reported to Hanoi. 'No more resources left, extreme fatigue and weariness of all concerned'. Cogny ordered that there should be 'no capitulation nor rout', while leaving the decision on a break-out to de Castries. The latter by this stage had reasserted his authority, visiting each one of his men and 'decorating' the most deserving without the medals which Hanoi had failed to deliver.

Three thousand Viet Minh, supported by howitzers, attacked Lieutenant Lucciani with his eighty men on Huguette 4. The position held for two hours, causing 'confusion and panic' among the Viet Minh and a change of commanders, but a counter-attack with only 100 Moroccans and paratroopers failed. There were now some 1,300 seriously wounded men in Dr Grauwin's care. On 4 May Major Pouget led a company of 8 BPC to Eliane 3 across the open battlefield, taking six hours to cover one mile. On 5 May de Castries told Cogny that Dien Bien Phu would run out of ammunition on 6 May. On that day, the garrison uselessly received the largest drop for three weeks plus 383 men of 1 BPC, of whom 155 were Vietnamese. Attacks on Eliane 3, Huguette 3 and 5 were held, but Viet Minh trenches came ever closer, and the mine on Eliane 2 was ready to be blown. Claudine, Dominique 4, Huguette 2 and 3, Epervier, Lily 1 and 2, Juno, Eliane 2, 3, 4, 10, 11 and 12 were held by units including French and Vietnamese paratroopers, the Legion, White T'ais, Moroccans and mixed groups, with the greatest concentration – 750 paratroops – on the Elianes.

At noon, just after de Castries had telegraphed his thanks to President Eisenhower for his message congratulating the garrison, the horrible blast and scream of Soviet Katyushas terrified the North Africans, destroying depots, bunkers and trenches. At 5.30 p.m. the main artillery barrage began again, eliminating weapons, ammunition and stocks of medicine.

The final infantry attack was mounted against Eliane 2 by a thousand men of 308, the Iron Division. Two hundred of them were destroyed by French howitzers before the Viet Minh counter-bombardment wrecked eight out of nine howitzers on Isabelle, eliminating any hope of defensive fire for Claudine and Huguette. The bearded axe-men sappers of the Legion lost, retook and lost

Claudine 5 again, all wounded or dead. Two regiments of 312 and 316 Divisions attacked thirty Vietnamese parachutists on Eliane 4 and 10. Bigeard's 6 BPC, for its part, died on Eliane 10, under Thomas, Allaire and Le Page. The mine buried in Eliane blew up; Sergeant Chubrier with five men, and Lieutenant Pouget with very few more, thrust back the mass of assaulting Viet Minh, but no reinforcements came. Eliane 3, 11 and 12 all fell. *Albatross*, the break-out, would have led to massacre and was cancelled.

At 9 a.m. on 7 May, the yelling horde submerged Eliane 4. At 10 a.m. de Castries, after giving Cogny his order of battle on the telephone, said, 'We're holding on, tooth, claw and nail.' Cogny replied that the battle 'had to be finished now', but without capitulation or a white flag. The last message from Dien Bien Phu was: 'We're blowing up everything. Adieu.' De Castries' bunker was taken at 5.30 p.m. by General Vuong Thua Vu of 308 Iron Division, de Castries in uniform with medals. Isabelle was blown up that night. One platoon, some tribesmen and a couple of Legionnaires got away. In Saigon, a call-up of 120,000 young Vietnamese brought in only 7,000, of whom 5,000 were 'unfit'.

Giap's proclamation after the battle included the words:

The Dien Bien Phu victory is the most prestigious which our Army has ever achieved . . . we have expanded our zone of resistance and further contributed to the success of land reform . . . This is due to the enlightened guidance of President Ho Chi Minh, of the Central Committee of the Party and of the government. It is due even more to the ardour and enthusiasm of the people's porters of the population in the north-west and of the rear area. In the name of the Army I warmly thank all the porters and the whole population.

When Giap gave the news to Ho Chi Minh, the latter is alleged to have said: 'However great the victory, it is only a beginning . . .' We shall see, in the next chapter, how prophetic and how chilling these words were.

The French prime minister, Joseph Laniel, announced the fall of Dien Bien Phu on the day it occurred. Next day, at Geneva, poor, battered Georges Bidault confirmed the news, proposing a general cessation of hostilities in Indochina. In Paris it was VE Day. The crowds shouted 'To the firing squad!' when Laniel and Pleven passed, but 'De Gaulle to power!' as the General saluted the tricolor at the Arc de Triomphe.

Of 37,000 French prisoners of war taken by the Viet Minh since 1946, 10,000 died in the concentration camps or on trek there. During the battle of Dien Bien Phu itself, the garrison suffered about 9,000 casualties, some 2,000 fatal, between 24 November and 7 May. On 8 May there were 8,100 survivors in all physical conditions left in the valley: 7,000 men and women, among them Ouled Nail North African prostitutes, then started under guard for the prison camps, many severely wounded before they had even begun a death march which covered 500 miles at twenty kilometres a day. They drank unboiled water and carried their own rations, fourteen ounces of rice per day and just ten peanuts every ten days. Only 3,000 men, including 885 wounded who were directly evacuated to Hanoi after the truce, ever reached their homes.

Medical attention in the camps was negligible. It is difficult to assess whether casual or contrived brutality by the Viet Minh was more damaging in the long term than brain-washing. The effects of brain-washing on Algerian troops led to the Algerian rebellion, and to the conversion of French officers to the totalitarian methods, although not the ideology, of Maoism. Both French and Algerians later applied against one another the lessons taught in the prisons of Tonkin. One of those lessons was that while 'the French had fought for their lives and for honour, the Viet Minh had fought for their country'.

That Giap should have accepted Navarre's challenge may demonstrate that, for the French, Dien Bien Phu was the wrong place to challenge him. French failure to abandon the place in December or January, when defeat could have been predicted, was a mistake. And it may be that Alessandri and Cogny's proposals for action against the Viet Bac bases and communications would have offered a better strategy.

Giap won for many reasons, the first being the disciplined fanaticism of his revolutionaries. But he also won because he was able to bring vastly superior quantities of artillery and ammunition from great distances into mainly hidden redoubts on heights dominating the French position, its airfields and the aircraft there or in the air. Although French intelligence knew what the Viet Minh possessed to within 10 per cent, they could not believe the Viet Minh were capable of installing it. Giap not only destroyed the flimsy fortifications which were all that French staff-work and an inadequate air supply force could permit, but the enemy's air power as well. It was upon that factor – bombing, reinforcement and supply – that the Expeditionary Force had relied for survival, if not victory. But because of France's special air role in NATO, the bomber component of their Air Force and Naval Air Force, in particular the dive-bombers to take out Viet Minh flak, was inadequate. At no time did they have more than seventy-five combat or one hundred supply aircraft.

As to the men, between 3,000 and 4,000 mainly T'ai, North African and Vietnamese deserters hid throughout the battle along the banks of the Num Yam River. Bigeard believed that with better troops – 'ten thousand SS,' he indiscreetly estimated – the French could have held the valley. General Cogny did not send in the two or three battalions which might have saved the first strong-points to be attacked, Anne-Marie and Gabrielle, because he believed in the pre-eminence of the Delta, not Navarre's concept of the offensive fortress, a fortress which did not even save the Delta in the end.

In a war supported, even encouraged, by the United States as part of an anti-Communist crusade, America finally chose not to deploy the '300 to 400 heavy aircraft' which, in General Catroux's words, 'would have smashed the Viet Minh siege organizations, and doubtless reversed the course of events'. The last part of Catroux's judgement is open to question. Although massive bombardment might have beaten the Viet Minh at Dien Bien Phu, it might not have saved the French position in Indochina. General Giap had fought the more intelligent campaign, as soldier, politician and statesman. But by its refusal, the United States took the first step in losing its own Indochina war.

Before we salute him as a twentieth-century Napoleon, whatever the strategic triumphs, Giap's tactical success owed much to French errors. Besides the original failure to predict the Viet Minh's ability to transport and install the artillery which destroyed the airfield and the almost non-existent fortifications, the French failed to 'collect and distribute' the air drops, to man the valley with heavy infantry rather than airborne units, and to withdraw the T'ai battalions at an early stage. And if, incidentally, Giap's guns were omnipotent, it is curious that the artillery at Isabelle and the two final quad-50s survived until almost the last minute.

We should also question his use of human-wave assaults on

Gabrielle, Anne-Marie and the Elianes, and the unnecessary Viet Minh casualties produced. Unless the commander-in-chief had secured an intelligence penetration of Cogny's, if not of Navarre's headquarters, he left a great deal to chance and, in the process, sacrificed tens of thousands of highly trained soldiers. Perhaps 'Geneva' was worth their loss in political terms, but one cannot presume that he knew that that would be so.

The question of Giap's skill as commander-in-chief is academic for Peking. We have seen that, as late as 1993, the Chinese claimed that the defeat was the brainchild of Wei Guo Quing, then commander of the Chinese military advisory group in North Vietnam. Some sources also insist that all the significant artillery employed in the battle was manned by Chinese crews. Others claim that each battery, or even each gun, had a Chinese 'advisor'. But this charge, and its implication that Giap was no more than a Chinese puppet, comes close to the criticism of the 'Vietnamese Tito', General Nguyen Son. Son, as has been mentioned, had served for twenty years in the PLA and had undergone the Long March; he condemned Giap as a 'military illiterate' without military training who had achieved high rank only through his political connections. This 'Communist by career, nationalist by faith', on his return to Vietnam, had disagreed profoundly with the leadership's reliance on Chinese military aid and returned to China in a rage, there to be met by false charges, including charges of rape, transmitted to Mao by Ho Chi Minh about his conduct in Vietnam. He was eventually shot in the back – well before Dien Bien Phu – on Route 4. However it is not easy to reconcile his reactions with his apparent position as Truong Chinh's protégé.

Dien Bien Phu fell on 7 May. The ceasefire was signed by some participants, but not by the US or South Vietnam, on 20 July 1954. In between, Groupe Mobile 100, the crack French 1st Korean Battalion was defeated on the southern plateau at the Chu-Dreh Pass, ceasing to exist. The Red River delta was almost completely penetrated by Viet Minh guerrillas and regular forces, while land communications even between Hanoi and Haiphong were under constant attack. Despite his terrible losses at Dien Bien Phu, Giap sought immediately to pursue southwards the beaten enemy, but he was prevented by Peking's conviction that such a move would provoke a reaction from the United States. Diplomacy and 'protracted war' would provide more certain and more enduring solutions. Given the depleted resources of his battered country, Ho Chi Minh found the argument impossible to resist and accordingly accepted less than satisfactory agreements at Geneva.

It is worth remembering that between 1945 and 1954 the French Expeditionary Force lost 91,000 men, 25,000 of French blood, and five officer-classes of St Cyr. It was, as Lartéguy said, thanks to them that South Vietnam existed at all. The Pentagon viewed the Geneva Agreements as leading to the potential 'loss' by the West of South East Asia.

XVII
Land Reform

At Geneva, under severe pressure from the Russians and from Chou En Lai ('We are here to re-establish peace, not to back the Viet Minh'), the Hanoi delegation under Pham Van Dong was obliged to agree to partition at the 17th parallel, with a demilitarized zone on either side. The agreements also provided for elections in the North and South by 1956, the withdrawal of French forces, independence from France for Cambodia and Laos, and movement of refugees for three hundred days between North and South.

The 17th parallel was not intended as a frontier between two Vietnams, but as a military dividing line between zones which would disappear after the 1956 elections. More than 750,000 Catholics and Vietnamese members of the Army of Indochina moved to the South, adding to the power base of Ngo Dinh Diem, Prime Minister after June 1954. Only 120,000 moved in the opposite direction. Among those bound for the South, however, were cadres and guerillas sent by Giap to form a stay-behind organization; the 6,000 or 7,000 Viet Minh cadres already there had instructions to stay in place.

To Ho, partition seemed like the concession of 6 March 1946 all over again. Before Pham Van Dong could give his government's formal agreement, Ho had to recommend the proposed measures to a seriously divided Central Committe of the Lao Dong Party in Hanoi.

To demarcate these areas within which forces are to be regrouped is not the same thing as to divide the nation. This is only a measure aimed at the successful reunification of the country . . . the former watchword 'resistance to the end' must be replaced by 'peace, national unity, independence, democracy . . . When people embark on negotiations, they have to reach reasonable mutual conclusions . . . the French have agreed to withdraw their Army . . . we are prepared to discuss the question of joining the French Union.

On partition itself, he added: 'Our compatriots in hitherto free regions now to be occupied by the enemy will despair . . . but in the interest of the whole country, in its *lasting* interest, they must be capable of enduring the present.' 'Uncle' Ho believed that the elections, which were never held, would reverse partition and open all Vietnam to Communist rule. His opponents in the Central Committee did not understand that nothing was final, that 'side by side with the armed battle, we are carrying on our campaign by diplomatic action and at international conferences'.

Ho added:

Our compatriots in the South were the first to embark on the patriotic war and have shown a high level of conscience. I am certain that they will put the interests of the whole country before local interests, permanent interests before immediate interests and that – hand in hand with the rest of our people – they will dedicate themselves unreservedly to the task of consolidating the peace, achieving unity, and securing independence and democracy throughout the land. The Lao Dong Party, the government and I are still keeping close watch on the efforts of our compatriots in the South, and we are sure they will reap success.

Giap had, by this time, acquire the sobriquet Nue Lua, 'Volcano under Snow' – power and energy concealed by cold composure, somewhat like the Iron Hand in the Velvet Glove. He began to attend receptions and public occasions, watchful, alert, commanding, a little apart from other ministers. He was smaller than most of his colleagues, solid, compact, with a wary gaze, the round face clear-skinned under a high forehead, cheek bones like polished apples.

Not only did the green or brown uniform with general's red tabs and stars distance him from his fellows in their meagre reach-me-downs. His own distinction, still and silent, matched even that of elfin Ho or gaunt Pham Van Dong. At home with his wife, who was to bear him four children, he read widely in French classics, Vietnamese translations from Russian, German and English, and Vietnamese poetry. (His French was almost comprehensive.) His private house was a former French villa which, over the years, filled with pictures, furniture, busts, and with grand-children whom he loved. His office was in the huge compound of the former French commissioner's residence.

As minister of defence, deputy prime minister and commander-in-chief, he led an army of nearly a quarter of a million men. Lack of funds, the requirement to relocate in the North his troops from the South, other than stay-behind agents, and to train them to beat off future assaults on the Motherland somewhat constrained him from expansion of his commands. Nevertheless, he established an Air Force with Soviet aircraft, a Navy (the Coastal Defence Force), while resupplying and reorganizing the Army.

The chief task, however, was non-military. It was economic and, above all, political. It was called 'building socialism', to be achieved under the pretence of destroying a 'feudalism' which had, in fact, almost ceased to exist after its abolition by the emperor Tu Duc in 1883. (Most land thereafter was either communal or bought and sold in the usual manner.) The objective, more or less imposed on Ho Chi Minh by Mao, was nothing less than the complete liquidation of anyone even remotely connected with landowners and the ownership of land, a Vietnamese copy of Mao Tse Tung's campaign in China after 1949. The programme may have cost half a million lives. It certainly rendered the country destitute.

In 1950 the first step was the introduction of the Chinese taxation system. This dragged the society down to the level of its poorest and most miserable members. The most significant of the taxes was a 'progressive' agricultural tax which, rising to 65 per cent in the case of a landlord with fifteen acres of paddi, was intended to wipe out the bourgeoisie as quickly as possible. The aim was also greatly aided by prohibiting landlords from collecting their rents.

The basis of tax assessment was the size of the holding, always pitched ludicrously high by 'people's estimates' obtained by pressurizing the landlord to accept false declarations of acreage or rice yield. Ruin was rapidly accomplished. Victims who sold their land had to return the sale price, although the buyers, usually 'poor peasants', kept the land. If the landlord gave the land to the government, his duty to pay taxes thereon still remained. The means to pay had, by then, been dissipated: jewellery, the herd, ceramics were all sold, only delaying, not preventing, the bankruptcies of these usually innocent and productive farmers.

Other taxes included one on trade which effectively killed a nascent, efficient private sector in many kinds of consumer goods, metals and power. Small businesses closed *en masse* and their owners hurried off to the 'corrupt' South. There it was not obligatory to wear ancient and dirty clothing as a tax-avoidance measure. In Saigon a chicken-in-the-pot or a cup of coffee were not the marks of a rich sheep to be fleeced, later slaughtered.

The land rent reduction campaign of 1953, the forerunner of land reform,* was preceded by the first dose of terror. The objective was to make the people live in fear not of God but of the Lao Dong Party, and to eliminate its putative opponents. In the lyrical words of a Viet Minh poet, it literally 'reduced to ash and smashed the bones of landlords, notables, opposition groups, middle-of-the-roaders and reactionaries'.

These 'criminals' were actually pre-selected, but 'discovered' through the arrest and torture of tax-debtors rendered impotent to pay taxes by the Maoist measures outlined above. The debtors in turn denounced the victims as instigators of deliberate failure to meet their duties. Those whose 'bones were smashed' were, in other words, those whose bones the Party wanted smashed: the ordained victims.

Denunciations gathered speed. The Party gave control to the peasants who in turn handed their distasteful work to gaolbirds, thugs, hooligans, the under-class. Chaos ensued. The thugs, drunk with power and the need to preserve their own lives, wildly denounced even Party members and cadres. The tortures then employed were those of traditional China: immersion, agonizing binding by rope, bastinado, gouging of eyes, hanging upside-down, fire, as well as hideous beating. Much blood was spilled, horror piled on horror. In every village there was mindless murder. Those arrested stayed in the camps and prisons for years. Most vilely, the Party had managed to implicate the peasantry as partakers in its own bloody crimes.

Public trials were then staged of dignitaries, 'compradors and capitalists', and wholly imagined 'traitors', all without proper defence and with maximum pain and humiliation. Thought reform followed. The targets were private enterprise, Confucianism, Buddhism, political freedom, French achievements and culture.

---

* According to Burchett, Giap and Truong Chinh published a two-volume work between 1937 and 1938 entitled *The Peasant Problem*, probably the ancestor of the authors' *The Peasant Question*. Copies of these volumes, most of which were seized by the French police, 'served as the basis for Communist Party, later Viet Minh, policies toward the peasantry . . . notably reductions of land rent and taxes as the first steps towards land reform'.

Truong Chinh, as Secretary General of the Party, acted as teacher and ideologue, Marxism-Leninism his instrument and religion.

Thought control, or 'control discussion', its methods ranging from violent abuse, pressure and threat, to 'logical deductions' demonstrating that, say, a polite observation was the consequence of the accused's role as a CIA spy, became a feature of Party life. 'Correctional training', the synonym for brain-washing or 're-education', was the next programme, usually involving confessions of error or crime as a means to inducing complete cooperation with Party policy, on land reform or other issues.

Land reform was temporarily halted in 1955 to avoid encouraging more Northerners to emigrate after the cease-fire and the Geneva Accords. The campaign began again about a year later and set the seal on the extermination of the rural bourgeoisie. Its principal technique was the seizure of such property as remained in private hands – domestic assets, *objects d'art*, buffalo, chickens, houses and land – on the basis of a 'classification' table, from landlords to landless peasant, manipulated by terror.

The first step, the land rent reduction project, was directed against the landlords. It specifically exempted and guaranteed the safety of rich peasants. These were delighted at the immunity and joined happily in the landlords' persecution. When the land reform battalions reclassified the remaining groups, moving the rich peasants and the 'strong middle-level peasants' to the landlord category, they laughed on the other side of their faces. The 'average middle-level peasants' then stepped nervously into their shoes.

Denunciation followed by tribunals at which the accused was forced to crawl on his knees to the prisoner's box and physically humiliated throughout was the standard method of presenting evidence, as in the terror and the public trials. As before, no proper defence was provided. Between 1953 and 1956, about five 'landlords' per village were sentenced to death, often executed by assassins untrained in small arms. Many more, boycotted, isolated, stoned, refused work or contact with villagers, died of starvation, their women and children associated with their guilt.

The Lao Dong claimed that 'since the masses had been given a free hand', land reform was not the Party's direct responsibility. But once land reform and the proletarianization of the countryside were in place, they launched a campaign for 'rectification of errors', proclaiming the resignation of Truong Chinh and of the responsible vice-minister. 'Party and Government began an orgy of self-criticism', although, in Ho's ghoulish words, 'one cannot wake the dead'. There is no doubt of the discontent, due to shortages, endless petty bullying, the absence of liberty, the horrors of land reform, which gave rise to the new campaign.

Giap was selected to make the leadership's apologia. This does not have the full credence of all students of Vietnamese Communism, who suspect that rectification was itself a part of land reform, total domination and control of the people now secured in the hands of the Party.

(a) While carrying out their anti-feudal task, our cadres have under-estimated or, worse still, have denied all anti-imperialist achievements, and have separated land reform and revolution. Worst of all, in some areas they have made the two mutually exclusive.

(b) We have failed to realize the necessity of uniting with the middle-level peasants and we should have concluded some form of alliance with the rich peasants, whom we treated in the same manner as the landlords.

(c) We attacked the landowning families indiscriminately, according no consideration to those who had served the revolution and to those families with sons in the Army. We showed no indulgence towards landlords who participated in the Resistance, *treating their children in the same way as we treated the children of other landlords* [my italics].

(d) We made too many deviations and executed *too many* [my italics] honest people. We attacked on too large a front and, seeing enemies everywhere, resorted to terror which became far *too widespread* [my italics].

(e) Whilst carrying out land reform we failed to respect the principles of freedom of faith and worship in many areas.

(f) In regions inhabited by minority tribes we have attacked tribal chiefs *too* strongly [my italics], thus injuring, instead of respecting, local customs and manners.

When reorganizing the Party, we paid too much importance to the notion of social class instead of adhering firmly to political qualifications alone. Instead of recognizing education to be the first essential, we resorted exclusively to organizational measures such as disciplinary punishments, expulsion from the Party, executions, dissolution of party branches and exile. Worse still, torture came to be regarded as a normal practice during Party reorganization.

The terrible atrocities committed during this campaign, the vast demands by the state for agricultural products and the increased taxes were not greatly compensated by the redistribution to landless peasants of only about one acre of land each and, to every group of thirteen families, a buffalo. Armed revolt broke out in Ho's own province, Nghe-An. Writers in Hanoi attacked the leadership, and dissension was rife in the towns and villages.

In the Quynh-Luu district of Nghe-An, 20,000 peasants armed only with agricultural implements took on the famous 225 Division. Elsewhere, numerous denouncers were publicly lynched, tongues were cut out, or the mouths of the so-called 'new' party members split by those whom they had denounced and who had then been released from prison. The calumniators had their mouths stuffed with excrement; informers were beaten by their former victims.

Articles and poems strongly critical of the régime's tyranny were published by young writers, all of whom were party members, earning them the title derived from China of 'The Hundred Flowers'. Most of the rebels, as in China, were 'sent to the countryside', areas rich in beriberi and malaria. The trigger for the movement was a poem:

> You who defeated invaders
> And did not bow down
> Under colonial domination
> Why do you bear with these villains
> Who shame our Fatherland?

There were many more. But collectivization, with all its evil incompetence, was at last achieved, producing progressively more inadequate rice crops.

It is ironic that, in these circumstances, Ho Chi Minh should have called in July 1956 for normalization of relations between North and South and early progress towards reunification. In August Giap told a German press correspondent that, should South Vietnam refuse consultations, a new Geneva Conference would have to be convened. This demand was not met by the British and Soviet co-chairmen of the 1954 Geneva Agreement.

XVIII
The Rise and Fall of Ngo Dinh Diem

In the South, on 4 June 1954 Emperor Bao Dai appointed the nationalist Ngo Dinh Diem as prime minister of Vietnam, a post Diem had refused twice before, regarding Bao Dai as a French puppet. It was unfortunate that the emperor did not nominate the magnificent Dr Phan Quang Dan, later arrested and tortured by Diem's brother, Ngo Dinh Nhu. Had he done so, South Vietnam might have survived. Diem, after all, that mixture of priest and mandarin, was elevated to supreme power by forces, including Cardinal Spellmann, the American churchman, hardly indigenous to Vietnamese culture.

By 1955 Diem had defeated the troublesome and divisive politico-religious sects, the Cao Dai and Hoa Hao, who were disloyally aided by the French, and the brigands of the 'mafia', the Binh Xuyen. (The Hoa Hao then temporarily merged their 'reformed Buddhism' with the Communists.) With American support, he had begun to extend his administration outside Cochinchina. In October, he had organized the dismissal of Bao Dai as head of state through a referendum rigged by American advisors, and established the Republic of Vietnam, with himself as president. The French Expeditionary Corps had been reduced from 175,000 to 30,000 men by July 1955 and all French troops departed by April 1956.

Diem, through a nationalism independent of and opposed to Communism, now had the task of creating a country able to compete emotionally, politically, economically and militarily with the totalitarian régime in the North, with its austerity, privations, physical suffering and absence of liberties. As a first step, he declared that he could not agree to the elections required for July 1956 under the Geneva Agreements, on the grounds, *inter alia*, that his government was not a signatory of those agreements. No elections were held.

It is not surprising that Ho and Giap, after their great victories and slim reward, could not placidly accept the annihilation of the chance of peaceful unification. Although their initial reaction took the form of little more than protest, the demand to end partition led to a personal appeal in 1955 by Ho Chi Minh for unification and 'final victory'. In September he founded the Fatherland Front, dedicated to unification through elections, a cause which his cadres in the South began to propagate. The appeal was to 'nationalism', concealing Hanoi's Communist aims.

However, his main concerns were in the North, with the horrors of Land Reform. Furthermore, Jean Sainteny, now returned as Delegate General, failed to persuade him to permit the French to retain, even in part, their business interests in the country. Nationalization without compensation was the general response. Hanoi began to sign a series of large economic aid agreements with China and the USSR and the first 'experts' arrived from Peking and Moscow.

Unfortunately, Diem's own land reforms, the main means by which he could have produced a united state, were inadequate, certainly far removed from the peaceful and democratic revolution that would have transformed and energized his people. The truth is that Diem was a conservative, nationalist and anti-Communist authoritarian, indifferent – even opposed – to radical reform, although strongly anti-colonial. He was incapable of compromise, and lacked administrative capacity. In the Mekong delta, 2.5 per cent of landowners still owned half the land and tenants farmed 80 per cent at high rents little reduced by his land reforms – peasants even had to return land given them by the Viet Minh. Industrially, private enterprise was a failure and the US – 80 per cent of whose aid went to the military – was reluctant to subsidize public projects, whether for infrastructure or not.

In the early years suppression of corruption earned commendation for the high standards of his government. Temporary authoritarian measures against the Viet Minh and their adherents were regarded as necessary and inevitable in the light of Ho's intention to impose Communism forcibly on the South. But they were heavy-handed, went on for too long, and became directed against *all* Diem's opponents, not simply the Communists. Death or life imprisonment was decreed for any 'crime against the security of the state'. This scatter-gun approach to criticism, including an absence of freedom of press and even speech, accompanied by a land distribution which affected only 10 per cent of tenant farmers, began to cause deep resentment. The government ignored or brutalized potential allies among both the intellectuals and the peasantry, thus sacrificing the support of the people, which Diem could so easily have acquired.

And under his brothers Canh and Nhu, and Nhu's wife, 'the Dragon Lady', with her lusts and sexual dissoluteness, corruption returned in coruscating excess, while at the same time in a blaze of moral hypocrisy the family outlawed the pleasures of brothel and cockpit loved by the Vietnamese man in the street. Because of Nhu's control of the security services and the administration, Diem did nothing to diminish his relations' arrogance and abuses, or the corruption and cruelty of the civil service. (No one, however, has denied the Ngo family's courage or its nationalism.) And by packing village councils with his 'own' Catholic officials, often refugees from Tonkin, he interfered with locally autonomous communities.

The Viet Minh were now strongest in the central highlands, north of the Cambodian Parrot's Beak, in Binh Dinh on the coast, in Zone D and its northern neighbour, Quang Ngai, containing the later infamous My Lai, and in Cochinchina. In response to the incompetence and injustice of some of Diem's officials, and to the exclusion of non-Communist nationalists from participation in public affairs, support grew slowly for insurgency. Diem's inability to meet the economic and social cries of the peasantry increased unrest.

In 1956, however, the British Ambassador was still able to assert that the southern pull for unification on northern terms was not strong, certainly not as strong as the fear of and the will to resist Communism. But that year propaganda by Viet Minh cadres, clandestine recruitment and assassination of officials ('extermination of the traitors') started. This resulted in even wider and more violent anti-terrorist measures on the part of the régime and then to counter-reaction by an enraged and frightened peasantry. A cadre said: 'Continue this until the situation is ripe and it will explode. We had to make the people suffer, suffer until they could no longer endure it. Only then would they carry out the [Lao Dong] Party's armed policy.' It has been estimated that between 1957 and 1960 at least 1,500 officials were murdered and 2,000 kidnapped, gravely damaging the credibility of Saigon: between 3,000 and 4,000 were killed in 1960–1.

Although Diem's persecutions of all not slavishly committed to him personally caused unhappiness, hatred and the spirit of revolution, it was not until 1959 that the Lao Dong decided to infiltrate armed cadres from North to South on a large scale – 4,000 in the first year. Their function was to take over, train and run the existing stay-behind organizations in the Cam Ran peninsula, the Plain of Reeds and the central mountains of Annam, with a view to control and unification. The decision was the direct consequence of a visit in 1958-9 by Le Duan, first secretary of the Lao Dong. In December 1960 Hanoi announced the formation of the National Liberation Front (NLF) as successor to the Fatherland Front; the members of this mass front organization were to be known as Viet Cong, or Vietnamese Communist, thereafter.

Some observers, however, point to the earlier Ben Tre rising, the declaration of former resistance fighters and the September 1960 mobilization in the South as evidence for lesser DRV hegemony and greater Southern autonomy than that generally asserted. Such views are incorrect. Hanoi's purpose in setting up the NLF was, according to General Vo Bam, 'to reunite the country'. It was not an autonomous southern Army, and the Ho Chi Minh Trail was begun in order to supply it from the North two years before *any* American advisers arrived in the South.

Already in January 1960, General Giap had said that the North had become a 'large rear echelon of our Army. The North is the revolutionary base for the whole country'. A South Vietnamese battalion was wiped out in early 1960 at Trang-Sup by Communist guerillas. The NLF's programme showed outstanding similarities to a speech by Le Duan to the Third Congress of the Lao Dong, but the DRV did not wish to invite possible US intervention by public claims to control it. In early 1962 the Lao Dong Party itself, while denying parentage of its southern infant, also established the People's Revolutionary Party (PRP), the controlling arm of the mass National Liberation Front; the People's Revolutionary Government (PRG) was not inaugurated until 1969.

In 1976 Jean Lacouture was publicly to recant earlier contentions about the NLF's autonomy, admitting that both it and the Provisional Revolutionary Government (PRG) were 'piloted, directed and inspired by the Politburo of the Lao Dong Party . . . in Hanoi', not the indigenous southern creations then claimed by observers such as Devilliers, Lacouture, and the wretched Burchett with his Bulgar wife and Moscow apartment.

It seems probable, in fact, that the NLF was not so much a coordinating organization for an allegedly pluralistic opposition, but the successor to a Viet Minh stay-behind *centrale* of Lao Dong cadres whom Hanoi wished to take more firmly in hand. But it is true that the insurgency had reached a stage when the successes of the Viet Cong had greatly widened their area of control on the analogy of the 'oil stain', the spreading influence of Giap's agitprop teams in the Viet Bac long ago. Terror was accompanied by 'hearts and minds' campaigns towards the ARVN (Army of the Republic of Vietnam) and the villages, as well as the establishment of armed guerilla and other units capable of attacks on small targets, as in Tonkin in 1944. The general's hand was in plain view.

These moves were not planned by Hanoi in 1956 when the elections had been expected. Later, disappointed by Diem's decision not to hold them, the leadership still hoped that his government would collapse under its own contradictions. There is evidence also from some of the statements of Le Duan and others that 'too active an insurgency, especially supported by actual northern intervention, would lead to a greater American military role. To maintain peace is a revolutionary slogan . . .' Even in 1959, the Lao Dong Party, guided by Giap's views, laid down that the political struggle had to remain 'the principal form of activity . . . permitting only self-defence and propaganda sources' in the military field.

But southern Communist despair at suppression of the Communist movement, alleviated by successful uprisings in a few provinces, including territorial control and defeat of ARVN units, convinced Giap of the value of militant armed insurgency, despite potential damage to the revival of the DRV's economy. These factors, and the fear that southern disillusion might damage the image of Ho Chi Minh and the Communist state, lay behind the formation of the National Liberation Front, the PRP, and the National Liberation Army, a force which grew to 10,000 men by 1961 and, by 1963, to 100,000.

Giap may in fact have tried to anticipate the shift to armed struggle. On 18 January 1959 he complained forcefully and urgently to the Indian chairman of the International Control Commission about 'the harsh prison system, mass poisoning and shooting of inmates, and burning down of prison buildings' at a 'concentration camp' in Phu Loi. The North Vietnamese alleged that there was a massacre, but in reality there were only twenty deaths which were exploited by the Hanoi propaganda authorities to provide the incentive for an increase in violence in the South, and the expansion of Viet Cong areas of control. But they did not immediately lead to the political and military changes of 1959 and 1960 earlier described, and the assumption of full control by Hanoi of the South.

During this period, Giap wrote *People's War, People's Army*, followed much later by 'anthologies' such as *The Military Art of People's War* and *The Banner of People's War*. Many passages, excluding the account of Dien Bien Phu, are almost intolerably turgid, as Ho Chi Minh had pointed out to him on previous occasions. The books do, nevertheless, clarify his theory of protracted war, and of revolutionary warfare's three phases, the preferred method of defeating Diem.

It will be recalled that his opponent, Truong Chinh, then Party Secretary, in emulation of Maoist tactics and exaggeratedly optimistic about Annamite and Cochinchinese affection for the Hanoi goverment, advocated a general uprising. This theory was pursued, without direct PAVN participation, until even the assassination of Diem in 1963 produced no explosion of violence among southerners against the status quo. At this point, Giap who had 'disappeared' for a short while in 1957 and whose political commissar had been made his co-equal in rank, resumed full status and authority, although still harried by Truong Chinh and his 'adventurist' supporters to undertake single actions involving up to 2,000 soldiers.

The number of infiltrators from the North between 1957 and 1960 was greatly exceeded by that for 1961 to 1963, approximately 25,000. Most of these were Viet Minh from the South who had gone to the DRV after the Geneva Conference in 1954, and were now returning to their old homes to arouse their friends and relations against the Americans advisors and their 'lackeys'. In this, they were helped by the badly administered first Strategic Hamlets programme, designed to separate the insurgents from the peasantry and from rural resources, a project based on the successful British exemplar in the Malayan Emergency campaign against the Maoist Communists. In Vietnam, however, it was shockingly planned, brutally executed and often opposed to ancestral custom.

The programme was also irrelevant. In Malaya there had been an enemy identifiable as 'foreign', a 'beast in view' against whom the Malays and most Chinese could unite. At the end of the road, also, the government in Kuala Lumpur had offered Independence, a goal in which not many under Diem any longer believed. In the shoddy 'prisons' of the Vietnam hamlets, it was the Communists who seemed to offer freedom.

An official American view in 1962 was that if the US presence and assistance programmes were maintained at current levels, Diem's military should be able to contain the Viet Cong military threat and might be able to mount offensives which would reduce its immediate gravity. If Diem stuck to his strategic counter-insurgency plan and continued to implement certain promising programmes, he might be able to prevent the Viet Cong from increasing their level of domination over South Vietnam's rural population and establish further control by Saigon over contested rural areas.

The Communists themselves were to conduct the insurgency in the South ostensibly as an 'internal war of national liberation'. Though the Viet Cong might mount an offensive or step up the pace of their operations, it was unlikely that they would alter the character of the struggle so as to risk a direct confrontation between the USA and 'Sino-Soviet military forces'.

The Americans, in an ominous glance towards the future, could not believe that the South Vietnamese government, *at least under Diem*, would take the political steps necessary to reduce the Viet Cong threat to a point where the United States could significantly diminish its present involvement in the struggle in South Vietnam.

Opposition to Diem over his oppression of the Buddhists, failure to introduce reforms, open dependence on the United States, incompetence, brutality and the corruption of his family, led on 1 November 1963 to his overthrow, undertaken with US connivance, and to his murder. (One pretext for this action was that he or his brothers were negotiating with the North Vietnamese through the French diplomatic missions in Saigon and Hanoi.) For all Diem's faults, even Ho Chi Minh admitted that only he provided any prospect for an alternative nationalist régime. Under squabbling and miserable generals, the republic and its Army now started to collapse: an ignorant American administration stared agape, or dumbfounded at its boots.

Giap in 1964 ordered the Viet Cong in the highlands to move on Pleiku in a drive to cut South Vietnam in two. This assault did not achieve its objective before the Tonkin Gulf incident, the start of US bombing and the arrival of American ground divisions further confirmed Giap's belief that victory against the massive techno-logical superiority of the United States could only be won by protracted war. Although the attack reached the coast in Quang Ngai, Phu Yen and Binh Dinh before being driven westward, it is hard to assess Giap's decision except as a rash failure in strategic planning.

But in advance of American involvement in 1965, the National Liberation Army had acquired control of a very large portion of the land and people of the Republic. The Viet Cong were moving in, local civil and military morale was at rock bottom, South Vietnam was almost beaten, the Chinese traders were considering habitual *renversement des alliances*. The landlords were shipping out their money, families and *objets d'art*. '*Ce pays est foutu*', as a French functionary had observed to me in the equally uncertain days of 1945. From 1961 safe road travel by day could not be guaranteed anywhere outside the immediate neighbourhood of the large towns; by night the dangers were greatly increased, a deterioration most apparent in the high mountain plateaux, the Mekong delta, Binh Duong, and to the north of Saigon.

XIX
Leadership and Army in the North

In 1963 party leaders in Hanoi who favoured an aggressive approach to policy gained influence as advisors to Ho Chi Minh, in voicing the tougher line adopted by Hanoi on its internal economic programme, the war in South Vietnam, and the Sino-Soviet dispute. Growing dissatisfaction on Ho's part with the impact of Soviet policy on North Vietnamese goals strengthened the hands of the militants, traditionally sympathetic to some of Peking's extremist policies and practices.

The North Vietnamese party hierarchy was divided into extremist and moderate factions, although it was characterized by a remarkable stability of leadership. There were no major purges, and a firm façade of unity had always been maintained – a stability resulting from the pre-eminent influence of Ho Chi Minh, who had ruled the party with an iron hand since its foundation. Ho kept himself above factional rivalries, using and encouraging them to gain his objectives. Exploiting his immense personal popularity, and carefully balancing one group against the other, he managed to avoid exclusive dependence on any one faction. At the same time, the existence of two groups with discernibly different views allowed him to change policy direction merely by relegating one group to the background while giving freer rein to the other. By using subordinates, moreover, to enunciate major policy lines, he protected himself in the event of a policy failure.

The factional line-ups centered on the personalities who some day hoped to succeed Ho, and personal rivalries and antipathies also played a role in the alignments.

The 'extremists' apparently took their cue from the powerful party first secretary, Le Duan. Other prominent Politburo members of the militant group were Truong Chinh, former party secretary-general; Le Duc Tho, chief of the party organization, department, Nguyen Chi Thanh, former top Army political Commissar;* and Hoang Van Hoan, former ambassador to China, with backing from

* See Appendix C.

162

Nguyen Duy Trinh, head of the state planning commission. In 1961 Nguyen Chi Thanh was sent to the Directorate of Agricultural Collectivization, but in 1965 he was appointed commander-in-chief in the South and died in 1967, either from wounds or from cancer.

In contrast to the moderates, the extremists viewed problems from a political standpoint, and played down the realities. Their speeches and pronouncements were strongly doctrinaire, emphasizing, for example, the efficacy of such things as 'revolutionary spirit' in the solution of problems. Some argued for the adoption of extremist policies espoused by the Chinese Communists. The increase in their influence marked the culmination of a drive to regain prestige that had been lost in 1956 when Truong Chinh was removed from his post as party secretary and took blame publicly for the collapse of the régime's land reform programme modelled on Chinese Communist practice. Moderate leaders had then been able to press ahead with more cautious programmes.

The leading spokesman for the moderates was Premier Pham Van Dong. His primary support came from Giap, a personal 'enemy' of Truong Chinh, who had pushed General Nguyen Chi Thanh in 1959 as more competent than Giap. The moderates may also have been backed by Pham Hung, identified with the Communist insurrection in South Vietnam and, on economic matters, by the conservative State Construction Commission chief, Le Thanh Nghi, who was relatively competent in industrial management and planning.

Ho's paramount influence in determining the ups and downs of the two factions was apparent in the Truong Chinh incident. Ho himself took over Chinh's position as party secretary to bolster the image of the party, but to maintain balance, he insisted that Chinh be retained on the Politburo and not exiled to the limbo that usually awaits Communists blamed for party failures. Although Ho took the title of secretary-general, the actual job went to one of the secretaries, Le Duan. In this capacity Le Duan gradually recouped the prestige of the militants. He formally took over the post in September 1960 and the title was changed from secretary-general to first secretary. In 1962 he appeared to be Ho's right hand and successor.

With Duan leading, party extremists overcame moderate foot-dragging and gained Politburo approval to push the régime's programme of economic self-reliance through expansion of heavy industry. The moderates' reluctance on this score stemmed from doubts about whether Soviet economic assistance could be counted on in the amounts planned. When the goals of the first five-year plan (1961–65) were announced, an ambitious industrial expansion programme was set forward which envisioned substantial Soviet and Chinese technical and material aid. North Vietnamese propaganda in 1962, however, suggested that the Soviets had been pressing Hanoi to orient its development towards the Soviet and Satellite economic structure through the bloc Council for Mutual Economic Assistance (CMEA). The Soviets presumably suggested that a substantial industrial programme was impractical in the overpopulated, under-developed and resource-poor area under Hanoi's control.

However the extremists adhered to the classical Communist view of state power based on industrial might. Le Duan rejected any economic arrangement whereby Hanoi would specialize in tropical goods, trading them for industrial articles produced by East European countries. The first secretary emphasized that North Vietnam must develop an independent economy, and specifically rejected a role in the bloc economy such as that played within the USSR by its Asian socialist republics. Le Duan also rejected suggestions by the moderates that Hanoi emphasize the production of consumer goods and raise its desperate standard of living before building heavy industry.

Le Duan charged that 'some comrades' erroneously believed that the question of industrial development was a 'purely professional' problem. Le Duan argued that it was in the truest sense a matter of the application of 'revolutionary spirit' and, as such, a proper concern for the Party, in which political objectives must be paramount. The militants appeared determined to push ahead firmly in the direction of industrial growth, even though the régime had cut back drastically on many of the initial goals of the five-year plan and was faced with a fourth straight year of serious shortfalls in agricultural production. Since North Vietnam was still essentially an agricultural economy, a failure in the industrial programme would not necessarily destroy the economy nor threaten the régime.

Ranking beside Hanoi's concern with its economic development was the determination to reunite Vietnam under Communist rule. Both militants and moderates shared this goal and submerged their differences over the tactics to be used in achieving it. But there was a heated debate within the Party in late 1962 and early 1963 over the proper tempo of insurgent war in the face of South Vietnamese anti-guerrilla efforts supported by the US. The moderates suggested that the Viet Cong concentrate for the immediate future on conserving their military apparatus and bases. The militant view that a more vigorous effort should be made to bolster Viet Cong strength prevailed. Considerable evidence accumulated that Hanoi was making a greater effort to stiffen Viet Cong military strength, with a view to helping the Communists regain the military initiative they enjoyed in 1960–1. More guerrillas and increased amounts of new material were infiltrated into South Vietnam long before the Americans even dreamed of despatching an US Expeditionary Force. In September 1967, Communist-initiated incidents reached their highest peak in over fourteen months.

In addition to their influence on strategy for the Viet Cong War, the extremists increased their voice in the formulation of general North Vietnamese military policy. One of the clearest indications of this was the emergence from obscurity of the militant, pro-Chinese Politburo member, Nguyen Chi Thanh. In 1961 Thanh had lost his job as political commissar of the army, apparently at the behest of the moderates. From mid-March 1963, however, he assumed the role of the régime's leading spokesman on military affairs, talking authoritatively on the insurgent war effort in South Vietnam, attacking the level of military efficiency and political indoctrination in the North Vietnamese Army, lashing out at the 'modern revisionists', and thus tending to align himself personally with Peking in the Sino-Soviet dispute.

During the same period General Giap and his chief subordinates in the Defence Ministry were almost entirely out of the public eye. Giap may have argued against the development of closer military ties with Communist China; he was known to have opposed such ties in the past.

A hint as to the growth of Chinese influence within the North Vietnamese military was contained in a rare public exposition of Hanoi's views on military affairs by assistant chief of staff Hoang Van Thai in the September issue of the party theoretical journal. General Thai repeatedly stressed the need for a programme of 'gradualism' in modernizing and improving the armed forces, declaring that it must be based on Hanoi's own industrial capacity. In the absence of a complete arsenal of modern weapons, he declared, a programme to raise the political awareness (revolutionary spirit) of the armed forces was a central and decisive task of the régime. He also argued at length that men, and not weapons, were the primary determinant of victory in modern warfare, remarks echoing Peking's pronouncements at the time on policy towards the armed forces.

Pressure by the extremist faction was partly responsible for Hanoi's public endorsement in 1963 of Peking's views in the Sino-Soviet dispute, playing on fears within the North Vietnamese Party that Soviet *détente* with the US would undercut Communist militancy in South Vietnam and Laos, the achievement of which remained a prime objective of North Vietnam. The extremists took the lead in Hanoi's public attacks on the Soviet-US atomic test ban treaty, calling for full-time, militant struggle by 'all Communists' in support of 'national liberation wars'. The latter theme echoed Peking's more direct attacks on alleged Soviet softness in supporting Communist revolutionaries.

Moscow may have warned Hanoi against pushing the war in South Vietnam to the point of risking massive US military retaliation. In a July 1963 article on the war, Nguyen Chi Thanh contemptuously dismissed those who were 'afraid of the United States and think that any stiff opposition to the US would bring out nuclear bomb blasts'. He went on to predict eventual victory for the revolutionaries by the classic methods of Communist revolution and rejected the Soviet concept of peaceful acquisition of power. Giap recovered influence after Thanh's death in 1967.

Ho Chi Minh clearly viewed Chinese Communist policies as more in line with Hanoi's own domestic and external interests, but when the Soviets supported the Viet Cong more vigorously, North Vietnamese support of the Chinese ebbed substantially. Ho Chi Minh again 'wrapped his Party in a mantle of neutrality between Peking and Moscow'. Neither he nor Giap ever forgot the centuries of Sino-Vietnamese hostility, Chou En Lai's duplicity at Geneva, or the certainty in their own minds that the main Chinese aim was to fight the Americans with Vietnamese proxies.

As for the armed forces, in 1954 North Vietnam emerged from the eight-year Indochinese war with an experienced cadre skilled in subversion, infiltration and guerrilla warfare. Using this as his base, Giap as minister of defence, launched an ambitious programme to develop a modern conventional Army. This had several important provisions: standardization and modernization of equipment, organization, training and discipline, establishment of compulsory military service, including a reserve force: development of technical services;

introduction of training for modern warfare; and, underlying the whole, a heavy stress on political indoctrination of the troops. Despite many frustrations and setbacks, some caused by the need to use the Army in agricultural and economic tasks, the goals he set forth were met.

The overwhelming strength of the People's Army of Vietnam (PAVN) was in the ground force troops numbering 223,000 in 1963, while the Air Force and Navy had only 2,500 and 5,000 men each. The main ground force elements were eleven infantry divisions/ brigades, one artillery division and ten independent infantry regiments, backed up by artillery, anti-aircraft artillery, engineer and other service and support units.

North Vietnam was divided into five military regions which primarily fulfilled combat support and administrative functions. Most of the forces were concentrated in the Hanoi-Haiphong area of the Tonkin delta, although there were sizable troop dispositions in each of the other regions.

The strength of the Army lay principally in its trained, competent and intensely loyal officer corps, combined with a disciplined, tightly controlled organization. Individual North Vietnamese infantry soldiers were highly adaptable and inured to hardship. Many had combat experience in Hanoi-inspired insurgent movements in Laos and South Vietnam. Participation in these 'local' wars also gave the Army command staffs in Hanoi valuable experience in planning, directing and supporting insurgent activities and actual combat situations. This training apparently added to the traditional strengths of the North Vietnamese Army: its proclivity for unconventional tactics, high degree of mobility, detailed planning and study of objectives, and its prowess in political and psychological warfare.

The army was and remained completely controlled by the Party and subservient to its political decisions. A major reorganization in 1960–1 was based on the political decision to intervene in Laos and South Vietnam. This decision remained a major influencing factor underlying the 1963 organization of the PAVN. The reorganization was an attempt to prepare the armed forces for prolonged guerrilla warfare, while at the same time presenting a credible conventional threat to South-east Asia and maintaining the internal security of the homeland.

North Vietnam then depended almost entirely on Communist

China for heavier firepower, better transportation and communications facilities, and standardized weapons and equipment:
arms and equipment had flowed almost continuously across the
border since 1949. Many weapons considered standard in the North
Vietnamese Army were, however, of Soviet origin, supplied by
the Chinese, although some items were of Chinese Communist
manufacture.

This flow provided generally adequate stocks of conventional
equipment. Hanoi's own arms and ammunition production capability
was limited, producing only small quantities of mortars, bazookas,
grenades, mines, small arms and ammunition, with a capability for
arms repair. While the overall programme for standardization of
equipment was quite successful, weak areas remained, the most
notable inadequacies being in heavy ordnance equipment such as
artillery and armour. Lacking an industrial base, Hanoi had to
continue to depend on outside sources for major items of equipment.

Backing up the People's Army was a 500,000-man militia, or
trained reserve. Only the elements of the militia considered
politically reliable were armed. The balance of this force was used
for local security missions or as informants, and the entire force,
organized on a provincial basis and dependent to a large extent on
local budgets, underwent two weeks' training each year. The militia
was intended to be the hard core of the trained reserves, to be built
up through a conscription programme begun in earnest in 1959 after
several years of experiments. Yearly call-up varied according to
national and local needs but men between the ages of 18 and 25 were
subject to two years' service in the armed forces, while those
between 25 and 45 served an unspecified time in the reserves.

General Giap had realized early that improved training was
essential in developing a modern army. A complete military school
system was instituted after 1957 and a separate General Training
Directorate on a level with the general staff was established in 1963.
Instruction in guerrilla warfare techniques was not neglected, but
conventional warfare training was stressed, with emphasis on
infiltration, camouflage, marksmanship, and field fortifications. This
formal training was supplemented by the combat training available
in both Laos and South Vietnam; Hanoi rotated as many personnel as
possible into Laos to take advantage of this experience. In general,
North Vietnam's military school system, as well as its training
philosophy, rested heavily on Chinese foundations.

Although North Vietnam had no combat aircraft in 1963, the foundations for the creation of an air arm had been laid. The 1954 Geneva Agreements had specified 'combat aircraft, jet engines and jet weapons' in the long list of forbidden military equipment. While Hanoi did not hesitate to ignore the Accords in building up its ground force, it apparently felt that there was not the same immediate need to create an Air Force in blatant contravention of the Agreements. Future acquisition of an air capability, however, was made easy by the foundation established in administration, logistics, transport and air defence.

The air command and administrative organ of the PAVN started as a small Air Studies Bureau of the general staff. Its primary functions were pilot training, air-base restoration and maintenance, and long-term development studies. An Air Force Directorate was first started in 1959. One of the early tasks of the fledgling air staff was airfield construction and improvement. A large number of sites had been inherited from the French, but most of these were overgrown or abandoned. Only twenty airfields with landing strips longer than 2,000 feet were serviceable, of which only five were considered capable of supporting even limited jet aircraft operations. Extensive improvements were made to at least ten, and perhaps twenty, airfields. Four new airfields were built, including one at Phuc Yen, about thirty miles north-west of Hanoi, with a concrete runway over 8,500 feet long. Although this field had been intended to serve as an international air terminal, it could also handle modern high-performance combat aircraft.

The air arm derived a new impetus from the Soviet airlift into Laos which began in late 1960 and lasted until October 1962. Soviet aircraft staging out of North Vietnamese airfields required sophisticated support in order to get heavy payloads off the ground. This support was given, with Soviet and Chinese help, in the form of strengthened runways, loading and reloading facilities, P.O.L. and cargo storage areas and maintenance facilities. When the Soviets withdrew from the Laos air supply operation, they left most of their equipment behind. The twenty-three transport aircraft included in this equipment more than doubled North Vietnam's aircraft inventory. China supplied MIG 17s and MIG 19s after the Tonkin Gulf incident, trained Vietnamese pilots, built roads, and supplied whole Chinese anti-aircraft units manned by Chinese.

With all this improvement, the main capability of the air arm remained in the field of transport, with a large increase in flights to airfields in the south of North Vietnam. These flights carried high-priority military cargo which, for the most part, was intended to support the insurgent forces in South Vietnam and Laos.

North Vietnam's Air Defence Command was directly under the general staff on the same level as the Air and Naval Directorates. It was divided into two elements: air warning and anti-aircraft artillery. Without tactical aircraft, however, only a limited reaction was possible by 1963. The sole active air defence capability (pre-SAM era) was light (37 mm) and medium (85 mm and 83 mm) anti-aircraft artillery, the medium guns defending urban centres, industrial complexes, and airfields. Approximately forty medium anti-aircraft sites, generally with eight guns each, were identified by American intelligence. The expansion of the South Vietnamese Air Force contributed to North Vietnam's sensitivity about its air defence capability: the country was extremely vulnerable to air attack, its small industrial base concentrated in only four centres.

The groundwork for North Vietnam's Navy was laid in 1955, with the establishment of the General Directorate of Coastal Defence, primarily a coastal defence force, with no real deep-water capability; its vessels included thirty Chinese Communist Swatow-class motor gun-boats and twelve Soviet motor torpedo boats. The Navy guarded against smuggling and illegal entry or exit, conducted some mine-laying, and participated in the transport of small clandestine forces, but it did not, until 1965, figure very prominently in Hanoi-supported guerrilla wars. It did, however, have a capability to counter attempted landings of small special-force teams, and was used to run guns and supplies to the Viet Cong. Although naval capabilities were limited by the small number of vessels and their modest sea-going characteristics, minor offensive action could be undertaken in the form of surprise torpedo boat attacks. The Navy, a minor element in Hanoi's military strength, was completely de-pendent on the Communist bloc for all arms and equipment. Local shipyards could not produce anything larger than district patrol craft for the foreseeable future.

XX
The Viet Cong

The Viet Cong, like the Viet Minh, waged political, economic, propaganda and military warfare – the latter, indeed, usually subordinated to political objectives to a degree unfamiliar in the West. Units of the People's Liberation Armed Forces (PLAF) included a large proportion of members of the People's Revolutionary Party who monitored and guided the Army's operations.

As in the Viet Minh, the 'lowest' level of the VC consisted of locally based guerrillas controlled by the PRP and responsible for small-scale action. 'Above' these were the regional forces, in company and sometimes battalion strength, still locally or province based. They and the guerrillas fought most of the smaller actions from 1957 onwards to which previous chapters referred. Both would then 'train on' to join the regulars of the PLAF. All lived more or less off the land, needed little heavy equipment or the internal combustion engine and, consequently, had plenty of fighting men and a negligible tail. For the same reasons, they could not fight pitched battles and were not mobile over large distances.

The Viet Cong's strategy was flexible within the parameters of protracted war. A *coup d'état*, coalition government preliminary to a Communist takeover, 'negotiations while fighting', or the organization of a general uprising – these various options were equally well served by the stimulation of anger and discontent, terror operations against Republic of Vietnam officials and ARVN outposts, the political conversion of peasants and the urban proletariat. Truong Chinh placed greater emphasis on self-generating revolt, but Giap knew that only a general military offensive would defeat his enemy, hence the emergence in 1964 of larger units than before.

If the Americans had not arrived, he might soon have succeeded on these lines through increased military strength and an improved political base, achieving command of the Highlands, the key to South Vietnam. The Delta remained a similarly sensitive area, but control of 'people' was always more important to the Communists than control of land, whether in the countryside or the cities and, in the existing military and political circumstances, more practicable.

This is not to say that the VC's and Hanoi's views on tactics in the South were unanimous. Some commanders preferred protracted guerrilla war with a view to controlling the countryside, the Deltas and lowlands being the chief areas of battle. Hanoi, on the whole, was more 'traditional', almost in the mode of Westmoreland. The final course, however, emerged as the old three phases: defensive infrastructure and organization, guerrilla warfare, and the final concentration of forces for 'the big push' in 1975.

George Tanham in *Communist Revolutionary Warfare* said that the first Viet Cong offensive tactic was the ambush, to obtain equipment, to discredit the government and to immobilize the people and the Army. Prior intelligence was obtained from the local population and through direct observation. 'Decoy' fire, booby traps, mines, 'hides' in paddi or beside roads, deception through W/T or false direction, blocks on railways, roads and waterways were all employed, countered later by enemy airpower, in particular by helicopters. To airpower the Viet Cong responded with improved camouflage, movement by night, better weapons, smaller groups, 'enticement' of aircraft by captured wireless to landing grounds defended by punji stakes, machine-guns and light anti-aircraft guns. They dug deeper, built underground artillery and other positions, deployed more widely, and 'used hand-to-hand fighting' as their response to air-power.

A second tactic was harassment or hit-and-run attacks against local militia, effective as a deterrent or 'frightener', one which also yielded useful equipment, and might even provoke an ARVN counter-attack which could then be ambushed, arousing even further lack of confidence in government.

The third offensive tactic was 'conventional' attack, but it differed from Western methods in aiming for casualties and fear, rather than terrain; the assaults were intended chiefly to demonstrate RVN weakness and usually not pressed home, broken off early. Since the VC had no heavy fire-power or air cover, first-class intelligence, detailed planning, reconnaissance and endless rehearsal were essential. The attacks were usually mounted just after midnight on villages or posts to take psychological advantage of the black night, preceded by sappers working against wall or wire.

Massed waves of troops armed with mortars, recoilless rifles and machine-guns followed in overwhelming numbers, producing ten times as many casualties in ARVN posts as among the attackers.

ARVN reinforcements were often unable to reach the garrisons because of ambushes and road blocks, at least before the introduction of US troops and air power. Battle ended at dawn, the VC either withdrawing under a covering force, or 'clinging to the enemy' to evade effective artillery or air power. Sometimes, for a variety of reasons, not always discreditable, the ARVN reinforcements would not get through at all to the battered positions. The government's reputation for protecting its people was thus further reduced.

The PRP Communist leaders in the PLAF decided whether to engage or otherwise, chose the battleground, even framed the main operational plan, leaving only details to the PLAF commander. They took part as officers or NCOs in the action, afterwards analysing, criticizing and devising measures to improve future strikes. Attention was paid to the deployment of anti-aircraft defences and much care given to the maintenance of morale, initiative and fighting spirit among the Viet Cong rank and file in the continuing terrorist campaign. 'Not to stand still' was a major VC objective.

Access to Viet Cong underground positions was usually through a network of tunnels reached by concealed entrances in the jungle or forest, and guarded by an outer defence of local guerrillas, ostensibly peasants carrying out their daily occupations. In the shelters below were stored the food and ammunition needed by the PLAF units and, above ground, were the mines, weapons and booby traps sited to destroy the enemy. These bases were autonomous, although linked with many others, with their own underground hospitals, weapons factories, training schools, armouries, manufacturing plant, work-shops and so forth. They were everywhere and were, consequently, one of the main reasons why the Communists won in the end. It is difficult to defeat an enemy one cannot see.

Bombing, sometimes lasting for hours at a time and using high explosives, demolition or napalm, could cause terrible damage to the surface above these underground bases, but frequently caused not a single casualty nor destroyed any of the installations beneath. Trenches, store-rooms and tunnels were shaken but left intact. Bombs, when they could be acurately aimed through the tree cover, were effective only against the civilian population, with the un-intended effect of drawing more recruits to the Viet Cong.

Giap described the struggle that he led as 'the model of the people's total war'. He was describing the NLF as the eventual successor to the little agitprop group which he had begun in the Tonkinese mountains against the French in 1944. 'Political activity is more important than military action and fighting less important than propaganda.' And in 1941 Ho himself had called on 'rich people, soldiers, workers, peasants, intellectuals, white-collar employees, merchants, youth, women . . . the cause of the national liberation front is sacred. Let us unite to save our nation from destruction.' Mao in 1938 had declared that 'the national patriotic struggle and the class struggle are welded into a unified whole'.

The NLF, like the old Communist Party of Indochina, knew better than to emphasize Marxism-Leninism; indeed it renounced the stigmata of militant Communism in favour of a nationalism aimed originally against foreign imperialism, advocating 'independence, liberty and unity'. (This innocent programme had been muddied by land reform and other brutally executed ideological concepts during the French War.) From 1955 the Lao Dong Party slowly threw off such restraint in its control of the southern insurrection. Nevertheless, outside the People's Revolutionary Party's middle and senior cadres there was little instruction in Communist theory, the appeal being for unification and liberation, anti-American and anti-landlord in tone, at least in the early days. There was a general ignorance of Marxism amongst both the private soldiers and the peasants, who were attracted to the front by nationalist appeals and by the infrastructure, including hospitals and schools, which it provided in the controlled villages. Their political education consisted of slogans hammered in by repetition by the *can bo*, or cadres.

Giap taught that power lay *in* the people from whom his soldiers were drawn, and within whose 'ocean' they lived and fought. Liberation lay through revolutionary violence: 'that gigantic creation of the masses, highly developed and invincible people's war . . . The people's war is absolutely superior to atomic war.' The cause put forward by the Communists was more persuasive to Giap's countrymen than Diem's arguments, backed as they were by Americans, who were presented as little more than successors to the French. The Communists as agents of 'progressive' change in an unhappy and corrupt society had the initial support of those who considered themselves 'oppressed'.

The oppressed in Vietnam today are only now perhaps beginning to understand that they, if not formally defeated, are not the victors either; history, in particular economic history, stranding them on an ebb tide.

The NLF and the PRP each had their own village organizations. These included sections for women, youth, guerrillas, propaganda, peasants, agriculture, education and so forth, and were, in turn, part of larger groupings embracing a number of villages. The PRP, as with similar organizations in Tonkin and in China, was defined as 'part' of the National Liberation Front. To strangers it would not necessarily admit to any formal ideology other than 'peace, democracy, and reunification, the isolation of America and her lackeys, the unity of all national and democratic forces in order to expand the bloc of national unity.'

By 1967 the NLF was represented in twenty-three international Communist fronts, including the World Peace Council and the Afro-Asian Conference; it had offices in most Communist or *Communisant* capitals, and in London, Paris, Rome, Stockholm, Zurich and Vienna. Its internal aim within Vietnamese was the subversion of the population and the creation of a strong National Liberation Army. Thanks to Diem's 'purification campaigns', the movement pushed on an open door, first of all in the deprived and frightened countryside, then in the cities among the middle class and the intellectuals.

In fact, as the People's Revolutionary Government (PRG), it became the shadow government of South Vietnam, led by the political commissars of the People's Revolutionary Party whose duties also included control or supervision of the PLAF, espionage, transport, terrorism, taxation, propaganda, all on a water-tight cell basis. The people, like their northern siblings, welcomed austerity as the price of self-respect, *vertuex quoique misérables*.

The Viet Cong, with their courage, 'ideals' and training, however unsupported by air power, armour and artillery, were able to outwit unmotivated South Vietnamese troops often led by cowardly and ineffective officers. Some of these would disobey orders, fail to accompany their troops into action, even disappear before major action – any form of abandonment to preserve their own skins. Their US ally had only the sketchiest and most incomplete control over their defections.

The first substantial Communist military contribution was in 1957: thirty-seven armed companies arrived in the Mekong delta, to be followed by Groups 559 and 759, responsible for enlarging the Ho

Chi Minh Trail and for the sea transport of men and supplies from the North. Between 1960 and 1962 the NLF regulars established firm organizational command in the provinces surrounding Saigon, including Zone D, and in the Mekong delta to the south-west. The guerrillas, certainly at night, were in full control of many villages. The regulars operated almost as freely. Murders of such government officials as were brave enough to reject Communist demands grew more frequent at both district and province level.

In the battle of Ap Bac, forty miles from Saigon, aided by US military advisors, 3,500 ARVN troops with artillery, tanks, fighters, bombers and helicopters failed to destroy two companies – about 250 men – of the NLF. The ARVN tank commander at first refused to advance. One subordinate officer destroyed his radio in order to pretend that he had received no orders. The tank commander deserted. The tank crews refused to go further, halted and were destroyed by dagger and grenade. One tank unit commander six miles away refused to provide support. Five helicopters were destroyed, eight were damaged. The government's artillery did not destroy a single NLF soldier. Giap said that the battle, which the Americans claimed as a 'victory', 'created new courage to pursue the enemy mercilessly and kill him'. He was exactly right.

In the jungles, mountains, scrub, brush and elephant grass of Vietnam, the guerrillas were for a long time the dominant factor, independent of, indeed rejecting, heavy arms and transport in favour of mobility. They lived in small scattered units, mostly off the land and by captured stocks from their enemies. Their weaponry included mines, machine-guns, grenades and machetes. The guerrillas, in bands of twenty or so, would unite for operations 'like a fan' which spreads out in the advance and closes like a dagger. They sought the destruction of men, not the acquisition of territory. Their technique lay in speed of attack, 'invisibility', and speed of withdrawal, in which they were rarely intercepted.

Planning their assaults with Viet Cong information from spies within the installations, they attacked fortified villages – including forts with wire and ramparts – but their preferred actions were ambushes, as Tanham described them. As well as mass attacks, very small sections, ten men or so, would take on much larger ARVN units with success, hardly ever seeking pitched battle. The frustration of the American infantry at these tactics was as acute as that of the French Army earlier, although it never led to the southern equivalent of Dien Bien Phu.

Withdrawals and evasion were perhaps the most difficult tasks. They would hide under water, breathing through bamboo tubes, they were sometimes caught by automatic fire in the open, liable themselves to Special Forces ambush and, always, to bombing and helicopter-borne machine-guns. If caught, interrogation involved torture, dragged through the paddi behind an armoured vehicle, beating, submersion, garrotting quick or slow. Viet Cong treatment of their American or Vietnamese opponents was no different. Nor were they above deliberately exposing their own villagers to enemy fire, the technique of indirect terror. On return to the burnt-out huts, they would point out to the peasants that devastation had only occurred because of their absence. 'Only we can defend you.'

'Camouflage' was a vital factor. Large sections of the Ho Chi Minh Trail, for instance, were unknown to the ARVN or the US until the tree cover was removed, while on the march each man was embellished with leaves and branches, changing with the vegetation. Men stuck to the shade on forest paths. Bunkers were concealed, sometimes duplicated, so that what appeared to be a bunker did not contain the enemy.

'Traps were real military works of art', said one American general; they enticed the government troops on from one ambush to another, with the attackers behind, in front, to left and right, firing only when the South Vietnamese were right upon them. Whole 'minefields' were invented, marked by English language signs with death heads. The PLAF moved a crashed US aircraft twenty miles towards a government post where they booby-trapped it at night. On occasion, 'self-operating' guns, operated from a distance, simulated an actual platoon. An entire Viet Cong company escaped from one village, unobserved by the ARVN because they were dressed in the clothes of the village women. Giap said: 'Confuse the enemy. Keep him in the dark about your real intentions, divert him. Sometimes what seems to be a victory really isn't, and sometimes a defeat isn't really a defeat.' And when the VC broke up railway lines, they removed the gravel bed as well as the ties and sleepers; when they dug pits, they took away the earth.

The Viet Cong, because they had to be self-sufficient, became the most effective guerrillas in the world, adapting the least warlike domestic articles to make deadly weapons, and were wholly dedicated to the destruction of the enemy. Most were imbued with their ideology and objectives; in 1966, 117,000 ARVN soldiers deserted against only 14,000 NLF defections.

According to Giap, South Vietnam was 'the model for the national liberation movement of our time. If it succeeded in defeating the special war being tested by the American imperialists in South Vietnam, this kind of war could be defeated all over the world.' Although they were paid very little – between 50 cents and US$ 1.50 for private soldiers and NCOs – the Viet Cong (all categories) probably numbered 200,000 in 1965 and 300,000 by 1967 when the PAVN strength in the South had reached 150,000. After the set-back of the 1968 Tet offensive, the Viet Cong assumed their subsequent minor role at only 20 per cent of the whole Hanoi-directed forces. (The ARVN's strength was then at over 500,000 men, and the US Army about the same.) By 1967 the Liberation Army had been greatly helped by very large quantities of US aid stolen, captured or sold on by South Vietnamese middlemen. General Nguyen Chi Thanh, earlier in the Party Military Committee and more apparatchik than soldier, commanded operations in the South with, as his chief of staff, Le Trong Tan, former commander of the formidable 312 Division and Giap's personal choice to prepare the Tet and preceding offensives. Thanh was no bad prophet: in 1964, on his advice, the Politburo had forecast that the US might send 'hundreds of thousands of troops' to South Vietnam.

The Americans invented an imaginary PAVN recruit, 'Nguyen Nguyen', and sent him down the Ho Chi Minh Trail to South Vietnam as a 'filler' for a Viet Cong (NLAF) unit. After a hideous four-month journey during which he contracted septicaemia in the foot, raw sores, malaria, beri-beri, and endured B-52 bombing, napalm and high explosives, he arrived at his destination and handed over four 82mm mortar rounds. 'Good job, Nguyen,' said the commander. 'Now go back and get four more.'

Although the VC and the NVA were mostly countrymen, few were naturally at home in jungle. Despite humidity, remorseless biting insects, heat, vipers, cobras and disease, including tuberculosis and pneumonia, the trail eventually became well organized and less dangerous. There was no doubt about the dedication of the men. Discipline, training and motivation were at a high level, and the leaders were mostly devoted. VC intelligence, tradecraft and guerrilla tactics were superior to the enemy's, although terrorism and cowardly brutalism, such as using women and children as a screen, defaced their record. Food and pay, of the PAVN in particular, if not generous, were better than that of civilians in the DRV.

Once the PAVN had started to strengthen the VC after the latter's huge losses at Tet, cultural differences began to show between southerners and northerners and between, say, southern cadres and regroupees from the North. There *was* dissension, but it was diluted by the ability of the Party to transfer loyalty to itself and away from regional, ethnic, family and other differences.

Equipment, weapons and supplies were adequate. There were certainly deficiencies, from anaesthetics to lasers and infrared, but tenacity was not one of them, nor was 'revolutionary will' or patience. As Giap said, 'The Vietnamese people's war of liberation proved that an efficiently equipped army, but an army fighting for a just cause, can with appropriate strategy and tactics, combine the tactics needed to conquer a modern army of aggressive imperialism.'

And, he might have added, provided also that public opinion in the homeland is under absolute control, that the government is not democratic but totalitarian, and that the enemy is neither determined to win nor employs effectively the technology in which it excels.

XXI
Rolling Thunder

The 'Special Forces' war ('Green Berets', etc.) of General Maxwell Taylor, President Kennedy's military advisor and later ambassador in Saigon, began in 1961. Except among the *montagnards*, it was únsuccessful. Although they acquired appropriate clandestine techniques, the Americans could not achieve the magnetic appeal of native revolutionaries. The so-called Staley Plan which accompanied it, intended to develop with U.S. Aid the Strategic Hamlet concept (the British tactic in Malaysia which so successfully isolated the guerrillas from any potential supplies or support) also failed, because the peasants did not want to leave their villages. When the ARVN burned them down and destroyed the crops, the villagers turned against the government, doubly so because the Vietnamese authorities, in 'building' the hamlets, did no more than 'drive a few people together and throw a roll of wire over their heads'.

The hamlets' housing was squalid or even non-existent: no compensation was paid; food was insufficient; officials trousered the aid; defence was so feeble that not only were two thousand hamlets attacked more than once in 1962, but 625 miles of wire and palisades were destroyed in that year alone although penetration was as often by tunnelling as by surface attack). Peasants' lives, however, were always spared by the VC. Only 2,500 out of 15,000 Strategic Hamlets demanded by Ngo Dinh Nhu had been erected by April 1963.

Staley's associated idea, dividing the country into zones of different degrees of security, could not be enforced. The Saigon administrators were incompetent, corrupt and indifferent. Embezzlement and a black market in American imports had become insupportable.

Washington recognized that 'indirect' methods were not enough. The Staley Plan ended in 1963 and, by Christmas 1964, the United States, with a quite inadequate number of 25,000 troops in-country, had nevertheless crossed a point of no return. US messages to Hanoi, via French and Canadian intermediaries, offering trade and reductions of US personnel in the South against an end to DRV intervention in the RVN received no response despite a plain threat of resulting US air and naval action.

By 1965 the Viet Cong's forces had reached 200,000 men, composed of regular divisions of three regiments each, mobile regional units, district, village and hamlet guerrillas, with 20,000 'political bureaucrats' devoted to administration, indoctrination and tax enforcement. Some 20,000–25,000 PAVN troops had entered South Vietnam either in coastal vessels or down the Ho Chi Minh Trail between 1961 and 1963, compared with a paltry few thousand infiltrated earlier. Another 15,000 had arrived by January 1966. The trail had its own camps, or stations, in bunkers, underground, or in camouflaged tents. One of these camps could hold 500 men. Supplies in very large quantities were stockpiled all down the trail.

Vietnamese, tribesmen, Lao, Chinese and, it is alleged, American prisoners under punishment worked on the road. By 1967 it was estimated that 80 per cent of Communist supplies came down it, only 20 per cent by the maritime route. General Westmoreland, the US commander-in-chief, said in 1966 that 'the transports no longer roll south on a narrow trail, but on a boulevard through the jungle'.

Increased PAVN and Viet Cong numbers, the weakness and chaos of the South Vietnamese after Diem's fall, attacks in regimental strength on ARVN installations, Giap's three-division drive from Cambodia to Pleiku in the highlands to Qui Nhon on the sea – all beckoned the Americans towards direct intervention in a country on the point of collapse.

A draft congressional resolution permitting President Johnson to commit United States forces to defend any nation in South-east Asia against 'Communist aggression' had been prepared by May 1964. It was postponed in mid-June. The Pentagon planners had also identified over ninety targets in North Vietnam to be struck by aircraft from US carriers, or from bases in Thailand and South Vietnam, whenever the decision should be taken.

In the meanwhile, a large clandestine US campaign against the North, employing South Vietnamese agents under CIA control, had been a complete failure – all or nearly all the agents turned, dead, captured or defeated. Certainly the operation could not be said to have remotely succeeded in the objective of matching the espionage, guerrilla, propaganda and assassination measures so ably conducted in the South by the Viet Cong. The hopelessness of these endeavours may be illustrated by the two Vietnamese agents who, dropped over the North from a US C-130, left delayed-action bombs behind them. The plane blew up in mid-air while, on landing, the agents triumphantly reported the deception to their Viet Minh ground controller.

Other operations included seaborne raids on the coast against radar and other targets by Vietnamese commandos. Concurrently, US 'electronic' vessels were employed to record North Vietnamese radar and to monitor other coastal installations from the Baie d'Along and other bays of astonishing beauty on the Gulf of Tonkin, projects also practised against targets in other countries and known as 'De Soto'. The North Vietnamese apparently believed that the two classes of operation were interconnected. It is not clear that they were not.

On 2 August 1964, after an earlier ARVN commando landing, the US destroyer *Maddox* on a De Soto patrol in the Gulf of Tonkin was attacked by three North Vietnamese naval motor torpedo boats. *Maddox* reported the incident, did not return fire, and continued to patrol with an additional destroyer, *Turner Joy*, in company. Air cover was provided from a nearby carrier. The president himself ordered that henceforward the force should attack and destroy any vessels which attacked them in international waters.

Confusion obscures subsequent events. On 3 August the captain of *Maddox*, whose sonar was erratic and not properly manned, reported that he had been attacked by enemy motor torpedo boats releasing twenty-two torpedoes. Wild firing broke out from both US warships. The commander of the US carrier's air patrol reported, however, 'No boats, no boat wakes, no ricochets off boats, no boat gun fire, no torpedo wakes – nothing but black sea and American fire power.' Even the president, some days later, commented, 'Hell, those dumb, stupid sailors were just shooting at flying fish.'

But nothing is certain. Secretary of Defence McNamara always insisted that an attack did at least take place. He denied connivance. Buu Tim, a former North Vietnamese Colonel who subsequently defected to Paris and has condemned the Hanoi regime on the BBC said the MTBs had indeed attacked the De Soto patrol at the instigation of stupid party, hacks who had defied Giap's orders that Vietnamese vessels should avoid US warships.

The president almost immediately ordered air strikes against some of the targets on the original list. Patrol boat bases and an oil depot were struck on 5 August in sixty-four sorties. Twenty-five boats were destroyed and the depot severely damaged. A congressional resolution was duly passed on 7 August, unanimously in the House of Representatives, with two dissentient votes in the Senate. One of those two opponents, Wayne Morse, said that 'its supporters would live to regret it'; it is true that many of them, including William Fulbright, the sponsor, later pretended that the resolution had been 'extorted' by lies and dishonesty.

Giap recognized the enormous potential damage that could be caused to the laboriously constructed North Vietnamese industry by US air power. That industry, nevertheless, was so small that its destruction, in the light of alternative Chinese, Soviet and East European supplies, might not in itself bring the DRV to halt its intervention in South Vietnam. He did, obviously, take full account of the damage that mines could deliver in the port of Haiphong and of the interruptions to production, movement and power inevitable from the bombing of plant, factories, oil storage, and road and rail communications. But when it became evident in Washington that air power alone could not defeat insurgency in the South, kept afloat since 1959 with Northern men and material, despatch of US ground troops grew nearer.

Before that occurred, McGeorge Bundy, the president's national security adviser, visited Saigon in January 1965, while Kosygin, the Russian prime minister, was coincidentally in Hanoi.

The Americans were already aware that units of the North Vietnamese 325 Division, one of the victors of Dien Bien Phu, were moving south. (By March 1965 three of its regiments – 32, 95 and 101 – had reached the combat area.) On 5 February, the Viet Cong made what Ambassador Alexis Johnson, deputy to Maxwell Taylor in Saigon, described as their 'greatest blunder' in mounting an attack with mortars and machine-guns on the South Vietnamese and American Special Forces base at Pleiku, killing nine Americans and wounding 146.

Bundy, still in Saigon, then recommended air strikes against North Vietnam, on a continuing, not a one-for-one basis. Providing grounds for a suggestion that one of the objectives of his visit had been to examine neutralization or a peace settlement, he specifically advised against a US withdrawal, 'surrender on the instalment plan'. The first strike, which was not particularly successful, against a PAVN base at Dong Hoi, capital of Giap's natal province in North Vietnam, just north of the seventeenth parallel, may have put a stop to any ideas that Kosygin had about persuading a stubborn and reluctant DRV to go to the 'negotiating table'.

'Pleiku' coincided with the sharpened conviction in Washington that South Vietnam was about to disintegrate, provoking a panic that earlier Viet Cong attacks – Bien Hoa, Binh Dinh province, the Brinks hotel and a VC divisional attack – had not been able to arouse. The administration had now persuaded itself that the fall of South Vietnam would be a catalyst for the complete communization of Asia under militant Chinese leadership, a perception which the actions of President Sukarno of Indonesia, under Peking's influence, had done nothing to dispel.

In April 1965 Le Duan and Giap visited Moscow, the Black Sea (where Brezhnev was on holiday) and Peking. The DRV secured a new agreement on Soviet assistance and resources to 'improve the defence of the North and support the war of resistance in the south.' From the Chinese they obtained specialists in air defence, railway defence and logistics, but not the pilots and other 'volunteers' whom they had sought.

In February 1965 NLF guerrillas had increased their activity with fresh operations in Binh Dinh and Quang Ngai on the coast of central Vietnam, scoring victories in Binh Gia (Phuoc Tuy) and at An Lac. Buddhist dissidence spread in the cities, and Military Assistance Command Vietnam (MACV) saw evidence of PAVN/NLF efforts on Route 19 – where the French Groupement Mobile 100 had been destroyed in 1954 – to cut off the central highlands.

In May and June attacks in regimental strength on the ARVN took place in the central highlands, against Song Be (Capital of Phuoc Long) and in Kontum and Pleiku provinces. An even larger assault was mounted against Ba Gia on the coast near Quang Ngai, and at Duong Xai; the latter in particular demonstrated the vulnerability of ARVN troops deprived of US air cover.

The North Vietnamese objective was to dominate South Vietnam militarily. The means to that end were to control the coast of Central Vietnam, especially south of Da Nang in I Corps, the highlands of II Corps and its links to the coast, and the region north and west of Saigon to the Cambodian border.

The programme of US bombing operations, *Rolling Thunder*, which soon followed the first attack on Dong Hoi in February 1965, continued for over three years on a graduated, escalating and strategically ineffective pattern, against hundreds of military and industrial targets in the North, most strikes personally authorized by President Johnson. The Americans did not, of course, target the dykes in the Red River delta, destruction of which would have flooded the Delta, destroyed the agricultural economy, killed most of the local population, filled the towns, including Hanoi, with water, and possibly won the war. Nor, until the end, did they mine Haiphong or bomb the main entry points for logistic supply along the Sino-Vietnamese border. But in 1967, when the programme was at last implemented with some ferocity, it was plain to acute observers in Hanoi that the country was tottering to defeat. At such times the DRV assiduously promoted 'peace initiatives', invariably without acceptable content, to which the United States invariably responded by stopping the bombing offensives: the initiatives had begun even before Diem's death with a letter from Ho, and continued, chiefly advocating neutralism on the Laos pattern, through Wilfred Burchett and Paris exiles in the years that followed.

After the US failed to react to earlier attacks in the South, Giap and his colleagues were disagreeably surprised by the post-Pleiku raids, 'Flaming Dart' I and II, and even more by an attack of 123 aircraft against a naval base. But, by April 1965, the joint chiefs told McNamara that 'the strikes had not reduced in any major way the DRV's military strength or seriously damaged its economy'. This statement would not have been true at the end of 1967, when 'virtually all military and industrial targets in the North had been destroyed or damaged', but still without decisive effect on Hanoi's will to fight.

The operations were designed to convince the South Vietnamese that they had allies ready to strike the enemy in its stronghold; to persuade Hanoi to lay down its arms; and, lastly, to eliminate the DRV's capacity to wage war, above all by the interdiction of communications across the demilitarized zone or on the Ho Chi Minh trail.

From the Tonkin Gulf incident in August 1964 until February 1965, the Chinese provided the sole military aid to Vietnam, in the shape of MIGs with Vietnamese air crews trained in China, bases and airfields, and the deployment of Chinese fighters near the border. From September 1965 complete Chinese-manned anti-aircraft units were stationed between Hanoi and the Sino-Vietnamese frontier. Such activities were intended as deterrents to US aggression, in particular, invasion, but were not a full response to earlier Chinese promises of a joint air defence. Mao did not want direct confrontation with America and saw the Vietnam War largely as helping the Cultural Revolution, the Sino-Soviet split, and the destruction of his internal enemies. 'Let there be turmoil in the world.' Although larger Soviet contributions in surface-to-air missiles and other weaponry followed, Chinese aid from 1950 to 1978 amounted to $20bn in *matériel*, and 320,000 anti-aircraft, engineering and other troops.

The first of the three US strategic aims described was almost irrelevant, yet was the only one achieved. Despite 25,000 USAF sorties in 1965, and 108,000 in 1967, the infiltration rate from North to South increased from 35,000 men in 1965 to 150,000 at the end of 1967. The Communist leadership not only kept its nerve but adapted the country to deal with the terrible damage that was being inflicted.

Power plants – the electrical generating system was eliminated by 1967 – oil storages, airfields, railway yards, bridges, factories, transport of all kinds were destroyed in stages from the southern provinces northwards with great precision.

Because of external aid, most of the transport was replaced and, because Giap created repair groups such as the 'Youth Shock Brigade against the Americans for National Salvation', the bridges were continually repaired with spare girders and adjustable parts, or by pontoon bridge replacements. In April 1967 a traveller saw only one undamaged bridge between Hanoi and Than Hoa in the south-east. Between Phu Ly and Thanh Hoa he saw electric light only twice, two bulbs burning. There was no piped water supply anywhere. In and around all towns and villages attacked, the traveller observed North Vietnamese anti-aircraft guns of various calibres, the acquisition and siting of which was another of Giap's achievements, together with the surface-to-air missiles round Hanoi manned by Soviet personnel. (Seven hundred aircraft had been shot down by the end of 1967.) As one pilot said, 'If that was a hospital, it was for sick flak gunners . . . a mass of sputtering, flashing gun barrels.'

Petrol was cached in drums along the road, virtually inaccessible to aircraft. Industry no longer existed, although small repair shops did. South of Thanh Hoa, on roads so broken as to be impassable to trucks, bicycles carried the large loads, between 140 and 400lbs each. Giap's youth workers received rations of rice, vegetables, soya nuts and bananas: they were paid only US $1.50 a month, but received clothes and lodging. Shelters were built, either trenches or single-man cylindrical holes in the streets, tunnels in the countryside. A home guard, providing rescue and first aid, was established. Urban populations, to their considerable discontent, were evacuated from the cities during the fairly well-defined periods of bombing, allowed back when the US laid off for meteorological and other reasons.

Since North Vietnam was an agricultural, not an industrial economy, industrial destruction did not have the same consequences as, for example, in Germany. Nor did the PAVN or the PLAF require the frills and furbelows demanded by the US Army, thus minimizing the loads which the Trail and other routes were required to bear. Inland waterways, less vulnerable to bombing, were increasingly employed.

It was thought that more draconian measures considered in Washington, such as mining the ports, would risk Soviet or Chinese intervention, a contention proved wholly incorrect in the bombings of 1972. And the real escalation, described elsewhere, of *Rolling Thunder* in the summer of 1967 had led by September to grave malnutrition, disease, hunger, the absence of replacement armour, armoured fighting vehicles, or artillery, hitherto visible in the streets of Hanoi *en route* to the South. The trains were coming in no longer. The DRV ceased to be capable of maintaining itself as an economic unit or of mounting aggressive war against its neighbour, but Washington shamefully or criminally either did not know or ignored the evidence.

'Peace initiatives', mostly illusory and all contrived, sidled once more upon the scene. At the end of March 1968, all bombing of North Vietnam north of the 20th parallel was discontinued, Tet being seen as final evidence of its failure, although most of the equipment in the February offensive had been in South Vietnam well before that event.

Giap, in any case, had long ago anticipated American lack of stamina:

It is obvious that our Vietnamese people have sufficient determination and capabilities and will certainly . . . defeat the US invaders' war of aggression, because our great national resistance has been glowing with just cause, has enjoyed correct political and military doctrine and the united strength of our people . . . and has enjoyed great assistance from the brotherly socialist countries and strong sympathy and encouragement from progressive people, including the American people.

The general remembered the eventual collapse of French will and knew that the Americans, too, would not endure an open-ended commitment to a lengthy war. He sensed the deadly force of public opinion, which, in his own country, was a factor of no consequence whatever. He knew, finally, that Johnson's Great Society programme and the Vietnam War were economically incompatible in a free environment.

As Pham Van Dong put it, 'Americans do not like long inconclusive wars: thus we are sure to win in the end.' Ho Chi Minh's comment in 1946 to the French, 'If we have to fight, we will fight. You will kill ten of our men and we will kill one of yours. In the end it will be you who tire of it,' was of even sharper relevance in an American context.

Giap's 'protracted war' was thus the only way to outlast the Americans. Far from 'persuading Hanoi to lay down its arms,' it is possible that the main effects of 'Flaming Dart' and the early bombing were to convince Hanoi that the United States really was bent on massive intervention and that Giap should, equally massively, expand his defence and attack capabilities, including DRV invasion of the South.

Had the initial raids been against 'Haiphong or the main entry points for logistic supply along the Sino-Vietnamese border', these arguments would not have applied, indeed *'la guerre de Troie n'aurait pas eu lieu'*, as Vietnam would have been in a situation of complete supply hopelessness and despair. But air power as actually applied (except in 1967 and 1972) and its incompetent execution offered no solution to the war in the South. No targets were permitted to be struck within thirty miles of Hanoi and ten of Haiphong. The DRV therefore concentrated their war material within these 'off-limit' zones, with total impunity, at least until US strikes were allowed there in 1967. In the torrid heat of that Hanoi summer, the DRV was first brought to its knees, then solicitiously helped to its feet.

As Dr Kissinger said, 'the US in Vietnam was engaged in a bombing campaign powerful enough to mobilize world opinion against us, but too half-hearted and gradual to be decisive'. Admiral Moorer, former chairman of the joint chiefs of staff, believed that *Rolling Thunder* in its gradualism did little more than grant time to North Vietnam to mobilize its labour force, disperse its targets and build up its air defences. It 'violated the principle of mass and surprise . . . forcing air power into an expanded and inconclusive war of attrition', the principal consequence of which was to increase innocent Vietnamese civilian casualties.

XXII
The First Combat Troops Land

In February 1965 General Westmoreland, an experienced Airborne infantryman, since June 1964 commander of the United States Military Assistance Command Vietnam (COMUSMACV), had sought a US Marine element to protect the airfield, port and other installations at Da Nang against Viet Cong guerrillas. President Johnson overruled US Ambassador (General) Maxwell Taylor's objections ('the use of white soldiers') to the proposal and, on 8 March 1965, the first American ground combat units arrived in the country.

They consisted of 3,500 men in two Marine battalions. Landing Team 3/9 splashed ashore on to a beach near Da Nang, opposed only by subsidized Vietnamese girls bearing flower garlands, the Navy's bright PR idea. Battalion 1/3 flew in later that day. They found green paddi, blue seas, rubber plantations in straight lines, palms and bananas, huge primary jungle, white sugar-sand beaches. Except in the highlands, they also found heat of an intensity few of them had even imagined, drenching humidity, and the disgusting stench of rotting vegetation, death, excreta, garbage and decay. In the dry season, the dust stuck to their bodies; in the monsoon, the rain outside met the sweat under their fatigues. Ants, mosquitoes, leeches tormented them.

Their orders were to occupy and defend terrain and facilities, but 'not to engage in day-to-day actions against the Viet Cong'. These may have been Washington's intentions but Westmoreland, who knew that Army Chief of Staff Harold Johnson had in mind the despatch of a whole division, did not see it that way.

In April the ambassador once again opposed the Joint Chief's proposal for one Korean and two American divisions to conduct active offensive operations against the enemy, initially in the central highlands. If US troops had to be deployed in action, Taylor favoured their location in coastal enclaves, as opposed to COMUSMACV's 'search-and-destroy' strategy of attrition. In the event, an increase of 18,000–20,000 combat soldiers was approved 'in a mobile counter-insurgency role from a secure base (Da Nang) to protect that base'. Taylor opposed even this as likely to increase US casualties, hence multiplying civilian opposition in the US to the war, and taking too much weight off the ARVN.

The Marines for the first months carried out extended patrolling and no 'aggressive' action, but the United States was nevertheless now formally committed to offensive ground operations.

On 20 April, at Honolulu, a further nine battalions were recommended. A total of three divisions, one in the Highlands, was under discussion. Commander in Chief, Pacific (CINCPAC, Admiral Ulysses S. Grant Sharp, and COMUSMACV both believed that the enemy would mount another offensive in the summer to cut the country in two and lead to an alternative government. Such parts of General Taylor's enclave strategy as were implemented did not outlast serious ARVN defeats in May and June.) On 27 June the first US Army 'search-and-destroy' operation of the war, supported by ARVN and Australian troops, began in Zone D, north-east of Saigon. At the same time, infantry bases were to be developed in five southern 'towns' and an enormous port and naval base constructed at Cam Ranh Bay.

In the North, enough Soviet equipment had arrived by 1964 to meet most of Giap's requirements. In April 1965, on his visit to Moscow, the general negotiated a further increase in the flow of arms. At home Ho Chi Minh led a recruitment (conscription) drive which not only brought back retired veterans from the Indochina War but enlisted a further 300,000 recruits for the PAVN. Air Force and Army training in the USSR increased and, in March 1965, the Chinese once more permitted transit of equipment through their country, banned in 1964 during the Sino–Soviet quarrels of that year. On the Ho Chi Minh Trail, two PAVN divisions (six regiments) set off for the central highlands from North Vietnam in July and August.

In December 1965 Ho ordered a dual strategy: strengthened defences in the North and increased action in the RVN on a guerrilla, rather than a large-unit, basis, together with a much larger propaganda ('political education') campaign. His decision for guerrilla rather than conventional warfare at that time was also General Giap's preference, in order to avoid casualties, disperse American forces, build up and train main-force units for the future. Nguyen Chi Thanh, Giap's old opponent and supporter of Truong Chinh, from his current post at the Central Office for South

Vietnam (COSVN) in the area known as the Iron Triangle, continued nevertheless to advocate large offensives. On at least one occasion, he launched a veiled written assault against the minister and commander-in-chief himself. But Giap had no objection to major attacks on particular bases, airfields and so forth, defending guerilla action not on theoretical grounds but because it was successful, plainly disrupting such pacification as existed, seizing initiative from the US Army and forcing the Americans back on static duties.

Giap said:

> Between 1960 and 1965, the war in the South developed from a political to an armed struggle, from an armed insurrection to a liberation war . . . from guerilla warfare to pitched battles and then to a combination of both. Armed self-defence troops developed in two categories: the regular forces and the regional forces formed the mobile force, the militia formed the static force. The people's war developed further with the mobile regular forces of the PLAF. Battles were fought involving large concentrations in which whole units of the enemy regulars were wiped out. The revolutionary war gained offensive power.

Giap was thus not against 'large concentrations', only allocating higher priority at that stage to mobile and guerilla warfare. Since he believed that his countrymen could outlast the Americans, that the political constraints in the US would eventually erode the will of the people and hence the administration, he insisted that steady, incessant 'knife wounds' were to be preferred to the losses endemic in mass positional warfare against a technically superior enemy.

In Washington, under-secretary George Ball consistently advised not that the United States should merely halt troop increases but actually 'get out' of Vietnam, before large numbers of GIs began to suffer heavy casualties in an unwinnable war. His subordinate Bill Bundy feared that, against the incompetence of the South Vietnamese ally, US intervention would only present America as a clone of colonialist France. He did not, unlike Ball, propose that his country should cut its losses, but both men were aware that *Rolling Thunder* had not diminished Hanoi's 'stoic determination' to maintain all its objectives.

As the president had publicly declared in 1965 that the United States would neither withdraw nor be beaten, to retire the 50,000 and 75,000 American combat troops that had arrived by the end of June and July 1965 respectively would have meant an unaccepable loss of face for this super-power. The ARVN, before the GIs' arrival, had been planning to abandon the Northern provinces, now 1 Corps including Huë and Da Nang, plus Pleiku and Kontum in the central highlands, as ARVN regiments had bolted or been cut to pieces in these regions. Future events cast their shadow before.

William Westmoreland was a tall, handsome man with the exaggerated features common in Americans. Giap was small, well-made, his face large and somewhat bloated. His intelligence was powerful but impulsive, violent and linked to the principles which won him victory over the French. Giap's strategy was based on ambush, surprise and secrecy of movement. He went to no military academy but seems to have absorbed Japanese combat tactics: night fighting, camouflage, indirect fire, harassment by sniper, the use of prisoners as hostages. He regarded ceasefires purely as occasions to better his position.

Westmoreland's strategy, on the other hand, followed that of Paul Haskins, his self-deceiving predecessor: the concept of attrition. It was summarized in a Joint Chief's paper: 'to seek out and destroy major Viet Cong units which, with the interdiction of DRV efforts to provide support, should lead to the progressive destruction of the Viet Cong/DRV main force battalions'. Unfortunately, the Communists not only avoided contact in situations unfavourable to themselves, but replaced their casualties as fast as they fell. Westmoreland's hopes of 'grinding down' the enemy were un-realized. Indeed, by December 1965, the Viet Cong and PAVN escalation rate was twice that of the Americans, and the latter's own casualties, although relatively small, would in time become intoler-able to the folks back home. Robert McNamara, secretary of defence, estimated in 1965 that 600,0000 US troops would be required by 1968, *without any guarantee of success*.

The alternative, advocated by the Marines and others, was pacification, in the sense of providing permanent security in hamlets and villages, combined with the destruction of such Viet Cong infrastructure as the omnipresent underground trenches, tunnels and 'fixed' installations in which the enemy really lived. The ultimate aim was to let the local RVN administrations function without continual Communist disruption. This the Marines began to achieve, 'taking-and-holding' before expanding their perimeters.

COMUSMACV opposed these practices on the grounds that they allowed the Viet Cong to operate freely *outside* the US or allied enclaves, particularly in the Central Highlands, and because the ferocity of Marine operations enabled an irresponsible press hysterically to emphasize civilian damage and to ignore the destruction of the Communist military base.

But the Communists could not be defeated until they had ceased to terrify the population. This could only be done by acquiring territory. Attrition, on the other hand, had no chance of ultimate success against an enemy that fought only on its own terms, disappearing into the jungle when it considered the odds in combat were unacceptable, and returning when the American Army itself consequently broke off and withdrew. Nor could it be effective against a pool of over two and a half million potential northern and southern fighting men. Nor could the population be won over without a coherent land reform programme and revolutionary social improvements. These, in their turn, could only be implemented within a society that, as advocated by the Marines and others, had first been secured militarily.

American troops, as well as engaging the main force, had therefore to protect the peasants in cleared areas where a rejuvenated South Vietnamese government, under discreet monitoring by US observers, could regain the respect and confidence of the people. As Saigon's agreement to any such comprehensive project was unlikely without coercion, a unified US/RVN command would be essential, like the Malayan Directorate of Operations. MACV had always rejected this concept, whether on the grounds of Viet Cong penetration or because the US staff preferred to fight 'an American war without the frustration of cooperating with the Vietnamese', until the establishment in May 1967 of 'Civil Operations and Revolutionary Development Support' (CORDS) under Robert Komer.

General Westmoreland issued nine 'good conduct' points for US troops. 'Do not seek privileged treatment; don't be brutal or noisy; do not show off your wealth; make friends with the ARVN and the people; be polite and respectful to Vietnamese women; alway give priority to Vietnamese; act as soldiers, always on guard; learn the language, study the customs'; and so forth and so on.

But the US Army and Air Force lived in air-conditioned bases, ate their own canned foods, treated the women as whores and the

ARVN often as cowards and traitors, threw their money about, sold their stores and equipment, immediately losing not the military but the psychological and political battle for those attributes later known as 'hearts and minds'.

XXIII
Let Battle Commence . . .

We have noted that the American military, for the most part, believed in attrition strategy. That strategy was to inflict casualties on the enemy, in this case the PAVN, such that the forces of the Democratic Republic of Vietnam could be driven out of the South without the need for an invasion of North Vietnam by United States ground forces. In that manner Hanoi would be 'unable effectively to support the war in the South'.

On 17 August 1965 the first major battle (*Starlight*) conducted by American troops since the Korean War was fought between 4th Marines together with an ARVN unit with sea and air support, and, on the other side, a battalion of the 1st Viet Cong Main Force Regiment numbering about 2,000 men.

The battle, on the Van Truong peninsula, took place among tunnels, caves, paddi, the bamboo of fortified hamlets. The stench from bodies in the tunnels blocked by Marine charges was suffocating. After a week, 668 VC had been killed and 109 weapons captured against forty-five dead Marines and 200 wounded; the Communists, however, claimed 900 out of 8,000 Marines killed.

Assuming the truth of the US figure, it was still not an encouraging ratio for the Americans when civilians were included, not withstanding that most of the latter were Viet Cong supporters. The protection of an US airfield, Chu Lai, the object of the engagement was, however, assured.

After much discussion in Washington, on 25 December 1965 the president halted the bombing of the North as a gesture towards diplomatic settlement. Hanoi, believing that they would be the victors in the end, saw the pause as United States weakness, which it was. They made no move to the negotiating table. Ground actions took place near Saigon, and an action originally code-named *Masher*, softened by LBJ to *White Wing* as less 'gross', was mounted on the coast above Qui Nhon during the Christmas bombing pause. *White Wing* was fought in the same area as Navarre's ill-fated amphibious landing, *Atlante*, during the battle for Dien Bien Phu in 1954.

In November 1965, *Silver Bayonet*, a major battle, had been mounted in the Ia Drang valley after the 33rd NVA Regiment had suffered heavy casualties in a failed attack on Plei Me Special Forces camp. The PAVN, in the Tay Nguyen campaign, planned an assault on the plateau containing Kontum, Pleiku, Binh Dinh and Phu Bon province, their aim, with 32, 33 and 66 Regiments, to destroy Special Forces camps and take Pleiku.

They were pursued by 1 Brigade of 1st Cavalry Division (Airmobile) under Major-General Harry Kinnard, later relieved by 3 Brigade under Thomas W. Brown (1 and 2 Battalions of 7th Cavalry and 2 Battalion of 5th Cavalry). 3 Brigade was known as 'Garry Owen', a song sung by the Irish Lancers and adopted by Custer's 7th Cavalry in the last century.

A PAVN deserter. who had been sustaining himself on bananas alone for five days, was now captured. This disaffected soldier allegedly told Colonel Hal Moore, a tall Korean war veteran, now commanding 1 Battalion 7th Cavalry, that three NVA battalions were on a mountain called Chu Prong, 200 yards from Moore's tiny helicopter landing zone: they numbered 1,500 men in three battalions to Moore's 450 men.

To prevent the NVA from rushing down the hill to overwhelm him, Moore sent his first company straight up the ridge. They met the enemy hand-to-hand among the trees at the edge of the rain forest, both sides using grenade launchers and automatic rifles. The Americans, well-trained although untested in battle, behaved well, but one platoon was surrounded in pursuing a PAVN section feigning flight: only seven men out of twenty-seven survived.

Moore's second and third companies fought similar infantry close-quarter actions near the base of the ridge, 'clinging to the belt', as the PAVN saying went. C Company were then jumped by a whole PAVN battalion advancing through elephant grass on all fours. Most of the hundred American officers and men were killed or seriously injured, only thirty unscathed. Out in the grass 'a Vietnamese and an American who had shot each other lay side by side. The American died with his hands round the throat of the Vietnamese.' A napalm attack landed among American, not NVA troops. The last PAVN assault, before 1 Battalion was relieved, was decimated by American M-16 rifles; wounded men drowned in craters filled with rain.

The bulk of the Vietnamese withdrew across the Cambodian border in the utmost disorder. Tim Brown, commanding the 3rd Brigade of the 1st Air Cavalry Division, to which Moore's battalion had been attached, assumed that in killing nearly a thousand identified PAVN troops in infantry encounters, the Americans had at least fulfilled COMUSMACV's attrition objectives. As artillery and air strikes from Huey helicopters or B-52s had been fairly ineffective in the trackless mountain wastes, the brigadier sought Westmoreland's authority to withdraw temporarily to reassess before a renewed attack.

The general refused: 'The newspapers will make it look like we retreated.' 2 Battalion, 7th Cavalry, relieving Moore's unit and less cautious than the 1st, now walked into a devastating PAVN ambush which killed 150 and wounded 120, almost wiping out the Third Company. Although the NVA lost 900 killed and 500 wounded, Cavalry losses in the whole battle were very high, nearly 300 dead. 'History repeated itself,' one of Neil Sheehan's sources said: 7th Cavalry had fought under Custer at the Little Big Horn. But this battle ended Giap's attempt to cut South Vietnam in two, from bases in Cambodia to the sea.

After this action, Secretary McNamara reported that Westmoreland had sought to raise the total of US troops in Vietnam to 375,000 by an increase of 40,000. It was this request and McNamara's prediction of 600,000 troops by 1968, coinciding with the Janos Péter 'peace' initiative, which prompted the Christmas 1965 bombing pause and its fruitless plea to Hanoi.

One of the most significant factors, incidentally, in the US pursuit of the war, was the responsibility given to a civilian Secretary of Defence for the actual *conduct* of war, at the expense of the professional advisors, the Joint Chiefs of Staff. This phenomenon had an increasingly adverse effect on US military strategy, policy-making and independent advice: 'business school' administration, systems analysis, body-counts and technocracy swamped diplomacy, strategy and politics.

And few thought of pacification, of retaining the US Army in the area, or flying in ARVN to hold and protect land vacated by the Communists who, of course, infiltrated straight back after 7th Cavalry moved on.

The 3rd Air Cavalry Brigade, now commanded by Hal Moore on promotion, moved on to the coastal plain of Bong Son, largely flooded paddi south of Qui Nhon, once a Viet Minh stronghold under the French. When Navarre had planned *Atlante* in 1954, he had expected to deploy here forty-five infantry and eight artillery battalions to clear a Communist bastion forty miles deep and 230 miles long, containing 30,000 Communist troops in twelve regular and six regional battalions. Navarre's landing behind Communist lines was successful. Thereafter the French Vietnamese troops acted with neither courage nor cohesion, later competing with the Saigon civilian administrators to loot and rob. The Viet Minh then forced Navarre to call in airborne troops from Tonkin, where they had been stationed as reserves for Dien Bien Phu.

In January 1966, the COMUSMACV offensive (*Masher/White-Wing*) numbered 20,000 US, ARVN and Korean troops, the Air Cavalry with its air and naval cover forming the southern wing. The heat, humidity and driving rain slowed the ground advance. The Bong Son plain was manned by a PAVN regiment from the 3rd or 'Yellow Star' Division, who had come in earlier by sea and down the Ho Chi Minh Trail, and by a Viet Cong regular regiment. These units were deployed in bunkers strongly built of rails and ties from an abandoned railway line, supporting packed earth. The sand beach and the paddi were covered by interlocking automatic weapon fire from within bunkers hidden in the coconut groves. As 2/7th Air Cavalry jumped from their helicopters, the unfortunate C Company again took heavy losses. Nor were the ARVN battalions any better off when they got to the paddi: 'You don't have much mobility in a full rice paddi', as an engineer said to Sheehan.

As infantry assault in these monsoon conditions would have involved terrible casualties, the battle was largely conducted by fire-power from aircraft and from the guns of the 7th Fleet offshore. Fifteen hamlets and one thousand houses were destroyed, at least a hundred civilians killed, many more – men, women and children – maimed. The PAVN and the Viet Cong, leaving behind fifty weapons and several hundred dead, retreated westwards, sensibly refusing battle.

1st Cavalry reported that between January and March 1966 'it had killed 1,300 armed NVA and VC, captured 600, and detained over 1,000 suspected VC'. Many of the coconut palms, which, with rice, formed the basis of the plain's economy through sales of copra and fresh coconuts, had been destroyed by five inch naval shells. The ARVN district chief then set to, selling copra on his own account through Chinese middlemen for the short period when he was not obliged to share the proceeds with the Viet Cong.

Although five out of nine Communist battalions were said to have been rendered ineffective, it would not be long before the Viet Cong returned to a destitute population deprived of half their livelihood, of nearly all shelter and of the lives of many members of their families. They returned also to thousands of refugees. These provided a haven for the VC infrastructure, and an enormous catchment area for Viet Cong recruitment; the peasants were filled with anger and hatred, directed equally at the Saigon government and their American friends who had disrupted, if not destroyed, their humble lives. By December 1966, Binh Dinh province contained eighty refugee camps with 120,000 refugees.

Nor were there plans for pacification in Bong Son. When the Air Cavalry and the ARVN Airborne had completed their pursuit of the Yellow Star Regiment and its Viet Cong comrades, the American and South Vietnamese troops would be withdrawn, 'in order to look for another battlefield'. If the PAVN and Viet Cong returned to the plain, the corps commander, in the most literal interpretation of attrition, would 'go back and kill more of the sons of bitches'. This was the logical conclusion to Westmoreland's belief that continual confrontation really would, in the end, erode the Communist enemy. Shortage of troops, US or ARVN, was no more than an excuse for his indifference to reform and security.

White Wing ended in March and was succeeded by Operations *Thayer and Irving*, which, waged with enormous expenditure of naval gunfire, B-52s and fighter bombers, were fought amongst the heavy populations of the Binh Dinh coast, and then into the mountains east of Kontum and Pleiku. No massive confrontations took place between the two sides, although the North Vietnamese lost heavily in men, *matériel*, burned and blown-up houses, tunnels, trenches and underground redoubts. Yet more refugees were created, up to one third of the province's population, while the Viet Cong and the PAVN avoided major contact with the enemy. The Americans claimed that the Communists 'had been driven from the coastal plain'. But when the administrators of the government of the Republic of Vietnam moved in to re-establish control, they found that security, without an adequate military force, was hard, sometimes impossible, to maintain in the hostile atmosphere of a secret Viet Cong infrastructure. After *Thayer II* 1st Cavalry reported that although most of the population in the province were *temporarily* released from control by the Viet Cong, 'the area of operations was still a power vacuum'. Nor, tactically, had any solution been found to the linked problems of brilliant Viet Cong intelligence pene-trations and the noise, visibility and preliminary fire of large US units on the move.

Over and over again, the US Army failed to eliminate an opponent who operated by ambush, withdrawal, and refusal to 'fight like a man'. A five-battalion Marine air and amphibious attack (*Double Eagle*) in January 1966, for example, against 352a PAVN Division on the border of Binh Dinh and Quang Ngai provinces, failed to find hide nor hair of the NVA who, warned in advance, had melted away.

However, apart from Buddhist demonstrations and an NLF-inspired general strike in Danang, the Americans and the South Korean Capital Division prevented the PAVN from creating a base in Kontum and Pleiku provinces in July and August 1966. Similar attempts to build another base in the north-west of Quang Tri were frustrated in battles along the demilitarized zone. These resulted in 342b and 341 Divisions being pushed back into North Vietnam with up to 1,700 casualties against 320 US dead.

Two or three PAVN divisions in Kontum and Pleiku, linked to 3 PAVN Division in Binh Dinh and 9 PLAF Division reinforced by an NVA regiment, were also defeated in their attempts to strike against three provinces north and west of Saigon in the summer of 1966.

In May 1966, nevertheless, addressing the Youth Congress at Hanoi, Giap referred to the defeat of the US imperialists' 'special warfare strategy'. He claimed victories in the dry season counter-offensive and scorned 'failed US attempts to isolate the South Vietnam battlefield or to strengthen the Saigon administration and Army'. He said that the Americans had not destroyed the Viet Cong. Giap claimed that 1,000 US aircraft had been shot down: American air supremacy had been smashed. Victory had been achieved over 350,000 US troops, many thousands of allied ('satellite') troops and 500,000 'rebel' (ARVN) soldiers; the ARVN had lost 70,000 men and the US 43,000. 'Those forces had been split into five or seven groups fighting each other. The North had further developed its role as the great rear-area of the large battlefield of South Vietnam'.

But the battle in the Ia Drang valley, like most of the actions fought by the US Army, was an American victory. No American, however, because of memories of the Chinese reaction to US 'victory' in the Korean War, considered mounting a strategic offensive against North Vietnam itself, the DRV, but only *containment* of the DRV's own strategic offensive in the South. Hence the emphasis on counter-insurgency, on the guerilla war in the South, and the consequent exhaustion of US military power on a secondary, if not irrelevant objective, the strategic defensive.

XXIV
The Bombing of the North

US air strikes, such as the bombing of North Vietnam from April to May 1966, were primarily armed reconnaissance against lines of communication (LOC), infiltration routes, dispersed logistic targets, and land and waterway traffic. The interdiction effort in the north-east section of the country was intensified while continuing pressure was maintained on LOCs to the south. All railway lines from Hanoi except that between Hanoi and Haiphong, were closed to through traffic, although extensive provisions were made to circumvent damage through bypasses, shuttle services, and water traffic. The constant interdiction of rail and road facilities and traffic caused the North Vietnamese to emphasize waterways for moving supplies southward. There was also high destruction or damage of watercraft during the period. Strikes against fixed targets (other than LOC targets) were few, and there was therefore little effect on national capacities.

Although the flow of men and material from North Vietnam into South Vietnam and Laos continued, perhaps at an increased rate, the US air effort below the 20th parallel had some adverse effects. Operations from a dispersed logistical base continued to cause management and control problems for Hanoi. The North Vietnamese, in attempting to circumvent the effects of the air strikes, continued to place major emphasis on construction and maintenance of LOCs. While the capacities of the LOCs still greatly exceeded observed traffic densities, the reduction in LOC capacities achieved by US air strikes lessened North Vietnam's capability to sustain an overt attack into South Vietnam and Laos. On the other hand, the capability of the PAVN to perform the missions of national defence, internal security, and to train and support forces in South Vietnam and Laos was not appreciably impaired.

The North Vietnamese leadership stepped up its propaganda campaign to bolster the morale of their populace. This suggested growing concern on the part of North Vietnam's leaders over the effects of the air raids on morale, but there was no evidence of any change in régime policies.

Although the economic impact of air strikes was limited by their restriction to targets of relatively minor economic significance, and by assistance from Communist countries, adverse effects of the bombing were confirmed by Hanoi. Increasing amounts of resources were drawn from agriculture and industry to counter the effects of bomb damage, thereby contributing heavily to constraints on growth in these sectors. Problems resulting from the reallocation of manpower and of inept management continued, with industry experiencing a decline in production. US air strikes on 19 and 23 April halted seaborne exports of coal from Cam Pha port, North Vietnam's principal coal export harbour, causing a substantial reduction for April. A prolonged reduction in exports of coal from Cam Pha would have had a serious effect on North Vietnam's foreign exchange earnings, 25 per cent of which were derived from sales of coal.

Some 2,500 vessels and 1,500 vehicles were destroyed or damaged, apart from fixed installations. Direct cumulative losses caused by confirmed bomb damage to economic and military facilities and equipment were estimated at approximately $59 million; measurable indirect losses amounted to about $10.1 million, made up principally of losses of foreign exchange earnings of $6.6 million and losses in the 1965 autumn rice crop of 3.5 million dollars.

But in the streets of Hanoi, the wandering food sellers still called their wares: thick glutinous rice to be eaten on banana leaf with coconut, beef consommé (*pho*) with noodles and onion, rice-cakes and doughnuts, little pork meat balls, *hu tien*, the Chinese seafood and pork soup. Champagne and other delicacies continued to arrive by air, from Hong Kong via Nanking, at the British Consulate-General.

The Hanoi radio international service in English broadcast the following at 05.32 GMT on 8 August 1966:

In order to calm American pilots, US military officials have described North Vietnam's surface-to-air missiles as ineffective 'flying telephone poles'. At the same time, the US command in Saigon has stopped specifying when American planes are hit by surface-to-air missiles over North Vietnam and, since last March, SAM hits have been merely listed under the general heading of groundfire or enemy fire.

The following is an account by the *Vietnamese Courier* on 28 July of how North Vietnam 'telephone poles' hit and destroyed the most up-to-date US aircraft.

The weather was gorgeous on this afternoon of 15 July. Flakes of snowy clouds sailed in the wind. The anti-aircraft missile fighters of unit X were at the ready. Since the American air pirates raided the periphery of Hanoi and Haiphong, these fighters have been boiling with anger and hatred and intensifying their training with a firmer determination to force the enemy to pay for their crimes. Today they will be able to fulfil their aspiration.

An order came from HQ: Target: a flight of enemy planes at 100 kilometres in the south-east! Everybody at the ready!

The whole battlefield bustled. Like an interrelated system, the reconnaissance, liaison, pinpointing organs worked harmoniously and accurately. Every fighter was absorbed in his duty. Enemy planes in many waves appeared on the radar screen, heading in the direction unit X had expected. They were only fifty-five, then forty, then thirty kilometres off.

The US air pirates split their formation in two, flew at different altitudes, and sought to sidetrack our observation. But such worn-out tricks could not deceive unit X fighters, who never lost sight of the enemy for even one second.

A wave of planes suddenly swooped down. Before they could drop their bombs, an order came from HQ: Target A, fire!

The missiles left the launching ramps and soared up in the direction of the air pirates.

'Got it, got it!' shouted the interceptors. An enemy plane was on fire, clouded in black smoke. It staggered for a while, then plummeted to the ground. The pirate pilot bailed out. When reaching the ground, he lay flat on his back, holding his head with his hands, then hurriedly covering up his body with leaves. But he was caught by the Vietnam People's Army fighters and the militia, coming from all directions.

The other planes either soared up or swooped down for an escape. But they all ran into a net of intensive groundfire: two more marauders paid for their crimes.

The battle ended swiftly and victoriously! Hanoi knocked down three more American jet planes and captured some more American air pirates.

It is now plain that Soviet technicians were present at most of the Sam sites, a charge hotly denied by Soviet interlocutors at the time.

XXV
Giap's Options in 1966

In spring 1965 Hanoi made two fateful decisions: the first to reject the opportunity for negotiations provided by a private Soviet proposal to reconvene the Geneva Conference, followed by the famous Four Points ostensibly to secure American withdrawal but patently designed to discourage negotiations. The second decision was to meet the prospective American build-up of ground forces by continuing the input of PAVN regulars, and to maintain offensive operations, a decision possibly effected by Truong Chinh, Nguyen Chi Thanh and 'the Chinese', and not approved by General Giap.

After the inconclusive battle of the Ia Drang valley, regular PAVN regiments had won no major engagements by November 1966. An operation across the demilitarized zone which began in June was stalled, no important ground was gained and only a small American force diverted from another area. No 'little Dien Bien Phu' was contrived before the US congressional elections. This was matched by the Binh Dinh operation (*Irving*) and the operation in Tay Ninh (*Attleboro*), which took a heavy toll in the long-held base area of War Zone C.

Giap was impressed by the ability of the US to move from one major battle to another. But he saw the war as part of a long-term revolutionary process that began twenty years ago. The North Vietnamese main forces were larger in 1966 than in 1965. The flow of men and *matériel* was adequate to maintain that level. The air and ground intervention of the US had not shaken morale. The Delta was relatively unaffected by US actions: the Communist forces were still intact. In 1965 General Giap had asserted, 'the essential problem, the decisive problem, was who would be the final victor on the battlefields of South Vietnam . . .' In purely military terms, Giap may, in 1966, have had doubts about future strategy.

Politically, Ho Chi Minh and his advisors faced similar ambiguities, including the surprising durability of the Thieu/Ky Government in the South. Hanoi could no longer count on permanent upheaval in Saigon. The DRV could, of course, have supposed that the work of the constituent assembly and national elections would produce a South Vietnamese government more favourable to the Communists as a negotiating partner. Or they may have thought that the development of a constitutional government would prove so disruptive that recent progress would be wiped out.

But the complete collapse of South Vietnam had not occurred, nor had any important southern figure defected to the National Liberation Front since Diem's death. Hanoi's particular concern was the possibility that more ARVN units might be assigned to security roles, requiring larger Viet Cong armed units to combat the South Vietnamese government's, Revolutionary Development programme.

The state of US domestic and international opinion was a main prop in Hanoi's calculations, which would eventually, they believed, drive the US to offer important concessions to disengage from the war. General Giap was convinced that French politics had been as important to his victory as the tide of battle. Since the North Vietnamese believed that American opinion and politics would, in the long term, prove decisive, there was a strong incentive to hang on until mid-1968, the date of the presidential election.

As to Hanoi's evaluation of international opinion, the vaunted 'Third Force' was not at that time a very effective factor. Some of the more strident voices – Nkrumah's, Ben Bella's, Sukarno's – were silent, and Hanoi paid a price for its close alliance with China. Their own intransigence repeatedly denied supporters the means to bring real diplomatic pressures on the US. Outside the Communist world, Bertrand Russell was currently Hanoi's loudest and most colourful champion.

A new factor was the crisis in China caused by the Great Leap Forward and the Cultural Revolution: the DRV could not fail to be concerned about the disruption of stable leadership in Peking. Hanoi was affected in two ways. Firstly, there was growing tension between Moscow and Peking, although Hanoi managed to steer clear skilfully, even profiting materially from Sino-Soviet competition. But given the uncertainties in China, some voices in Washington believed that China might force Hanoi to 'take a stand' against the USSR.

The second effect was to make a less reliable deterrent. The North Vietnamese had noticed that China's international role as Hanoi's champion had been greatly diminished by Peking's domestic troubles. China's *military* potential had not diminished, but there was a growing impression, particularly in Japan, that the danger of

Chinese intervention was receding, depriving the DRV of a high card. China's nuclear missile caused international apprehension, but Hanoi realized that this was far in the future.

The Americans used to regard the USSR as a counterweight to the Chinese. A rise in Soviet influence accordingly meant a rise in the possibility of negotiations, but in 1966 this was not thought realistic at that stage of the war. Although the Soviets saw the Vietnam War as causing strain on US resources and a deterioration of the Western position in Europe, they feared the consequences of escalation. And as neither China nor Russia had enough influence to force decisions on Hanoi, Russia had little choice but to wait for the moment when Hanoi was vulnerable to their advice. This advice would be for Hanoi to move towards a negotiated settlement, but one which the Soviets could not guarantee.

The North Vietnamese themselves had no wish to be entangled in the quarrels of their enormous partners but, however much they disapproved of the Cultural Revolution, they certainly believed that Chou En Lai and even Lin Piao would not allow its effects to damage Hanoi's interests. There had, of course, been no indication in 1966 that Mao's hostility to Moscow would lead to later Chinese détente with the US.

Hanoi had three options. The first was to change the character of the war through escalation by their own forces, or with Chinese help, the latter unlikely so long as the situation in China was unstable. Nevertheless, Chinese Communist volunteers would continue to be stationed in North Vietnam as a form of anti-US deterrence.

The second was to opt for 'protracted war' – guerrilla operations primary, operations in small units, terrorism, sabotage, etc., answering the question of superior US mobility and fire-power in large engagements. A guerrilla strategy was consistent with a policy of long-term resistance, in which the war-weariness of the enemy became the main objective. PAVN regiments could be broken down into smaller units, or retained intact to tie down American forces. Hanoi, Washington hoped, might even withdraw certain units in a bargain for US withdrawal.

The Americans did not know whether a reversion from a 'higher stage' of revolutionary warfare to a lower could be accomplished without damage to the morale and structure of the fighting force. According to General Giap, 'guerrilla war must multiply. To keep itself in life and develop, guerrilla warfare has necessarily to develop into mobile warfare. This is a general law.' The issue of guerrilla versus mobile warfare had been under debate in Hanoi, although expressed as 'offensive' versus 'defensive' operations. The main proponents of the 'offensive' were Le Duan and Le Duc Tho, both of whom had led or would lead the Central Office for South Vietnam (COSVN).

There were, of course, 'doves' who did not believe that the United States could be defeated militarily: theirs was the third option. That was a basic shift in political strategy, to obtain by negotiation or reciprocal action a US withdrawal or diminution of the war in the expectation of gaining Communist objectives by other than current DRV means. But the North Vietnamese feared that negotiations would deny them the gains they had won on the battlefield.

In 1966 Washington believed that Giap would press for greater emphasis on guerrilla tactics, while building up his major units for the future, with General Nguyen Chi Thanh at COSVN as a more fervent advocate of large-unit operations. Washington, or rather the Board of National Estimates of the CIA, was right.

XXVI
The Spokesman

In December 1966 General Giap told Jacques Decornoy of *Le Monde* that the Vietnamese were determined to continue their struggle until they won completely. Final victory would be theirs, both military and political.

For more than two hours, Giap developed his theme without stopping even to catch his breath.

This smiling man, who sometimes burst into laughter, literally sparkled, spoke French, and developed his train of thought with impeccable logic and skill. This former professor of history manipulates Vietnamese history better than any other Vietnamese and, in this country, references to past experiences are important. He talked in terms of military and political strategy, enumerated, classified, listed, put events back in sequence and context, and was not afraid to repeat himself for emphasis.

He said that his country was dealing with a big aggressor, Yankee imperialism, the largest imperialist power in the world, whose military and economic potential was enormous. This self-styled *gendarme* of the world nourished secret aggressive designs. Imperialism was strong, but faced with the peoples of the world, and with Giap's people, it had its weaknesses. The Americans could be defeated and had been, in Vietnam and elsewhere – China, Korea, Cuba, Laos.

In Vietnam, Giap said, when the French Expeditionary Corps was defeated at Dien Bien Phu, the US played an important part. Arms, bombs and ammunition bore American markings. Nevertheless, America did not then intervene militarily. Washington weighed the pros and cons.

Since Geneva, the Americans had gone through various stages, from defeat to defeat. In the first stage, they maintained a neo-colonial policy under Diem, which proved a bloody dictatorship with an Army of 200,000 men. As US policies brought defeat, they began 'special war' from 1961 to 1964, open military intervention, equipment for 500,000 men, and economic aid. By the end of 1964, American advisers numbered about 30,000 and were practically in charge, using recent experience in their struggle against the 'emancipation' of the Phillipines, Greece, Malaysia. Washington was confident of victory, but 'special warfare' was defeated. At the end of 1964, the 500,000 men equipped by the Americans could not stand up against the tide of the popular movement by the people of the South. In the current stage, the Americans were testing localized war with infantry, the 7th Fleet, invasion of the South and the bombing of the North.

The American troops were sent to avoid a débâcle: they believed that, with this new strategy, the people of North and South would capitulate. They could not believe that the people would be able to stand up against the bombers. The Americans caused many losses and problems, but the DRV was holding on.

In the South, the Expeditionary Forces had gone from 50,000 men to more than 400,000, counting 'satellites'. With 500,000 'marionettes', that made about one million, counting the 7th Fleet. Well, then! With one million men, including 350,000 Americans and the 7th Fleet, plus strong air-power, have they been able to reach their goal? No. Johnson said that they must expect a hard and a long war, that 'pacification' was not very successful. The Pentagon said that 'the war was going to last a long time'. Westmoreland told you that he lacked supplies and manpower . . .

Westmoreland's first goal was to annihiliate the liberation forces, but the liberation forces had not been wiped out and were growing bigger.

The second goal was 'pacification', to win the people over. The US thought that they could do this with the 'almighty dollar'. A feudal Vietnamese adage says that 'with money you can buy anything, including witches and fairies', but 'pacification' had not been accomplished. Johnson's famous Second Front had not materialized.

The third objective was to reinforce the 'puppet army'. The goal had not been reached. Did Ky's government enjoy greater prestige than previous governments? The Americans ruled in Saigon. The war was American. It must have surprised the Americans, as they built up their own strength, to find that the strength of the puppet army diminished. The puppet troops had lost their capacity for combat since the arrival of the Americans.

The fourth goal was to isolate the South. But the South and its fourteen million inhabitants had the strength to build up the ranks of the Liberation Army.

The fifth objective was to increase the bombing of the North to bring the people to 'a peace table', strange peace table, where the guests were invited by bombs. We have not capitulated. We are still holding on. We are more determined than ever to fight the aggressor. The Americans believed that if they bombed the North, they would force capitulation because the losses would lead to chaos and collapsed morale, all to improve the morale of the marionettes.

We are an independent, sovereign, Socialist country with a fighting history. The Americans are violating the most elementary international laws by bombing the North, and the Vietnamese people as a whole are more determined than ever to fight as a consequence of this criminal aggression . . .

If we understand why the Americans have not yet won, we will understand why *we* will win. If we employed the formal logic of the aggressor, the US would have already overwhelmed our resistance efforts. Why has this not happened? Because the Vietnamese people have strength too and the Americans have weaknesses.

If one goes a step further, one can see the truth. Our army was inferior to the French in manpower, equipment, armour and aircraft; President Ho often jests saying that 'we lost no tanks or planes'.

Remember the French Revolution, remember Valmy and the badly equipped soldiers facing the Prussian regulars; and the ill-equipped soldiers won. To understand us, think about those heroic hours of the French people. There is one major difference between US technical strength and our own. The Americans are facing us after we have reached the twentieth century. The national consciousness of our people has reached a high plane, and technically the difference is only relative. With their moral strength, the people of Vietnam can use their technical strength to defeat the enemy. The fact that the Americans with 500,000 marionettes are going from defeat to defeat is beyond current imagination. We are proud of the struggle of our people; they are writing the most glorious pages of their history.

Let us speak a bit of these Vietnamese people who have a history of struggle against aggressors. In the thirteenth century the Mongols were beaten by us three times. In modern times we have fought the Japanese, the French, and now the Americans. When the Americans sent troops as part of their 'special war strategy', they had already lost the rescue operation. Things had got out of control. Manpower, might and military tactics are not the decisive factors in this war. That the Americans constantly have to increase their strength and manpower shows that it is not a classical war. The specialists on 'special wars' said that to win a war of liberation, you need odds of twenty-five to one, at least fifteen or ten to one. McNamara tried to secure these odds; he increased his manpower, but so did the liberation troops. They say that when the odds are three to zero, alarms should ring. Measuring strength is not an arithmetic problem: with odds of three to one or five to one, they said they could win if technical strength were improved, but even with this improvement they failed.

This is a war of aggression against an entire people. American public opinion will see the injustice of the war more clearly each day.

Strategically, when their troops arrived, the Americans did not have the initiative. They were losing the 'special war'. The entire population of Vietnam had been politically and militarily mobilized for twenty years. Then the Americans had to disperse their forces, in Saigon, on the high plateaux, at Tourane and elsewhere. Everywhere they must disperse troops from their bases. That is why they lack manpower. If they keep the terrain, they must disperse. If they do not disperse, they cannot keep the terrain. There is a basic contradiction between 'searching and destroying' and 'holding'. They cannot seize the initiative. Now the Americans are settling down to carry on a long war. They do not know whether to establish bases in depth in the country or on the coast; they wonder if they can cooperate with the puppets, or if the missions should be divided.

Tactically, the American troops, besides not knowing why they are here, lack ideals. Nor can they fight as they have been taught, but must do so under the unfavourable conditions imposed upon them by the Army of Liberation. They are not cut out to fight on the Asian continent and even less well suited to fighting in the tropics. But that is not the main point. The main point is that, even with better tactics, they will lose the war with a whole people against them. They are facing the strategy and tactics of a people's war.

Their troops were to reinforce the puppet troops, to act as a political booster, to lift the morale of the Saigon régime. The puppet army will however, collapse. It is already an American war. But even if the Americans took over the country and increased their manpower to 750,000 men, they would also fail. Our people will not break. The greater the escalation, the more stinging the defeat.

At first, the Americans wanted to annihilate the forces of the Front. Then, after 'Honolulu', they engaged in clean-up expeditions to control populated areas. They tried many things, impeding the life of civilians with artillery and Air Force. But although manpower is not lacking, Ambassador Lodge has admitted the failure of 'pacification'.

Vietnam is one. All the people rose up as a sacred duty. We support our compatriots in the South with all our strength; we declare that we are the ones who stand by the 1954 Agreements.

There is no path open to us except to fight. The Americans say that they want a political solution, while trying to settle the problem with arms. Well, then, in order to convince the Americans, we must win a victory. We want freedom and independence, we want peace, but a real peace, not one under the boot of the aggressor, which is the American version of peace. The Americans will only abandon their aggressive goals if they are forced to. We will not shrink before sacrifice because we are convinced that, only through these sacrifices will we win this sacred war of independence and progress along the lines of development. The day the Americans see that they cannot win the war, they will give up.

That day in Lisbon, Vo Nguyen Giap's book *War of the People, Army of the People*, published in Portugal by Sera Nova, was seized from every library in the country by the PIDE (the Portuguese political police).

XXVII
Pacification versus Attrition

Attrition has been described as 'killing the enemy's trained soldiers in the hope that someone will negotiate'. But a Senate committee in 1951 said that 'American policy' in all other wars had been 'designed to win the conflict at the earliest possible moment with the least possible loss of human life', whether American or enemy. In Vietnam, apart from strategic error, attrition also 'influenced American idealism and eroded public support for the war'.

In January 1967, when the journalist Wilfred Burchett asked for Giap's views on 'pacification', both assumed that this would be mainly conducted by ARVN troops. The general replied that, since Saigon had tried uselessly to pacify South Vietnam for the past twelve years, further efforts by 'those puppets' would only lead to disaster. He agreed, nevertheless, that pacification was indeed a threat to the progress of his own operations in the South.

In a statement that year, of almost Alice-in-Wonderland complexity, Giap said, however, that pacification had been forced on the United States by his own guerrilla actions. It was to be welcomed because it prevented American concentration against PAVN and VC main forces. It diluted the American/ARVN numerical advantage into frantic efforts at Pan-Vietnam defence. The Allies had become mindlessly, even hysterically, reactive without coherent strategy or even tactics, slaves of counter-insurgency, a contention that must have reassured Westmoreland.

A more conventional assessment is that to confine attrition almost exclusively to US combat units was to relegate the ARVN to static security duties. Two military commands, effectively conducting different strategies, made it even easier for Westmoreland to downgrade pacification as a lesser objective.

But by August 1966 General Westmoreland had in fact begun to include among his objectives 'maximum support to area and population security' and allocated, at least nominally, a 'significant number' of American battalions to that role. In September, the 25th Division from Hawaii, under Major-General Fred C. (Frederick Carlton) Weyand, a hero of the Korea War, carried out Operation

Lanikai, in Long An province by the Parrot's Beak, which conformed to the objective. It was mounted with ARVN as well as US troops, discouraged the creation of refugees, and restricted air and ground fire-power against villages. The engagement was a qualified success, resulting in the unusually high number of 105 VC defectors.

But although the battalion concerned began to settle in the pacified area, it was taken away after only two months to fight in a main-force action code-named *Fairfax* in Gia Dinh. (From 1966 to 1967 the division's other battalions were also reallocated.) The Viet Cong moved into Long An again, while the US battalions continued tos be engaged elsewhere in direct confrontations with NVA and PLAF units. Westmoreland, in other words, in order to keep the enemy out of populated areas like Long An, followed his policy of attrition. 'Search and destroy' occupied the overwhelming majority of American troops, pacification reverting to the often corrupt and incompetent mercies of the government of Vietnam.

In October 1966 McNamara reported depressingly to the US President on both pacification and the condition of the ARVN. His recommendations included greater emphasis on the former, new restrictions on the bombing of the North, and increased pressure on the Saigon generals to reform both the ARVN and the condition of their society, in order to produce some semblance of efficiency. He had become increasingly doubtful, even pessimistic, about the course of 'McNamara's war' and, in early 1968, resigned, to become President of the World Bank.

Very little was done to implement his proposals. One thousand Americans out of a force of 22,000 were killed and wounded during Operation *Attleboro* in the Tay Ninh jungles during November 1966. From January to May 1967, first Operation *Cedar Falls*, then Operation *Junction City*, were implemented with extensive and effective use of armour to clear the Iron Triangle jungles, a few miles north-east of Saigon and a constant menace to the capital. The Triangle also periodically contained the Central Office for South Vietnam (COSVN), then General Nguyen Chi Thanh's head-quarters. But COSVN was very mobile, occasionally reappearing even in Cambodia.

One PAVN regiment and two or three Viet Cong battalions were in the region, opposing the 25th United States Division and an ARVN battalion which also disposed of massive artillery support from a dozen 'fire-bases'. The North Vietnamese forces avoided a major confrontation, although losing three times the American casualties; Viet Cong and PAVN returned to the Triangle, vacated by the US and the ARVN less than a month after *Cedar Falls* ended. In February John Deane's 173rd Airborne and first Division Brigade struck south in Operation *Junction City*, inflicting really severe casualties – over 1,900 men wounded or killed – on the 'anvil' of *Cedar Falls*. But again the VC came back.

These sweltering battles were fought in rain or implacable heat by the PAVN, with mortars and 75mm recoilless rifles against 90mm and 105mm American artillery, helicopters, tanks and APCs, US infantry using M-1s, M-14s and M-16s. The North Vietnamese infantry charged in human waves to the bugle, in front, behind, on the flank. They never beat the 25th Division and, as they died in their thousands, their bodies were 'dumped in open trenches . . .'

Morley Safer, in *Flashbacks*, comments that the paddi, eucalypt forests and rubber estates of Binh Duong and Hau Nghia had been turned into a moonscape. 'The people endured in relocation camps or in underground, stinking, infested tunnels . . . that neither courage, nor determination, nor sophisticated gases could eliminate. If the war could not be won in the Iron Triangle, then the war could not be won.'

These extraordinary tunnels at Cu Chi were less than a kilometre from the US 25th Infantry base at Dong Zu. The Americans were always visible and their movements were always known . . . the Viet Cong never fired until they were within twenty yards range.

The Americans did not find COSVN. That body had transferred itself again into Cambodia. They did, as we have seen, carry out an effective attrition operation. They deprived the 'fish' of their 'ocean' by the forced expulsion of 6,000 Cochinchinese who had provided the Viet Cong with intelligence, food, income and the other facilities essential to guerrillas and main units alike. They destroyed, on a very large scale, trenches, tunnels and subterranean installations. A joint US/ARVN action near Kontum at this time also caused major losses to PAVN and VC, while a revenge attack by a Viet Cong division was bloodily shattered by B52s using high explosives and anti-personnel bombs, and artillery barrages.

Giap's claim that *Junction City* alone had led to the deaths of '13,000 allied soldiers' was either based on extremely inventive reporting by his commanders, or was a plain propaganda lie. In reality, perhaps 3,000 PAVN/VC and 2,000 US/ARVN were killed or wounded, the majority of the Allies wounded rather than killed. The VC lost hundreds of tons of ammunition and equipment. Giap's plan to isolate and overwhelm Saigon itself was temporarily defeated. Some 500,000 pages (40 lb) of secret PAVN documents were captured.

But the American assaults on the three Viet Cong/PAVN divisions around Saigon in II Corps, although holding off the thrust on the capital from Phuoc Tuy province and War Zones C and D, divided US strength between III Corps, other areas such as the central highlands, and the VC concentration in I Corps, the northern part of South Vietnam. In I Corps Giap fought in phase two mode, attacking US camps and bases, thus reducing the US technological and numerical superiority in airpower and ground mobility which could have been devoted to III Corps. He also forced the Americans everywhere to fight on terrain – jungle, mountain, and marsh – which had been selected by Hanoi and not by General Westmoreland.

Now Giap started to exert further pressure on I Corps, infiltrating more North Vietnamese units across the demilitarized zone (DMZ). This led the Americans to devise in 1967 a barrier right across the country and into Laos, to be equipped with mines, lasers, fire-bases and so on. (A similar plan had been proposed by ARVN General Cao Van Vien in 1965, to be coupled with seaborne landings in North Vietnam.) Because of the diversion of troops needed to man or support it, and because of the volume of fire directed from the DRV at the work force, the barrier was never finished. Although incomplete, it did help to channel PAVN infiltrators into corridors where some at least were dealt with, even if it did not 'cut off the North's front from its rear'.

Had this measure been executed, a tactical US offensive along the DMZ into Laos and against the Ho Chi Minh Trail might have been the only successful way to 'isolate the battlefield', without taking the land war into North Vietnam. (It would have, incidentally, almost halved the size of the Expeditionary Force). It could, in other words, have broken the PAVN's assault on South Vietnam, deprived the Viet Cong of support, and led to a negotiated settlement, even to victory. By cutting off Hanoi's military roots, it was the latter-day equivalent of that earlier alternative, aerial mining and bombardment of Haiphong and the Sino-Vietnamese land and sea entry points.

The sheer numbers of Viet Cong and NVA troops in this area produced in Robert O'Neill's opinion, 'a similar effect to that achieved by Giap at Dien Bien Phu'. The threat obliged the Americans to create strong points which, however, were so tightly beset that they could not be used for aggressive patrolling or for any other purpose than to defend themselves under siege. Unlike, however, Dien Bien Phu, the Americans had a monopoly of air-power and great superiority in artillery up to 175 mm, which at least enabled them to gain their tactical objectives, if at great cost. MACV was also helped by sensors code-named 'Igloo White' which either hung in the branches of jungle trees, or, simulating bamboo shoots, buried themselves in the earth, recording voices or move-ment and transmitting them by indirect means in Thailand or at sea to the bombers overhead.

Fighting had taken place in I Corps (Quang Tri province) since September 1966, when a French airstrip had been upgraded in the Khe Sanh valley – tiger country and the home of the Bru minority. The Americans already had a Special Forces camp in the valley. The commander-in-chief then ordered the deployment to Khe Sanh of a Marine Corps battalion, allegedly as a preparatory move for any US thrust into Laos. The Marine general commanding Fleet Marine Force Pacific, General Victor (Brute) Krulak, believed that Westmoreland's real purpose was to use the Marines, who also deployed five more battalions in the north of the province, as a magnet for PAVN and VC units, which were then to be destroyed by US bombing and artillery. Krulak saw therein evil consequences for pacification.

Westmoreland believed that Giap's plans included a major attack in 1967 and 1968 across the demilitarized zone and down the Ho Chi Minh Trail into the three or four northern provinces of I Corps. When Giap's forces, which included two PLAF regiments (272 and 273) and two PAVN regiments with new heavy mortars, rocket-launchers and other Soviet and Chinese equipment, started a variety of engagements in the jungles and along the demilitarized zone, the Americans regarded their assessment as confirmed.

Battles took place in October and November at Loc Ninh, lasting a week, at Song Be, Con Thien, and Dak To in Kontum province. Dak To lasted nearly three weeks and caused 300 US casualties against 1,200 VC and North Vietnamese. These battles have been subsequently categorized by Giap as part of the second phase of his winter and spring offensive, preparatory to the Tet offensive, the third phase or 'Second Wave'.

US and allied forces taking part were the 1st Air Cavalry, the 173rd Airborne, the 4th US Infantry Division, six ARVN battalions, plus 800 B-52 flights with 22,000 tons of bombs in the Con Thien action alone, not to speak of heavy artillery and the guns of the 7th Fleet. But at Con Thien the Vietnamese had relearned the use of heavy artillery, including Russian Katyushas and guns with calibres up to 152 mm.

'First Khe Sanh' took place in April 1967. The American objective was to take and hold three hills, 861, 881 south and 881 north, in a ridge which dominated the airfield and the Khe Sanh valley, and which were held by PAVN Division 325c. The battle resembled those at Church Knoll and Hunter's Hill south-east of Kohima, and at Aradura, during the British campaign in Burma from April to June 1944. Each time the Americans climbed to within twenty yards of the summit, like the Punjabis, Sikhs, Queen's and Gurkhas against the Japanese, they were repulsed by mortars (82 mm in this case) from pits behind bunkers, and by automatic fire from within them.

These bunkers, invisible to the Americans under the tree cover, two-man or four-man, had their own telephones, drainage systems, living quarters, shelves and matting floor. The overhead coverage on the smaller ones consisted of six-foot layers of bamboo and grass. The larger bunkers had log roofs eight-foot thick with four feet of packed earth. They were invulnerable to mortars, napalm, 250lb and 500lb bombs (except direct hits), or to rockets and cannon. Very little damage was caused by the artillery, whether 105, 155 or 175 mm. It was not until the Marines were ordered off hill 881 south and their assaults replaced by 750lb, 1,000lb and 2,000lb bombs with delay fuses that the high explosives could penetrate the bunkers and explode them.

Even then, in the torrential rain and fog, the paths reduced to liquid mud, the 18th PAVN Regiment not only escaped from 881 south to 881 north, but were there relieved by 95th Regiment from 325c Division. When the Marines after bombardment by 2,000lb bombs, advanced up 881 north, they were met by heavy rain and a roaring gale. To conquer these three terrible hills, the Marines required seventeen days, each day fought hand-to-hand and bunker to bunker, with hundreds of corpses rotting and corrupt in the vile monsoon. Over 150 Americans died; 700 PAVN soldiers were killed, against some of the best and toughest assault troops in the world. Giap had again obliged the US infantry to fight on his terms, in his own territorial circumstances, so alien to American training and ethos. He had also forced the Marines to abandon littoral pacification, allowing almost *chasse gardée* to the Viet Cong and their NVA supporters on the coasts.

From May to August 1967 Task Force Oregon, later to become the US 23rd or Americal Division, conducted search-and-destroy operations (*Malheur*) against fortified villages in Quang Ngai province. (The Americal was later accused of indiscipline, the distribution of the chemical defoliant Agent Orange after its earlier prohibition, even of war crimes.) These strikes led to the burning of whole hamlets, and to forced evacuations of peasants, which had, by that time, almost reached the status of policy. The Allies claimed to be too weak on the ground to remain in the villages after battle and guarantee Annamite security. Another operation, *Dragon Head*, in north Quang Ngai, by the same formation, led to similarly large numbers of refugees, the torching of houses, 'the depopulation and destruction of large sections of the province'. The press naturally played down or even omitted to report the VC's trenches, caves and tunnels in the hamlets, but as most of the peasants were under the harshest Communist duress, it may be thought that the villagers had no option but submission to 'Victor Charlie'.

In these and in the Binh Dinh operations, the Viet Cong suffered considerable losses but, by exploiting their knowledge of terrain to escape the US advance, usually evaded the most bruising encounters with their enemy.

XXVIII
'Negotiations'

Attrition seemed to have buried pacification. Opposition grew among the generals – Weyand, Krulak, and Lewis Walt, Commander Marines Vietnam – to General Westmoreland's plans, especially over pacification, dispersal and the very survival of their own men in pursuit of an unnecessarily dangerous and ultimately fatal strategy.

The more effective attrition, some of them thought, was that affected by Hanoi in hand-to-hand or close-quarters combat, which reduced the American advantages of artillery and air-power. Attrition caused US casualties which, Giap knew, would lead to the same failure of will in Washington as the French killed and wounded of 1954 had brought about in Paris.

It was not that any of these senior officers wanted to let the PAVN and Viet Cong lie at ease but they wanted to maximize air-power against them, using ground troops only where they would not reduce the effects of pacification or otherwise diminish US interests and advantage. Reform and pacification, they said, were the only practicable means of restoring the authority of the government of Vietnam. The strategy was, or should be, to secure bases and expand therefrom, depriving the Communist enemy of local support in their mountains, jungles and forests. They would force upon the enemy dependence on the long, difficult trails and railways from the North.

But neither they nor Admiral Sharp saw much virtue in aerial interdiction of the Northern supply routes, only, or chiefly, in intervention against Haiphong, the ports and the 'marshalling' entry points along the Sino-Vietnamese border. That proposal was put to Averell Harriman, the millionaire elder statesman, pusillanimously wrong on every political issue of his long, disastrous public life. His response – 'Do you want war with the USSR and China?' – was sadly refuted for the United States six years later by the inaction of either power during the Easter and Christmas bombings of 1972.

In late 1966 McNamara had proposed a bombing halt. The joint chiefs of staff had opposed a curtailment even of the current emasculated *Rolling Thunder* against potential concessions by Hanoi. In 1967 a CIA survey of the 1966 bombing programme offered the president no comfort; in May, Robert McNamara advocated the limitation of US bombing to the North–South infiltration points. In August, on the contrary, LBJ lifted restrictions on the bombing of the North, opening Hanoi, Haiphong and targets near the Sino-Vietnamese border to air strikes. The new policy was instantly successful in reducing the supply southward of fresh Soviet and Chinese *matériel*, a phenomenon ignored by planners presumably 'frighted by the false fire' of a Sino-Soviet hostile reaction, which never came.

As for negotiations, in 1963 President Johnson had seen J. Blair Seaborn, the Canadian representative on the International Control Commission (ICC) whose duty was to monitor in Vietnam the application of the 1954 Geneva Agreements. Seaborn was asked to tell the DRV prime minister, Pham Van Dong, that the USA would recognize Hanoi and help it economically if the North Vietnamese were to stop their aid to the Viet Cong. If Hanoi did not agree, bombing and naval bombardment would follow.

The prime minister could only agree if the Viet Cong were permitted to join a 'neutral' government in Saigon and if the Americans were to leave South Vietnam altogether. Seaborn saw Dong again on several occasions. He repeated to him Johnson's offer on 13 August. Dong told him to come back with American proposals based on the Geneva Agreements. U Thant, former Burmese secretary-general of the United Nations, then independently arranged for a DRV/US meeting in Rangoon, an idea supported in parallel by Khrushchev, but which collapsed after Khrushchev was removed from power by his own Politburo in Moscow.

In a March 1965 speech, the president then offered the DRV participation in the US-funded project to create economic development along the Mekong River. Pham Van Dong again insisted that until the bombing ended, and until a 'neutral coalition government' could be founded in South Vietnam to include the Viet Cong, no talks of any kind could be held or offers accepted. Another Canadian diplomat in the ICC, Chester Ronning, with Washington's partial and wary agreement, saw the prime minister in March 1966. Pham Van Dong demanded an unconditional end to the bombing before Hanoi would agree to talks, 'which could, however, then lead to formal negotiation' based on Hanoi's earlier preconditions.

Also in 1966, Janusz Lewandowski, Polish delegate on the ICC, told the Italian ambassador in Saigon that he had received a 'specific peace offer' from Ho Chi Minh, who was 'ready for compromise and would take steps towards an agreement'. The North Vietnamese, he said, no longer demanded that the Americans leave South Vietnam immediately, nor that the Viet Cong 'take part' in the government, nor even that that government be dissolved. They demanded only that the bombing be 'suspended' and that the VC should *have a role* in any negotiations. After talking to Henry Cabot Lodge, the US ambassador, Lewandowski assured the North Vietnamese that Washington would protect ('take account of') the Viet Cong's position in any consequent agreement. Hanoi then agreed to talks in Warsaw between their officials and the American embassy, but 'because of continued US air raids near Hanoi', Pham Van Dong then cancelled them.

According to Wilfred Burchett, the approach had been a Soviet project anyway; a European Communist official thought that Lewandowski had even been acting 'on his own', at least without proper authority.

In January 1967 two Americans from the Centre for the Study of Democratic Institutions in California were invited by Ho Chi Minh to Hanoi. On their return Messrs Baggs and Ashmore were able to annouce that Ho had asserted that, provided the US halted their southern build-up and stopped the bombing, 'everything could be negotiated'. Johnson, although he sent the DRV a temporizing letter proposing reciprocal restraint, refused to see either of these two men. In a separate letter to Ho, the president emphasized that unless the NVA ceased infiltration into the South, he would neither halt the bombing nor take any other conciliatory measures. This was a reversal of an earlier plan to stop the bombing and then undertake reciprocal PAVN/US withdrawals from the South.

Harold Wilson, then Prime Minister of the United Kingdom, at this point proposed that he should exploit Kosygin's visit to London in February 1967 to bring Soviet influence to bear. In the middle of his talks, Washington appears to have altered proposals which had already been given, via the UK, to Kosygin, and then issued a revised draft on Sunday 12 February, to which the US demanded DRV agreement by the following afternoon. With such ridiculous notice, no agreement could be obtained. The US air-raids began again. Kosygin went back to Moscow.

Another channel to the North Vietnamese was opened by two
Frenchmen, vetted by Henry Kissinger, then a don at Harvard, who
subsequently arranged their visit to Hanoi. One of the two had
known Ho Chi Minh from the latter's visit to Paris in 1946. They
proposed to Pham Van Dong in Hanoi that the US bombing could
end provided that the PAVN did not exploit the 'halt' to gain
advantage. President Johnson publicly endorsed the proposal on
condition that the bombing pause led to 'meaningful' discussions.
There was a certain tergiversation on the Communist side but, in
any case, President Johnson and the PAVN increased their respective
escalations at about this time without apparent reference to
Monsieur Aubrac of the FAO or Monsieur Marcovich, a biologist.

This approach, like the others, could therefore be described in the
words of Stanley Karnow in the context of the Wilson initiative:
'simply another refusal by the belligerents to shift to the conference
table before they had improved their battlefield postures'. Other
intermediaries, from India and elsewhere, hot for the Nobel Prize,
were to raise their snouts over the next few years.

In 1965 the Hungarian foreign minister, a former bishop called
Janos Péter, had falsely and arbitrarily told the American secretary
of state that, if the USAF stopped bombing the North, negotiations
could begin. This led to a cessation of bombing over Christmas, but
to nothing else. A KGB plan, purporting to emanate from Hanoi
temporarily persuaded both Adlai Stevenson and the UN secretary-
general, U Thant, that the North Vietnamese were willing to come
to the conference table. Adam Rapacki, the Polish foreign minister,
put forward similarly baseless proposals to the United States in the
'Marigold Plan'.

In fact neither China nor the Soviet Union, nor the North
Vietnamese, were prepared for anything less than the unconditional
withdrawal of United States forces from South Vietnam.

For his part, by the end of 1967 Giap intended to make no
concessions to bring the conflict to an early end. He was as
determined as ever and confident of ultimate victory. A 'quick
victory' was an essential component of US military strategy. But
Giap saw that America had limited its military objectives in Vietnam
in order to prevent the war from interfering with 'political,
economic and social life' in the metropolitan United States, or with
US foreign policy elsewhere. He drew the correct conclusion,
although he also, as a Marxist, erroneously believed in major

political contradictions between Saigon and Washington, none of which became militarily significant.

This in no way deterred him from accepting the contrived farce of Burchett's Paris 'intermediary' in late 1967, which brought about the most significant bombing halt of all, significant in the respite it provided for a potentially defeated DRV.

XXIX
Giap's New Strategy

In January 1967 Giap had rejoiced that the United States had failed either to annihilate the PLAF, to pacify the South, to strengthen the Saigon administration, to isolate the South on land and sea, or to force the North to negotiate under American bombs. In September, he professed even greater confidence that dispersal had been forced on the Americans, that they had to fight the protracted war which was the war that Vo Nguyen Giap sought, that search-and-destroy had been a failure, that the US was now on the strategic defensive.

Giap's essential view was that the US had been thwarted in its plan quickly to attack and destroy the Communist main forces. Because of its world-wide military commitments, the US could put only a limited number of troops into South Vietnam. It had originally counted on quick victory at a relatively small price, but its failure to achieve this had forced it unwillingly to fight a prolonged conflict. In such a long-term struggle, the advantage remained with the Communist side, better able to persist. There were basic US weaknesses, which would eventually bring about US defeat in a protracted war.

One basic weakness of was, he said, the inability of the South Vietnamese Army (ARVN) to perform adequately either as a combat or as a pacification force. This had forced the US to send additional troops to Vietnam and to spread its forces thin in an effort to take up the slack caused by the ARVN's failure. Giap confidently predicted that the performance of the ARVN would not significantly improve and, in fact, would further deteriorate, forcing the US to divert more forces from their primary task of seeking out and destroying the Communist main forces. The problem facing the US was so great that putting another 50,000 US troops into South Vietnam would be like 'throwing salt into the sea'. Even another 100,000–200,000 US troops would not suffice to alter the 'stalemate'. A perpetuation of the 'stalemate' was more advantageous to the Communists than to the Allies.

Even more important than US weaknesses was the role of Communist tactics. General Giap had long believed in guerrilla and unconventional warfare. While praising the regular Communist forces in South Vietnam, he emphasized unconventional tactics such as lightning raids on urban centres, sporadic mortar and rocket strikes against air bases and camps, and harassment of allied lines of communication.

If Communist forces could remain in the field, keeping the Allies spread out and unable to concentrate their forces, they could inflict casualties and avoid head-on clashes with more powerful US units. In time, the Allies would tire of the war, and the Communists would gain an acceptable settlement.

Giap emphasized a tactic which he himself used successfully in the French war: concentration of main-force units in a single strategic area rather than dispersing them less effectively throughout the country. Such an area, according to Giap's theses, was carefully chosen, close to a safe haven from which troops could be quickly withdrawn or reinforced, and for which resupply was relatively easy. Giap found the Quang Tri-Thua Thien area, just south of the demilitarized zone, such a strategic area: here this concentration of main-force troop strength tied down large numbers of US troops in areas of Communist choice, forcing the US to react by drawing down allied troop strength and fighting capacity in other areas. Giap claimed that such a strategy enabled the Communists effectively to counter superior enemy strength without attempting to match it man for man. It also relieved US pressure on other areas and enabled Communist local guerrilla and regional forces, in conjunction with limited numbers of main-force units, to operate more effectively in widespread areas of South Vietnam.

The relative *concentration* of Communist main-force units advocated by Giap directly contradicted General Nguyen Chi Thanh's arguments when directing the fighting in the South before his death in July 1967. In mid-1966, Thanh called for a widespread build-up of main-force units as the only way to challenge the build-up of US forces in South Vietnam: for the first time Giap now openly identified himself with the opposition.

Giap departed further from Thanh in asserting that the war could be won through main forces which did not 'necessarily possess a strength equalling that of the enemy'. The build-up of main forces 'must conform to the conditions of each region and battlefield', i.e., where the US position was strong, Giap warned against over-committing Communist assets. To the Americans, however, Giap seemed to be constructing a rationale for the then current Communist tactic of building up forces in the highlands and northern part of South Vietnam, while maintaining Communist strength only at current levels in some other areas, II Coastal Corps and the region north-east of Saigon. To the extent that heavy losses and interdiction of supply lines inhibited a significant build-up of forces in certain areas, the strategy had been forced on Hanoi.

Giap also applauded the 'independent fighting method' of elements of the Communist armed forces, including mortar and rocket attacks on allied base areas and command raids on enemy strongpoints by small, high-grade, 'crack, special units', complementing the 'coordinated warfare' long the standard tactic of Communist strategists.

General Vo Nguyen Giap anticipated that the US might further escalate the war against both North and South Vietnam. 'The US might also even invade North Vietnam, or expand the ground war into Cambodia and Laos', bomb North Vietnam's populated centres, further strike its lines of communications, blockade the coast, and bomb the dams and dikes. Greater efforts would be needed for the Communists successfully to counter the expected increase in US military activity. In the North, Giap called for better military training, an expanded militia force, improved air defence and more strenuous efforts to keep open the lines of communication. In the South, he called for more coordination between the various elements of the Communist armed forces.

But his main intentions lay elsewhere.

From September 1967 to January 1968 the Viet Cong had suffered severe losses, particularly in Phu Yen, Khanh Hoa and Binh Dinh provinces, where the 'liberated' areas greatly shrank. ARVN and allied forces were not so active in Quang Ngai, Quang Nam and Da Nang, but they still inflicted heavy casualties on the VC that PAVN infiltration could not make up.

During 1967 the Viet Cong also pretended to be weakening in order to mislead the RVN and its allies. In reality, men and weapons were moved into South Vietnam in considerable quantity. Hanoi believed that the US would increase its strength in South Vietnam during the summer of 1968: the Communists wanted to increase their own strength first. Hanoi also planned to put the greatest possible pressure on the US during 1968, the year of the US presidential elections.

Although his fate remains controversial, 'officially' General Nguyen Chi Thanh had been recalled to North Vietnam because of the failure of his strategy. Giap 'reconsidered' the South Vietnamese battlefield: Thanh had been mistaken in occupying rural areas, and trying to hold on to them, resulting in the elimination of Viet Cong troops by ARVN, and by B-52 bombers. Delegations from Communist China, North Korea and Cuba had visited the South Vietnamese battlefields and, upon returning to North Vietnam, had reported unfavourably on the situation. Before Thanh's removal, or death, serious thought had therefore been given in Hanoi to Soviet pressure for negotiations with the United States.

As for the Communists' opponents, Giap believed that co-ordination between allied and ARVN troops was loose. Allied troops only tried to protect their own bases. ARVN troops were widely scattered because of their use in the rural reconstruction programme. They could easily be separated and destroyed. The US would support government troops only with air and artillery, not with infantry.

Giap ordered the following new three-phase strategy:

Phase one: Attacks on, and protection of, rural areas would be limited. At the right time, a general offensive against South Vietnamese cities would be launched. Except in important cities like Saigon and Huë, only one half of available forces, experienced local combat units, would be committed. This general offensive would cause ARVN to pull back to protect the cities, leaving the rural areas to the Viet Cong. The Viet Cong would thus achieve complete victory in the rural areas without the need to fight there.

Phase two: If the general offensive failed, Viet Cong troops would retreat, surrounding the cities and villages to create a chaotic situation, to exhaust the economy and break the piastre. At the same time, the Viet Cong would decoy as many US troops as possible into the Khe Sanh area, thus reducing US strength in other areas.

Phase three: Because of the pressures generated by phase two, the government of South Vietnam would probably agree to accept a coalition government with the National Front for the Liberation of South Vietnam. Simultaneously with the demand for a coalition government, North Vietnam would launch a *decisive battle*, with a view to providing political support to the Front element in such a government. This battle would occur in either the Kontum–Pleiku area or the area around Saigon, Binh Long, Phuoc Long, Phuoc Tuy,

Bien Hoa, Tay Ninh and Gia Dinh provinces, important battlefields because of their closeness to supply routes from Cambodia.

The Viet Cong would fight in Kontum and Pleiku provinces because the North Vietnamese high command could easily support that area across the Laotian/Vietnamese border against the strong US/ARVN forces there in those two provinces.

In order to carry out the new strategy, all activities in the southern part of Laos should be increased so that most regular North Vietnamese Army units (other than coastal defence units, anti-aircraft units and units guarding important installations) could infiltrate into South Vietnam. *All forces would be used to attack US troops, to lure them to the Khe Sanh area, away from the decisive battle areas.*

Although in the past Viet Cong/North Vietnamese Army troops had fought against US troops, the new 'surprise' strategy required them to avoid such combat, only to besiege and hold them in defensive positions at bases.

Giap's strategy was approved by the Politburo. Le Duan took it to Moscow. The Soviets approved it and changed aid policy from a 'passive' policy to accelerated despatch before October 1967 of weapons, armour and experts to the DRV. In general, and despite reverses, Hanoi believed that the northerners were now better led and trained. Their mobility had improved, and so had their morale. The Americans were unhappy in the jungles and mountains of the tropics. Opinion in the US was turning against the war. The ARVN were penetrated, corrupt, undependable and often cowardly. US troops had too large an administrative tail and did not stay long enough in-country to deal with the conditions they had to face.

The offensive was preceded and accompanied by the deification of 'Nguyen Van Be', acclaimed for deliberately blowing up himself and sixty-nine US and ARVN soldiers with a claymore mine, amongst a 'whole heap of mines and grenades' in the Plain of Reeds in the Mekong delta. When it later emerged that Be was alive and well in an ARVN detention camp near Saigon, the saga had assumed an unbreakable truth, formally embodied in stories, plays, statues, poems, the 'christening' in his name of both a Northern fertilizer factory and a production line of sewing machines.

But when his brother defected to the South on hearing 'the big lie', he nevertheless acknowledged that the 'soul' of Nguyen Van Be, however falsely, had seized the spirit of his fellow fighting men moving against Con Thien, Khe Sanh and, as the ultimate targets, Saigon and the provincial capitals of South Vietnam during the Tet offensive.

XXX
The Battle of Khe Sanh

The first battle of Khe Sanh had been fought by the Marines in April 1967. In the thick jungle and elephant grass of that foggy, beautiful landscape between the Mekong and the South China Sea, they had struggled for mastery of 'the three hills'. Here lay South Vietnam's northernmost province, just below the demilitarized zone. Khe Sanh and Dien Bien Phu resembled one another in holding relatively similar geographic locations in their respective 'countries', and in their strategic situations on major roads (Khe Sanh on Route 9) with access to Laos. They were like one another in little else, certainly not in the air-power and artillery deployed, nor in their commanders' intentions.

Among those drenching mountain jungles, under the vast Dong Tri hills, were a strengthened airfield and a Special Forces base. In the latter, since 1962, the Green Berets had worked, lived, drunk, eaten rodents and other animals with the Hre and Ca Bru *montagnards*, and copulated with their women.

In 1966 a company of Marines had marched in, to be upgraded to battalion in 1967. Two French Catholic missionaries and some Cochinchinese nuns completed the cantonment, together with some French coffee planters in the immediate neighbourhood. In happier days the French hunted tiger in the valley, coming all the way from Tourane, now Da Nang.

More fighting took place in June 1967. In the autumn US aircraft overhead received information of urine, footsteps, sweat, cooking fires and vehicle sounds transmitted to the reception point in Thailand by 'sniffers' and sensors in the trees and undergrowth below. A very large PAVN force was closing on the Marines from down the Ho Chi Minh Trail. One of the NVA divisions, the Hoang Minh Thau or 304th, had engaged at Dien Bien Phu. Another, the 325c, had been in the fighting at 'First Khe Sanh'. Three artillery regiments with one hundred guns supported them, and regiments from two more divisions, 320 and 324, were thought to be proceeding down the trail or on subsidiary roads behind the first 20,000 men. Among the 20,000 was a squadron of light PT-76 tanks, driven in some instances by women, who later played a noisy role in the rout of the Special Forces camp at Lang Vei on 6 February 1968.

Lang Vei was a brutal firefight, ending in the capture and total destruction of the camp by the NVA. Two hundred out of the 500 indigenous troops were killed and ten out of twenty-four Americans in Captain Willoughby's Green Beret command. Six thousand Lao, *montagnard* and South Vietnamese stragglers poured into Khe Sanh where, fearing penetration by VC, Colonel Lownds held them off until interrogation established their bona fides.

Although Marine strength at Khe Sanh eventually reached 5,000 (1st and 3rd Battalions of 26 Regiment, 1st and 2nd of 3 Regiment), plus three hundred ARVN 37th Rangers, the Marine generals were not in favour of occupying the post. One officer observed that 'when you're there, you're not anywhere . . .' Westmoreland, however, more or less saw the place as a future 'hedgehog', or, in Cogny's phrase, a 'mooring point', for raids against the trail or Laos.

He believed firmly, furthermore, that the North Vietnamese divisions now moving against Khe Sanh were intended to create a second Dien Bien Phu, there to defeat the United States and then to take Quang Tri and other northern provinces as an inducement for the US to negotiate. 'Westy' foresaw a spring offensive which involved a crossing of the demilitarized zone by other PAVN divisions. He moved 101 Airborne and the Air Cavalry Division north to the coastal plain, planned to send General Creighton Abrams to a new overall command at I Corps, despatching there '40 per cent of all the infantry and armoured battalions in South Vietnam'. He would destroy Giap with American fire-power, invade Laos from Khe Sanh, *and* land Marine divisions on the coast.

Initially, his prediction seemed to be confirmed by a PAVN officer defector who, on 20 January, told his interrogators at Khe Sanh that the People's Army would swamp the garrison, move eastwards, take Quang Tri and drive south to Huë in Thua Thien province. This anti-aircraft lieutenant with a white flag, who had been passed over for promotion, then divulged the operational plan for Khe Sanh, the main assault on which would not develop until the temporary ceasefire at Tet.

But still, the difference was enormous between Khe Sanh and Dien Bien Phu, the cornered French in their valley with complete NVA artillery superiority, the inferior quantity and quality of French colonial troops and *matériel*, totally inadequate French fixed defences, and an Air Force that in the end could not penetrate – with reinforcements and supplies – the overwhelming Viet Minh anti-aircraft screen.

Not only Giap, but several American officers also attested with hindsight that the PAVN move was a trap, feint or diversion, intended to immobilize and disperse major US and ARVN forces away from the cities when the Tet offensive broke out. Giap's actual words included: 'Khe Sanh was not important to us, or only to the extent that it was to the Americans . . . only a diversion but one to be exploited if we could cause many casualties and win a big victory'.

He also said, in September 1967, that the object of this and other northern battles was to draw US forces away from the populated areas and thus damage pacification. 'The Marines are being stretched as taut as a bowstring over hundreds of kilometres.' Westmoreland believed this statement to be disinformation, and went on sending his troops to the frontier, even at the cost of defending the Mekong delta, where Giap had thought the Allies were 'doing well'. Giap had already created a surprise move in November 1967 to disperse his enemy yet further by the major PAVN engagement in II Corps against the air base of Dak To in the central highlands. This, as we have seen, led to US casualties and to the participation of no less than sixteen ARVN and US battalions when, as later emerged, the populated areas demanded a full allied presence.

In fact, at Khe Sanh the Communists lost 10,000 killed and an unknown number wounded against only 500 Marine casualties. The PAVN soldiers fell principally to the terrible Operation *Niagara*, 75,000 tons of high explosive, anti-personnel and napalm projectiles from B-52s, together with mortar, howitzer and 175 mm cannon fire from within and without the garrison perimeter. The reeking corpses piled up in the undergrowth.

The 'diversion' did enable the allies to hold out in Quang Tri, Huë and many other towns which would have been defenceless had 101 Airborne and 1st Air Cavalry not been 'dispersed' there. Conversely, had not the decision been made to stand at Khe Sanh, 304 and 325 might have participated in the Tet offensive against helpless northern coastal towns. Though Westmoreland was right in that regard, he may still have believed that the main DRV objective was Khe Sanh, and not the uprising in the cities.

The Marines held five hills at Khe Sanh. On one of them, 881 south, a 'tattered American flag' was hoisted daily – over fifty new ones were flown in during the siege from private citizens in the States – and a bugle played 'To the Colours'. The Marines stood at attention, saluted, dived for cover and were lying in their trenches before the PAVN mortars came in.

NVA shelling and sniping began in the first part of January. On 16 January another Marine battalion, the 2nd of 26 Regiment, arrived and was posted on hill 558 to support 861. On 20 January, 304 Division drove the Marines in a fierce engagement from 881 north to 881 south. Next morning, an artillery barrage began against hill 861 and the airfield, from 881 north, which had been lost the day before to the NVA. A huge ammunition dump at the base was struck by rockets, flinging mortar, artillery and tear-gas shells widespread, many exploding. North Vietnamese shells landed among blazing gasoline. The PAVN took Huong Hoa (Khe Sanh village) with sixty US casualties. The defenders awaited their fate, as in that other siege at Kohima, twenty-three years before.

But reinforcements, replacement shells and medicine were soon flown in by helicopters and C-130s, and the wounded were flown out, quite unlike events in that Naga village. B-52s and fighter bombers attacked in 'boxes' every five minutes, from the great carriers of the 7th Fleet, from Strategic Air Command, from Guam, Okinawa, Thailand, with 'a daily explosive power of five Hiroshima bombs . . . so accurate that they fell within two hundred yards of Marine positions', while hitting their most precise targets. Defoliants exposed PAVN troops on the move to aerial attacks: some, because of electronic espionage picked up from the MACV targeting network by Soviet vessels, could be warned in time to shelter in tunnels and caves, but most were totally and systematically obliterated. Certainly no mass North Vietnamese infantry attacks could now be mounted against the hills or base. All was confused disruption in the shattered wasteland.

On the American side, although North Vietnamese artillery was often 'inaccurate and sporadic', one tenth of the garrison, despite their own underground bunkers, were killed or wounded by PAVN mortars or by 105 mm and 155 mm cannon. As at Dien Bien Phu, the guns were hidden in camouflaged revetments and caves in the looming hills, invisible from air and ground. The People's Army trenches, as at Dien Bien Phu, but without their intricacy and number, were coming closer. Fog prevented aircraft landings. Even parachute drops carried risk and danger for the crews. In Saigon they began again to whisper of 1954.

On 1 March 304 Division hit the Rangers, but by late March, the PAVN, crippled by American fire-power, had started to move out of the battle. Although the North Vietnamese could still harass the base with gun-fire and small infantry assaults, improved weather at the end of the monsoon permitted even deeper US air devastation and even worse DRV casualties. Colonel David Lownds, calm, professional and laconic, and his magnificent, outnumbered Marines, had outfought both the enemy and the world's press. 'Dien Bien Phu' and the other disasters forecast day by day in the hysterical US media to terrified readers and viewers, had not happened . . . Khe Sanh went quickly off a screen which it had monopolized for two months without cause.

On 15 April the base was formally relieved. 'Strewn with rubble . . . troops living a life more similar to rats than human beings . . . the trees were gone, everything was gone . . . it was all rubble, bodies, nothing . . .' It was worse for the North Vietnamese, but Giap was not the general to mourn for 100,000 cadavers homeward bound, up to half the NVA fighting strength, without substantive success at Khe Sanh or any other battle in this particular campaign. Yet the rumour that he was in personal command of the battle seems improbable, not worth the tons of high explosives allegedly dropped by B-52s on his supposed HQ.

After the war General Palmer said, 'Strategically, by attacking everywhere Giap had superior strength nowhere . . . he failed to mass his forces, a strategic error which he committed knowingly, but an error none the less. Military victories are not won by violating military principles.'

26 Regiment had held for seventy-seven days. Their divisional commander, General Tompkins, had flown in daily at real personal hazard, and they had also been visited regularly by General Cushman. They had built 510 bunkers, miles of trench-lines, hundreds of minefields and trip flares, plus a maze of variegated wire. They had disposed of night observation devices, ground survival radar, starlight scopes and had almost unlimited B-52 support when the weather was right. The PAVN had been foolish: outgunned and outfought, they had tried to slug it out at a time when siege deployment made them sitting targets.

XXXI
The Tet Offensive of 1968

Tet is Vietnam's spring festival – New Year's Day and Christmas combined – an affair of peach blossom, kumquat trees, gladioli, exchanges of presents, discharge of debt, homage to ancestors, a day of family and hope, the lunar New Year.

According to General Westmoreland, North Vietnamese documents captured in October 1967 had indicated that General Vo Nguyen Giap's 'protracted war' of attrition and conservation of forces was about to be varied. Giap had exhorted his men to 'make a maximum effort on all fronts, political and military, in order to achieve victory in a short period of time'.

In January 1968 Pham Van Dong, prime minister of the DRV, was reported to have said that 'our purpose is to cause many US casualties through a programme of all-out attacks, and to erode the US will so that *anti-war influence will gain decisive political strength'*. The planning and positioning of PAVN and, mostly, VC troops for the forthcoming assaults on population centres were under way.

In his State of the Union message on 17 January, the president of the United States made clear his policy on a bombing halt and on 'talks'. The latter should follow 'the San Antonio formula . . . The bombing will stop immediately if talks take place promptly . . . and the other side must not take advantage of our restraint, as they have done in the past.'

A PLAF notebook captured in November 1967 and released by the Americans to the press included the following:

[COSVN] has ordered the entire Army and people of South Vietnam to implement general offensive and general uprising in order to achieve a decisive victory . . . use very strong military attacks in coordination with *uprisings* of the local population to take over towns and cities. Troops should flood the lowlands. They should move toward liberating the capital city, Saigon, take power and try to rally enemy brigades to our side. Cadres should say that these orders came from the NLF, *not* from the Lao Dong Party and Uncle [Ho].

Operations were under the overall control of General Tran Van Tra, of the Central Office for South Vietnam, COSVN. The first steps in the programme had already been taken, the battles at Con Thien, Dak To, Song Be, Loc Ninh in the autumn, and now Khe Sanh.

Nguyen Van Thieu, president of the Republic of Vietnam, had ordered a thirty-six-hour ceasefire beginning on 29 January, in response to the Viet Cong's seven-day truce from 27 January to 3 February, which the Communists had no intention of honouring. Half the ARVN had been given leave and, as important, the curfew in Saigon and elsewhere was lifted for the holiday. Intelligence, such as that in the National Liberation Front notebook, was discounted.

The Communist order of battle during Tet varied from province to province, although the full organization of the National Liberation Front was brought to bear in every province in terms of food and supply storage, population control, and intelligence. Local preparations began in early January with the arrival in villages of small parties of PAVN and VC on foot, by bicycle, or in the Bomb attack from the 'truck filled with flowers' at the Saigon Presidential Palace. The sappers who caused such damage in Huë did not arrive there until two days before Tet itself. The Front's official warned the villagers of the struggle ahead, prophesying that a 'general uprising' would soon be mounted to bring down the government of the Republic and defeat the Americans. Main force NVA and PLAF units, in up to regimental strength, did not appear until the last minute.

Attacks in the countryside began in late January against government and military vehicles and with bombs and satchel charges against government officials and their bureaux. Catholics and other supporters of the republic were forcibly abducted, most never to return except to fill mass graves. In several provinces, both government soldiers and civilian officials ran for their lives, only coming back after US artillery and air support of ARVN or US infantry formations had driven the guerrillas out of 'the populated areas'. The uprising took many lives through assassination, shelling, air-attack or hand-to-hand.

Although the PLAF were eventually thrown out, and their subsequent repeat attacks in May and August were defeated, the majority of peasants were still impressed by their showing, frightened by their brutality and mobility, and far from confident that they would not come back again from the tunnels and their caves in the hills. The people no longer had much confidence in their ARVN protectors. They resented the damage caused by American fire-power and some of them even believed, in the absence of Front attacks on US bases, that there was an NLF/US concordat. They dreaded their fate, whether as dead or wounded victims in this 'war without end', or, as refugees, deprived of their possessions and far from home.

On the other hand, the allied reaction to Tet was so vigorous, affecting the efficiency and morale of even some crack Northern units, that local opinion occasionally preferred to hedge bets. (In any case, earlier VC action in most places had not gone much beyond the laying of mines, planting punji sticks and so forth, violent US responses to which only brought deeper opposition to the Americans, always hated more than the ARVN by the southern peasantry). Sir Robert (Bob) Thompson the British counter insurgency expert believed that the bulk of the southerners, lacking any loyalty, cause or principle, were never more than fair-weather friends to either side. And why should they have been? Where had ideology led their country?

The first Tet attacks began on 30 January against Hoi An and Da Nang in I Corps, and a whole range of targets: Dak To again, where the PAVN cleared mines with their hands, Ban Me Thuot, Qui Nhon, Kontum, Pleiku and Nha Trang in III Corps. In Saigon, however, fireworks, rockets, crackers and other *feux de joie* continued at midnight to mark the spring festival. Rumour said that next day would see penetration of Saigon city, but American parties were in full swing.

According to Hanoi's official history, the difference in the timing of some of the attacks between 30 and 31 January was 'because New Year's Day in the South was 30 January but, in the North, one day later'. That makes little sense. It is nevertheless true that one reason for Communist failure in Saigon was that the attack was launched before the designated time, totally upsetting planned events.

The large but undistinguished American embassy came under assault at 03.15 on 30 January. A Viet Cong platoon of twenty sappers dressed in brown and blue with red arm-bands breached the high wall of the compound, trying to burst into the Chancery with bazookas and demolition charges, killing two US military police-men. They failed to enter the building, killed one by one by M-16s and grenades in a long close-contact battle with military policemen and Marines in the compound, just before US airborne forces were landed by helicopter on the roof. The Vietnamese police contribution was minimally helpful.

The upright, impassive, white-haired US ambassador, Ellsworth Bunker, was escorted to a safe place in dressing-gown and pyjamas, returning to his home when the embassy battle was over some six hours later. (He and his wife, then ambassador in Kathmandu, used to commute to one another by air.)

Can Tho in the Delta, Bien Hoa – the large military air base north-east of Saigon – and Than Son Nhut – Saigon's military and civil air base – all came under fierce attack, and in Saigon a whole series of satchel bomb, rocket, mortar and automatic weapon raids were flung against the presidential palace, ARVN headquarters, officers' quarters, hotels and public buildings. Fighting in Cholon and the suburbs against PLAF and PAVN troops 'holed up' in shacks, apartments, or in underground and other safe houses, was chiefly – and creditably – conducted by Saigon Army and police units, with US air and artillery support. The ARVN, for the most part, offered stout resistance and, in Huë, they followed their enemy from bunker to bunker, although they were subsequently denigrated by their American colleagues.

In all, according to Peter Braestrup's *Big Story*, the Communists 'attempted to take thirty-six of forty-two province capitals, sixty-four of 242 district capitals . . . it was touch and go at Than Son Nhut. Huë, My Tho, Vinh Long, Ben Tre, Kontum and Quang Tri'. But, except for Saigon, Huë, Dalat (the hill station housing the ARVN military academy), and Phan Thiet, the worst was over within five days. On 25 February, when Huë was recaptured, city fighting had ended. Khe Sanh, as we have seen, was not completely relieved until mid-April.

Strangers had been seen in the Dong Ba market at Huë on the evening of Tet. The first mortar attacks, initially against military targets, the An Hoa Gate, the Citadel and the Imperial Palace began at 02.00 next day and culminated in the raising of a vast NLF flag over the Citadel at 08.00. Massacres of wounded and nurses began. Two thousand prisoners released from the city gaol were armed by adolescent NLF soldiers and went about dragging political enemies from their homes and murdering them. Thieving and looting were general.

Corpses piled up in the streets, including those of American civilians, German doctors, French missionaries, as well as more than 2,000 Vietnamese civil servants and opponents of the Viet Cong. The victims were thrown into mass graves which they themselves had been forced to dig, some after atrocious torture, decapitation, butchery, some limbless, or with their arms bound or tied together in groups of ten or fifteen.

Eighty per cent of the city's houses, pagodas, temples, gates and palaces were destroyed or damaged by the battle. The town, with ten of the bridges across the Perfumed River broken, was little more than a mass of rubble, the streets littered with filth, dead rats, broken glass, bodies everywhere. The entire Imperial Palace, the Citadel, the Ngo Man Gate were all grievously damaged. The Citadel had been penetrated through the drains or up the banyan trees outside the walls.

About three regiments of Viet Cong (PLAF), 2,000 men each, plus Sappers who had entered the city surreptitiously before Tet, took part in the battle, assisted by some 600 young collaborators recruited in Huë during the battle, and the criminals released from prison. US and Vietnamese Marines (seven battalions), elements of the 1st ARVN Infantry Division who clung to their post in the old Citadel, the 1st ARVN Airborne Battle Group and the 1st US Air Cavalry Division opposed them. The Allies were supported by artillery, including white phosphorus shells, and by airborne bomb, rocket and cannon fire, at least when the fog did not make aerial assistance impossible.

The Viet Cong evaded air and artillery fire by fighting hand-to-hand, or at least in as close combat as possible, 'clutching their enemy to them'. Many PLAF actions were at night in small groups with B-40 and B-41 rocket propelled grenades, skirmishing was the preferred tactic by day, snipers ubiquitous throughout the town. The rear and flanks of advancing allied troops were under permanent attack by small-group action; major ground assaults were well coordinated with PAVN artillery.

The Allies should, of course, have been aware that the assault at Huë was about to take place. Intelligence failed, as so often in this war and, in particular, the 1st Air Cavalry Division did not make that immediate intervention which might have frustrated the 'invasion' that wrecked a beautiful and historic city, killed 2,000 innocent civilians, 200 ARVN soldiers and fifty-three Americans, and wounded many more. The battle for Huë, when the Viet Cong and PAVN withdrew, had lasted twenty-six days: over 2,600 PAVN were killed.

Of ARVN units, the 1st Division in Huë had become outstanding, defeating better-equipped PAVN units, one company (Black Panther) holding for three whole days and losing all but nineteen men. One bombardment liaison officer had to call down fire, with the tears streaming down his cheeks, on his home and family; he died in a PAVN counter-attack shortly afterwards.

After the battle, 1st ARVN, by holding ground taken, secured the pacification of the coastal plains around Huë. General Ngo Quang Truong said: 'We used to go in quickly and return. Now, when we go in, we stay as a result of those battles.' Denis Warner, one of the most intelligent observers concluded that, although the RVN could not go it alone and survive in a full-scale war, a phased American withdrawal might be feasible so long as US air-power and some artillery could remain.

At Bien Hoa ARVN ignored intelligence that one PAVN and two VC regiments were in the vicinity, one armed with 122 mm rockets. Heavy US and ARVN fire, however, broke up bewildered VC teenagers and although only 30 per cent of local government forces were deployed, the Communists suffered very heavy casualties indeed before withdrawing in panic. In Pham Thiet, the chief VC attack was against a relatively unimportant suburban post. In Nha Trang only small posts were attacked, permitting an effective counter-offensive. Kontum's ARVN garrison was too small and the town was saved by US power. At Quang Ngai the Communists started too late and their artillery bombardment was wrongly timed, but here the ARVN did not behave well. In Da Nang the northerners shelled a refugee camp. Their infantry were later trapped in the air base compound – the whole assault was a day early, so most of their troops had not yet arrived.

A captured VC document subsequently admitted that the Communist 'mole forces' inside the cities were often too small to ensure that the 'invaders' hit their targets in adequate strength. Surprise, because of errors of timing, was not generally achieved nor, even in Huë, did the expected general uprising occur, and certainly not coincident with general offensive. COSVN tried to pretend that that aim could best be achieved in future by 'protracted flexible pursuit of the goal.'

Although thirty-five VC and PAVN battalions were employed in the Saigon area, many PLAF and PAVN communications went badly wrong: units got lost, two companies finding themselves in the middle of the racecourse. Formations lost wireless contact with command and with one another. Combined operations were slow and ineffective; troops did not know local geography. Units failed to concentrate, for fear of air attack. Main-force strengths were inadequate for victory against 'massively reinforced defence structures'. Reinforcements did not get through. The soldiers for the general offensive included too many guerrillas unfamiliar with urban conditions or with concentrated American fire-power. There were too few 'quislings', and the political and military inner-city infra-structure was ill-prepared. Sappers and 'moles' were not embedded deep enough in the sensitive target areas, an error COSVN tried unsuccessfully to correct in their May offensive.

But when Ben Tre was levelled, an American officer, in a much derided statement, admitted that 'it had become necessary to destroy the town in order to save it'.

XXXII
What Giap Wanted from Tet
and What Giap Got

As an example of VC planning, it is interesting to note that plans for the attack on Da Nang were outlined to senior cadres there as early as 22 January. Although the PLAF realized they would be out-numbered and wiped out if they tried to stay in the city, they thought that they must make the assault as part of Giap's overall plan for the general offensive. It was understood that if the first phase of uprisings in the cities should fail, phase two, or main-force action in the western highlands and Khe Sanh, would follow.

High-ranking cadres in touch with underground elements in Da Nang city had been selected to incite the masses and the penetration agents to support the Communist general offensive, the 'seventy-six-day plan'.

Senior Colonel Vo Thu was in overall command, his deputy, Senior Captain Hien, in charge of special action. Political officer Lieutenant Colonel Duc served as chief of staff and Captain Pham Duy Dai, member of Special Zone Headquarters, was officer in charge of military affairs and sappers.

Da Nang was divided into three operational districts, each headed by a district committee member. Secretary Sau Hang was in charge of District 2 (Da Nang centre), with the key role of taking over the RVN administrative installations. District 2 VC cadres would automatically constitute the Da Nang city provisional executive committee, with Sau Hung as mayor, once the RVN administration had fallen.

The plan for the attack on Da Nang was that forty youths of both sexes, aged 16–17 and carrying birth certificates to avoid the need for RVN identity cards, would infiltrate the city between 24 and 29 January, under Captain Hien, led by liaison agents and armed with silenced pistols, submachine-guns and TNT. Their mission was to reconnoitre ARVN and RVN installations and to observe RVN intelligence personnel, the latter to be captured or killed during the general offensive. The VC recognized they would be greatly outnumbered by the ARVN and allies in Da Nang, probably wiped out if they drove deep into the city and stayed there long. If they did not attack the city, however, they would lose face with the masses, having failed to carry out their part of the general offensive.

Two local main-force battalions, R20 and Q16, would attack and occupy RVN posts around the city. One North Vietnamese Army battalion belonging to work site 2 would be held in reserve. Only a few elements would thrust deeply into the city, and would then immediately withdraw to the outskirts to rejoin the other units for a prolonged siege designed to pressure the local authorities into negotiating.

In the meantime, the 'special action unit' would coordinate with other specialized elements in inciting the population to go out into the streets to struggle against the RVN, demand the creation of a coalition government, destroy the fuel dumps and power plants, and steal weapons and ammunition to arm young men and women who had distinguished themselves in previous struggles. These developments would result in the formation of a 'dissident army' headed by Pham Duy Dai, the 'uprising' in Da Nang appearing to be a mass movement against the RVN.

The attack would begin on the night of 29/30 January 1968. A later order changed the date to the night of 30/31 January, but it was launched as originally scheduled. The assault was, in fact, abortive, since the VC had been penetrated beforehand and an RVN police agent warned of the coming attack. Although a VC company succeeded in getting inside I Corps HQ, heavy US bombing only 200 yards from that headquarters forced the VC back under helicopter gun-ship pursuit.

The Communists attacked thirteen of sixteen provincial cities in the Mekong delta. They were defeated by the Mobile Riverine Force (MRF), a 'brigade' in assault boats with revolving armoured turrets containing 40 mm cannon shipped in 60-foot long monitors and artillery barges. These vessels, in support of ARVN 7th Division fighting hand-to-hand, took three days to recapture My Tho. Ben Tre, the town that 'had to be destroyed in order to be recaptured', took thirty-six hours to 'save' and to drive out, with artillery and air strikes, a reinforced PLAF regiment of 2,500.

Seven provincial capitals were attacked in the central highlands. At Qui Nhon on the coast, although ARVN had already seized the Communist operational plan, VC sappers still managed to take their objectives. The battle for Ban Me Thuot went on for nine days, the city centre changing hands four times before ARVN 23rd Division under the able Colonel Dao Quang An regained control, in a fine example of good Vietnamese leadership. But one ARVN general, in the Delta, refused to leave his headquarters and a province chief wore mufti under his uniform.

In Chau Phu on the Cambodian border, after a thirty-six-hour battle the invaders were driven out by Special Forces Detachments of the Phoenix project and by Navy SEALS (Sea-Air-Lands, units conducting unconventional and clandestine operations) of an intimidating toughness.

Total US and ARVN casualties were between 8,000 and 12,000. The Communists lost up to 50,000 dead, 'corpses stacked like cord wood' outside one unit headquarters. Tet was a military victory for the ARVN and the US Army. Huge damage had been inflicted on the Viet Cong infrastructure, organization and order of battle, but none of this was remembered against the instant and adverse perception within the continental United States of a political defeat for American and allied forces.

Giap announced that Tet had demonstrated that North Vietnam

was stronger in 1968 than at the time the US committed massive forces to the war . . . now there was a new US strategy, one of defence. And that was our biggest victory: to change the ideas of the United States. The Tet Offensive had been directed primarily at the people of South Vietnam but, as it turned out, it affected the people of the United States more. Until Tet, they had thought they could win the war but now they knew that they could not. Johnson was forced to decrease military activity and discuss with us around the table how to end the war.

Giap thought that that balanced his 50,000 dead, 12,500 civilians killed, 22,000 wounded, nearly a million refugees.

In late February a request by Westmoreland for an additional 200,000 US troops, 'contrived' with the chairman of the joint chiefs in order to bring about a call-up of the reserves, was presented to the president without reference to COMUSMACV's proposed 'new offensive strategy', which included attacks on Laos, Cambodia – to 'seal the borders and assault the sanctuaries' – and on North Vietnam itself. LBJ ordered the new defence secretary, Clark Clifford, to reassess US strategy in Vietnam. Since 'search-and-destroy' and attrition had not worked, early staff papers recommended 'a population strategy and the concept of an RVN war with US assistance, instead of a US war with dubious RVN assistance' – i.e. Vietnamization. The secretary of state's final recommendation was for 22,000 men only, plus a call-up of reserves, all contingent on better South Vietnamese contributions, political and military. No reference was made to Cambodia and Laos.

At the end of March 1968 Johnson halted all bombing of North Vietnam except immediately north of the 17th parallel, the de-militarized zone. He announced that he would not himself be a candidate for re-election to the office of president. Westmoreland was removed as commander and succeeded by his deputy, General Creighton Abrams, himself becoming Army chief of staff, not limogé, but kicked upstairs. Clifford's recommendations indeed eventually emerged, under President Nixon, as the formal project of 'Vietnamization'.

Although search-and-destroy continued and, after the May offensive against Saigon, MACV paid more structured attention to city defence, pacification and de-Americanization were thenceforth to become the major themes.

Three days after the president's announcement in March, the DRV agreed to talks to decide 'the unconditional cessation of bombing and all other war acts'. Hanoi had adopted the strategy of 'fighting while negotiating' but while Washington sought a mutual withdrawal from South Vietnam of both US and North Vietnamese forces, the Communists would not accept anything less than unilateral US withdrawal and NLF participation in a coalition government – a negotiated settlement which handed South Vietnam to them bound and gagged.

In Paris the chief US negotiatiors, Averell Harriman former ambassador at Moscow and governor of New York, and Cyrus Vance, later to become President Carter's secretary of state sat down with Xuan Thuy on 18 May 1968 for talks which rapidly got bogged down, but, in one form or another, trailed on until 1973. On 31 October 1968 the president stopped all 'air, naval and artillery bombardment of North Vietnam'. Plenary peace talks began in January 1969, although the North Vietnamese immediately, and regularly, violated the three 'undertakings' they had made as conditions for the bombing halt.

Perhaps, in the end, Giap had better judgement. 'We wanted to carry the war into the families of America – to demonstrate that if Vietnamese blood was being spilled, so was American . . . more and more Americans renounced the war.' Despite his failure to create general uprisings, that is what he did, greatly helped, of course, by Washington's response to China's 'ping-pong diplomacy' and the eventual withdrawal of US troops. Nevertheless, it is true, to paraphrase Winston Churchill, that 'never was so massive a political gain achieved by so unsuccessful a military undertaking'.

XXXIII
General Abrams Takes the Chalice

General 'Abe' Creighton Abrams, a tough, explosive fighting soldier who took over from General Westmoreland in July 1968, judged that MACV's concentration on troop destruction between 1965 and 1968 had failed to provide a shield of security for the people of South Vietnam – the 'pacification' advocated by the Marine Corps.

As for attrition, its principal measure, the 'body count', had become distorted. Duplication, 'estimates' or guesswork, and imprecise monitoring from the air on the one hand, and enemy body-recovery on the battlefield, death by disease, etc. on the other hand, had all tended to make this concept unreliable. Commanders even falsified their claims in order to acquire merit with superiors.

A more serious limitation on successful allied attrition lay in Giap's orders to his generals to control their losses – through timing and disengagement – to a level replaceable from southern or northern resources. That level, however, was also one which Giap calculated would require American replacements on a scale ultimately unacceptable to United States' public opinion.

The US joint chiefs even believed that Hanoi and the VC, by their actions, were determining an attrition rate acceptable to the North. MACV figures for 1965–7 showed enemy losses of 344,000, although total PAVN/PLAF strength had risen by 80,000. Local recruitment and infiltration from North Vietnam had produced 424,000 more men over the period. Attrition therefore had not even taken place, nor was substantive attrition forecast for 1969, whether by Westmoreland, McNamara or by the National Security Council.

In the towns and countryside the people's loyalty was not secure. The defeat of enemy units in the field could not be enough without southern social, political and economic reform, in particular land reform (not really enforced until 1970), nor without long-term protection of hamlets and villages from their VC tormentors by night as well as by day. Westmoreland believed that he did not command enough men for pacification *and* for the main force operations behind which pacification could be achieved. But, in fact, the latter was not a concept to which he gave priority. 'Popular allegiance' should have been projected as the major aim, not simple military victory, in a war waged against a general who had already demonstrated that there was 'no such thing as a single strategy. Ours is always a synthesis, simultaneously diplomatic, military and political measures.'

Neither was allegiance brought nearer by the terrible damage inflicted by allied fire-power on land and people in populated areas, often as a substitute for land-power. This was especially so in uncontrolled harassment and interdiction operations or in 'specified strike zones' (free-fire zones). For example, more tons of bombs (admittedly under strict MACV monitoring and circumspection) were dropped between 1965 and 1968 than during the entire Second World War whether in the Pacific or European theatres. And as between 2 per cent and 5 per cent of these loads failed to explode, the resulting explosives often provided the Communists with raw material for their own ground devices, booby traps, mines, etc.

Most of the blame for casualties in the villages, no matter how heavily defended they were by Viet Cong intruders above and below ground, naturally fell upon the Americans and the South Vietnamese. It was very hard for the latter to carry out a 'hearts and minds' operation while attacking Viet Cong installations defended by civilian 'human shields'.

Corruption, arrogance and incompetence amongst RVN officials, until Bob Komer's CORDs programme began to bite, embittered the people and hampered the war effort. Too much US aid went to the 'fat cats', even to the PLAF. The 'Open Arms', or *Chieu Hoi*, a programme of incentives for surrender produced non-existent 'defectors from the Viet Cong', rewards for whom crammed the pockets of officials. Only in Catholic, Hoa Hao or Cao Dai regions was policy buttressed by a cause in which people believed.* There was no Uncle Ho in South Vietnam, and the massive corruption of a Communist state was ignored among the petty squeeze and bribery of Cochinchina.

Refugees, official and otherwise, numbered some three million

---

* In 1971 10 per cent of Vietnamese were estimated to be Roman Catholic. Two million reformed Buddhists formed the powerful Hoa Hao sect in the Mekong delta. There were also about one million Cao Daists, a sect synthesizing Buddhism, Christianity, Taoism, Confucianism, Animism and ancestor worship; it had its own pope, and venerated the spirits of such great Europeans as Victor Hugo and Shakespeare.

by 1967, many living in crowded, insanitary camps with vilely inadequate facilities, driven from the countryside to the coast and towns by US/ARVN artillery, bombing and infantry 'sweeps', chemical spraying, forced labour, conscription, VC imposed taxes.

The exodus was sometimes the result of deliberate US military policy, to drive civilians out of battle areas in which they provided the commissariat and became 'the Ocean' for the VC 'fish'. Their departure also enabled the Allies to exploit unrestricted fire-power. 'It deprived the guerillas of local support and freed innocent civilians from terrorism', or such was the theory. But compulsory or voluntary relocations created miserable and resentful people, potential allies of the VC, and deprived the government of any intelligence potential. Relocations, furthermore, removed workers from agricultural land and, above all, showed that the government could not protect or maintain its own people. These evident disadvantages to pacification did bring about a change of policy, at least in terms of actual generation of refugees, but the change was honoured by ARVN and US commanders as much in the breach as in the observance.

Britain and Malaya had won their war against Chinese Communist terrorists by many expedients – including brilliant intelligence – of which a combined command, the 'Directorate of Operations' under Field Marshal Lord Templer, incorporating all government departments, was the most significant. The inability or unwillingness of either Westmoreland or Abrams to impose a similar concept on their Vietnamese or Korean colleagues had vast consequences. Westmoreland's view on probable VC penetration of a combined command are an illuminating comment on the problems faced by MACV, affecting attrition, pacification and the eventual result of the war. We have already noted that even a unified command would have been ineffective unless harnessed to a cause such as 'independence' (*merdeka*), which the British were able to offer to Malays and local Chinese. No such bright vision was available in South Vietnam or, rather, the Communist version was more attractively presented.

Nor did 'Westy' much encourage another project favourable to pacification, the Marine Combined Action Platoons. These consisted of Vietnamese Popular Force platoons of thirty-eight men with a Marine rifle squad of fourteen, who lived together in villages for whose security they were responsible. By the beginning of 1968 some eighty of these platoons, the Americans learning from and stiffening the Vietnamese, had been established in I Corps. Their security performance in the hamlets was much better, and their casualties much lower than in conventional Army units. They began to gain the confidence of the villagers and started to show that Cochinchinese and Annamites could defend their own people as well as the Viet Cong could disrupt them.

The Marines believed that once the villages were clear of the enemy, the Communists could be handled by main force infantry and US/ARVN fire-power outside the pacified areas. But without pacification, search-and-destroy was an endlessly self-renewing process. General Westmoreland, however, disagreed, and, as we have seen, the Marines were deployed to Khe Sanh and to other bases every bit as 'static' as those in the 'pacified villages' so criticized by Westmoreland.

In the social field, most projects – civic action, Strategic Hamlets and rural development – failed because prior security had not been achieved. In May 1967, however, an organization was established called Civil Operations and Revolutionary Development Support (CORDS). This agency, although subordinate to the theatre commander of COMUSMACV was staffed from all US departments of state, military and civil, and led by a noisy, ebullient and quite remarkable former CIA officer named Robert Komer, much later to become deputy to President Carter's secretary for defence.

Komer founded mixed teams to work in the capital and in the field with the Saigon authorities, at all levels from hamlet to province. Although actual results were not substantial in 1967, CORDS fairly rapidly began to coordinate RVN and US pacification programmes in forty-four provinces and 250 districts, trained the Popular Forces (PF) and police and, so far as was possible, eliminated corruption ('non-existent defectors, etc.') from the *Chieu Hoi* 'Open Arms' project.

The Phoenix programme, originally a CIA operation to identify and attack the VC infrastructure – terrorism, recruitment, intelligence, supply, and so on – was eventually incorporated into CORDS. It was susceptible to private enmities, to Saigon's unpopularity among the people, to fabricated intelligence, to corruption stemming from a reward system. Komer regarded it as badly managed and not particularly efficient. But its CIA chief, Bill Colby, claimed that by 1971 it had produced 28,000 VC prisoners, 20,000 killed and 17,000 defectors.

Stanley Karnow once suggested to 'Blow-torch Komer' that cash payments to each VC of US $500 would be a cheaper system of winning the war in the South than wasteful and extravagant US programmes. Komer replied: 'We've worked it out: US $2,500 each.' But he, too, was reluctant to recommend the course set by General Templer in Malaya – to dismiss the incompetents, seize control of the establishment, to command and intervene – fearing charges of 'colonialism' and 'imperialism'.

Like Westmoreland, he believed in mass and might, and until 1970 he could not see past his computers to the sordid realities of crooked province chiefs, cowardly generals and corrupt officials. Although by that year he had managed to replace the worst civilians, all of their military counterparts still remained in place, lacking adequate protest from MACV.

Giap claimed in 1968 to Madeleine Riffaud of L'Humanité that 'the Pentagon' realized that, after Tet, the war was being lost. Nevertheless there was a vacuum in the countryside. The Saigon government was able to fill it by a People's Self-Defence Force of 1.5 million which, with Regional and Popular Forces (RF and PF), attacked the VC where the PLAF had become exposed during Tet. Several small, successful US/ARVN operations took the place of main-force sweeps and massive fire-power. Clear-and-hold pacification operations were beginning to work.

After Richard Nixon's accession to the presidency in 1969, the prescriptions of Dr Henry Kissinger, now national security advisor, were followed. Washington sought to concentrate on the protection of the people, the gradual reduction of 'some' US troops and the strengthening of the ARVN. A target date of 30 June 1972 was set for the end of major US military action and the completion of Vietnamization.

General Abrams' new plan was designed to combine pacification and main-force fighting, the security of the population being its chief objective, plus the neutralization of the Viet Cong infrastructure in order to 'blind' the PAVN and PLAF. He sought a substantial reduction in provocative and counter-productive fire-power. Unfortunately, due to the US command structure, many of his more traditional corps and divisional commanders were able virtually to ignore these instructions, convinced that they were inappropriate to the standards of the United States Army, based on their own perceptions and the past efforts of their formations.

The Marines, with grave losses, fought main-force battles in Quang Nam province without ever achieving peaceful and secure local government. Huge battles were also launched in 1969 by the Americal Division in Quang Ngai. Others took place in the Delta under the 'body count'-obsessed General Julian Ewell and his 9th Division, in the A Shau valley of Thua Thien and at the bloody Hamburger Hill under General Zais.

Enormous numbers of refugees continued to be generated. Huge quantities of ordnance were expended, with vast civilian casualties and ruinous consequences to farms and villages. No decisive military gains were made. At Hamburger Hill, in a grinding ten-day battle, 500 Communists were killed, but the 101st Airborne lost fifty killed and 400 wounded. When the Americans had taken this feature, of no military significance whatever, they abandoned it.

Giap had again enticed the Americans into a series of pointless battles, to the pitiful neglect of a pacification campaign which had just begun to show results. The president's response on a visit to Vietnam in July, was to 'make the reduction of casualties General Abrams' first duty . . . the primary mission of US troops was to enable the South Vietnamese forces to assume full responsiblity for the security of South Vietnam.' Vietnamization had really begun: US troop strength was reduced from its peak in January 1969 of 542,000 to 472,000 in January 1970, 336,000 in 1971 and 45,000 by July 1972. As a strategy it was not designed to win the Vietnam War; it was a political device to cover US support for a war which had lost US metropolitan approval, even to cover the abandonment of honour should such be required.

As Kissinger said, General Abrams was 'doomed to a rearguard action . . . his purpose was increasingly logistical redeployment and not success in battle . . . he could not possibly achieve that victory that had eluded us at full strength, while US forces were constantly diminishing'. Nevertheless, despite all that has been and will be said, Abrams did at one point have a relatively stable Saigon government, an improved American pacification policy, and an enemy that had almost abandoned large-scale offensive operations: his task should not have been a hopeless one.

But during these years the US military effort was further diluted by drug use, disobedience, cowardice, misconduct, desertion, murders of officers and NCOs, and confrontation between blacks and whites. These attributes were not necessarily unique to Vietnam;

they were the consequences of the permissiveness of the times, the unpopularity of the war, boredom, and the collapse of civility in the metropolitan United States. Nevertheless, in 1971 drugs from the 'Golden Triangle' of Laos, Burma and Thailand flooded a market controlled in Saigon chiefly by black deserters, their customers unwashed, long-haired GIs so unsuited to battle that their principle gesture as they shambled through the streets and brothels was the 'peace sign'. As Lartéguy said, 'they had been corrupted by Saigon in the same degree as they had corrupted Saigon'.

XXXIV
The View from Hanoi in 1970

Communist statements and documents in 1969 bore a more sombre tone after the 1968 Tet offensive. Cadres were excoriated for their shortcomings, particularly political, exhorted to do more, and then reproached for failing again. In mid-1969 COSVN Resolution 9 seemed to admit that Communist capabilities had been considerably reduced. It contained the most explicit catalogue of Communist liabilities to appear in a high-level Communist document, a theme repeated in captured documents and in the testimony of Communist prisoners and 'ralliers'. Finally, in December, General Giap pointed out that the Communists had ignored many of the cardinal precepts of fighting a 'people's war', and declared it imperative to repair these faults even if it meant going on the defensive temporarily.

In South Vietnam, in order to avoid the heavy casualties associated with large-scale military actions, Giap resorted to tactics designed to conserve manpower, relying increasingly on small-unit, sapper and shelling actions against South Vietnamese security forces and allied positions. Five main-force regiments were sent to the Mekong delta to bolster the Communist position. There was a concerted effort to halt the erosion of guerrilla and local forces; indeed, in some areas it appeared that PAVN main-force units were being broken up and assigned to lower echelons.

The Communists seemed to fear that they had overemphasized military action, neglecting the political and subversive base. They began a significant restructuring of their apparatus in South Vietnam, to consist of, firstly, the movement of cadres into government-held territory, often under the guise of defectors; secondly, the transfer of experienced cadres from military to political bureaucracies; and thirdly, the tightening of the party structure by raising standards and conducting purges. The Communists also stepped up efforts to subvert the South Vietnamese people and military. Many operatives were assigned strategic or long-term responsibilities, instead of tactical functions. Finally, the Communists tried to refurbish and strengthen their mass organizations.

Despite Hanoi's obvious concern with its problems, the

Communists believed that their basic strengths and advantages would ultimately prove decisive. They saw themselves as the only valid representatives of Vietnamese nationalism; in their eyes, the Saigon régime could not sustain itself if deprived of US support. RVN military and political gains were not considered by Giap to have been either crippling or irreversible. He believed that Hanoi's infrastructure was more durable than that of the RVN. Hanoi was worried, nevertheless, by the political stability achieved in South Vietnam and by the RVN's expansion of presence over a greater area and a larger number of people than for several years. Militarily, Giap attached considerable importance to controlling the adjacent Laotian and Cambodian border areas, which could continue to serve as base areas and sanctuaries.

Even if US support were withdrawn only gradually, Giap believed that the RVN could be undermined sufficiently to enable the Communists to move from their 'rice roots' positions to seizure of power. They counted heavily on their abilities in guerrilla war, terrorism, political organization and agitation to exploit South Vietnamese vulnerabilities. Hanoi was heartened by President Thieu's failure to rally greater political support, by the RVN's economic difficulties, and by the general war-weariness of the people of South Vietnam. Giap drew encouragement from attempts by opposition figures in Saigon to exploit popular grievances and aspirations for peace, and by their increasing boldness in criticizing the Thieu government. None of these vulnerabilities proved decisive so long as US troops anchored the military effort and shored up the Thieu régime. Now that the US was moving out of Vietnam, Hanoi counted on better opportunities for the future.

Although Hanoi saw the Vietnamization programme as fragile and likely to become more so as US troops withdrew, they recognized that it could work enough to give the RVN a chance to hold its own without a substantial US military presence. The longer it held, the greater the possibility that both the Viet Cong and the South Vietnamese population could believe it to be successful.

By early 1970 the Communists had not subjected the ARVN to major tests, considering that developments provided insufficient evidence of the US timetable for withdrawal or the ARVN's ability to fill the gaps left by departing US units. Hanoi was waiting until more US units had departed, providing better opportunities with lesser risks. But Hanoi would either have to engage the ARVN seriously, or face a considerably prolonged struggle.

Giap saw the RVN's pacification effort as an integral element in Vietnamization. Since late 1968 the RVN had sharply reduced the population controlled or influenced by the Communists. Communist access to local manpower and supply had been restricted, the mobility of many Communist units limited, and local cadres exposed and demoralized. Hanoi believed that RVN pacification progress was essentially fragile, to be rolled back once US forces were out of the way. However, further contraction of Communist-controlled areas would limit Giap's ability to confront the RVNAF, to launch major attacks on population centres, or even to wage a prolonged struggle. He planned to devote increasing resources to countering the pacification effort.

By early 1970 Hanoi's presence in Paris and the return of chief negotiator Le Duc Tho, evidenced continuing interest in negotiations. Although Hanoi probably had little hope of reaching an overall political settlement, including a coalition government, it saw some point in probing the possibility of an arrangement which might hasten US withdrawal or fix a timetable for a withdrawal. At least Hanoi hoped that that might sharpen US–RVN differences and stimulate anti-war sentiment in the US.

XXXV
Laos and Cambodia:
The Trail and the Sanctuaries, 1970-1

Melvin Laird, secretary for defence, believed that Vietnamization would 'work'. Dr Henry Kissinger, the national security adviser, was less optimistic, seeing a race between reduction in United States military power and an equivalent improvement in that of ARVN, an honourable disengagement the uncertain prize. The alternatives were either withdrawal or escalation, neither universally acceptable to the American *Zeitgeist* in 1969 and 1970. The administration therefore adopted the dual track of Vietnamization and negotiation. DRV responses to the latter included a peace proposal of ten points that was unacceptable to both South Vietnam and the US and the formation of the Provisional Government of South Vietnam, or PRG.

Le Duc Tho, Kissinger's DRV interlocutor in the Paris talks, unyieldingly demanded total American withdrawal from South Vietnam, gibing, 'Before, there were over a million US and ARVN troops, and you failed . . . Now, with only US *support*, how can you win?' (Reconcile yourselves, in other words, to the admission of defeat.) But America had to give President Thieu time to 'replace the US Army', or risk the worldwide consequences of US scuttle.

In April 1970, although denounced as illegal by Prince Sihanouk, the Cambodian leader, the North Vietnamese drove *en masse* into Cambodia in order to create another front of 100,000 men from which to attack South Vietnam. Washington could either stop them or abandon Vietnamization. ARVN performance in the consequent incursion into Cambodia under American advisors was competent, but, without advisors *sur place*, their 1971 drive into Laos ended in retreat.

The Hague Convention of 1907 had decreed that 'a neutral country had the obligation not to allow its territory to be used by a belligerent. If the neutral country is unwilling or unable to prevent this, the other country has the right to take appropriate counteraction.'

President Nixon had ordered a campaign of bombing, Operation

Menu, against the Ho Chi Minh Trail, and the ports and existing North Vietnamese sanctuaries in Cambodia which formed the infamous Harriman Expressway. The operation was not declared to the American people. In April and May 1970, in a move against strengthened PAVN control over the sanctuaries which was making the defence of South Vietnam unmanageable, joint US/ARVN forces in a series of multi-battalion operations mounted cross-border attacks with a total strength of 20,000 men, supported by US air-power. Fourteen major North Vietnamese bases in Cambodia were assaulted, 800 bunkers destroyed, weapons and supplies destroyed and NVA operations badly disrupted.

The North Vietnamese initially withdrew deeper into the Cambodian jungle but, as in the Iron Triangle earlier, they soon returned to the bases, although in reduced strength.

Time had been gained for Vietnamization. The ARVN had demonstrated that they could conduct mobile operations far from their bases; US military intervention had been in collaboration with, but independent of, ARVN units. The Americans withdrew their cooperation in Cambodia after domestic criticism back home, but Thieu held the border areas and operated deep into the country.

Time had also aided the US withdrawal from South Vietnam, to the theoretical benefit of the latter's development and that of its armed forces. But 'Cet animal est très méchant: quand on l'attaque, il se défend': British liberal pundits including William Shawcross and Bamber Gascoigne found MACV's defence of its men and its South Vietnam strategy outrageous.

A less successful offensive was mounted in 1971 against the town of Tchepone in Laos, Operation *Lam Son 719*, named after an ancient Vietnamese victory over the Chinese. ARVN troops involved were the 1st Infantry Division, the Airborne Division, Rangers and Armoured, later the Marine Division, all led by the equivocal General Lam, I Corps commander. US troops held staging areas in South Vietnam, providing air and artillery support.

The objective was, once again, to buy time for Vietnamization by disrupting PAVN supply lines and staging areas on the Laos sector of the Ho Chi Minh Trail. Viewed as a rapid, in-an-out raid, some observers considered *Lam Son 719* a success. The terrain, however, with its mountains and forests, differed from much of South Vietnam and made it difficult for the ARVN to gain advantage from their customarily superior ground and air mobility. At least the NVA was placed on the defensive, but ARVN supplies depended on narrow jungle tracks to South Vietnam, with armour confined to the 'road' and secured by fire support bases on the flanks.

Here, the PAVN were ready with 130 mm and 152 mm guns supporting mass infantry assaults. ARVN divisional staffs were weak, incapable of coordinating their troops' offensive.

In fact, US bombing and support for Hmong and Meo tribesmen and, earlier, for the Lao government under Prince Souvanna Phouma had been going on since 1964. But *Lam Son 719* confronted a PAVN force of 20,000 men, including a tank and an artillery regiment, nineteen anti-aircraft battalions and twelve infantry units, with reinforcements close to hand. This was heavy odds for untested soldiers.

After the Cambodian incursion, Congress had precluded the presence of US ground forces, either there or in Laos. Using Khe Sanh as a supply base, the ARVN 1st Division alone, therefore, with its 21,000 men and only US air support – much hindered by the North Vietnamese air defence – captured Tchepone, now ruined by bombing. Instead, however, of advancing against other targets or disrupting the Ho Chi Minh Trail system for the duration of the dry season, the South Vietnamese then started to retreat home, fearing the arrival of PAVN reinforcements.

Giap decided to attempt a victory against the ARVN that would not only devastate the 1st Division, but ridicule the entire concept of Vietnamization. He had 36,000 troops to do it with. Thousands of ARVN soldiers were killed and a great deal of heavy equipment was either destroyed or abandoned in what became an ARVN rout down Route 9. Many thousand PAVN troops were also lost, to the ARVN and to US fighter-bombers, but General Vo Nguyen Giap took heart that his troops 'could defeat the best-equipped South Vietnamese units. We had not been certain we could do this before Vietnamization created a strong Vietnamese Army . . . Our Army had to learn how to organize large-scale battles. So 1971 was a big test.'

The ARVN did not behave very well in Laos, but Kissinger believed that the offensive 'delayed the start of the 1972 PAVN offensive for several months, until towards the end of the dry season . . . it enabled us just barely to blunt the North Vietnamese offensive in 1972. Without the attrition caused by the incursions into Laos and Cambodia, this would have been impossible.'

Saigon had gained more time, but *Lam Son* had exposed grave deficiencies in the ARVN which was, evidently, in no position to challenge North Vietnamese base territory. A simultaneous operation against a position in Cambodia called Chup was, in Kissinger's words, 'similarly inconclusive'.

Opposition in the United States to the war, which now included *fainéants* such as Ramsey Clark, former Attorney General as well as Averell Harriman and former Secretary of Defense Clark Clifford, began to press for unilateral withdrawal, echoing Hanoi's demands for the abandonment of the Thieu government.

Kissinger then proposed fresh elections under an international commission in the South, to include the Communists; President Thieu was to resign beforehand. Thieu agreed in September 1971. Le Duc Tho ('Ducky') did not, evidently expecting that imminent Communist military action would soon break the dissolving American will and bring about US surrender on DRV terms.

Laird implemented Vietnamization by providing ARVN with very large quantities of equipment, armoured fighting vehicles and personnel carriers, 500 helicopters and 500 fixed-wing aircraft (fighter-bombers), large and small calibre artillery, encouraged by Sir Robert Thompson, who told him that Vietnamization, provided that US aid continued, would keep the ARVN going. Thompson told Nixon at this time that 'the future of Western civilization is at stake in the way you handle yourselves in Vietnam'.

By 1970 ARVN and most Regional and Popular Forces were equipped with M-16 automatic rifles. By early 1972 the PSDF (People's Self-Defence Force) numbered about four million men, the RF/PF 550,000, and the Army 430,000, eleven infantry divisions of 120 battalions, twenty armoured battalions and fifty-eight artillery battalions, 1,000 aircraft.

It was unfortunately also true that South Vietnamese troops often lacked discipline and the *will* to win. Pay was low, the bureaucracy was frequently incompetent, corrupt and indifferent to the men's interests. Leadership, often by officers lacking respect for or the affection of their soldiers, was sometimes very bad. Nor did upper-crust graduates care for the welfare of their men, or show understanding of 'social inferiors, bumpkins, peasants' far from home and worried about their families.

The desertion rate was high in ARVN combat units, but less so in RF and PF formations serving in their own provinces and villages. Fire-power in battle counted for less than PAVN/PLAF tactics of superior concentration, VC penetration and treachery through the 'open arms' programme, insufficient 'fighting' units in relation to the administrative tail, little regimental or unit pride. Owing to the sloth and inefficiency of ARVN military policemen, deserters could usually take refuge without detection in their own distant villages.

ARVN theft, refusal to pay for commodities, assault on innocent villagers, looting, 'tolls' on road and river traffic, smuggling in the Delta, deprived them – at least in comparison with the righteous VC – of popular support. Heavy artillery fire and air bombardment again created the resentments against which Abrams had ruled. ARVN operations in the Delta and elsewhere all too often generated huge refugee displacements and the destruction of farm animals and crops. Intelligence sources were also lost in the process on a thoughtless scale. But, after battles in the U Minh forest south of the Bassac, and in the northern delta, four PAVN Regiments did no more than survive.

The RF/PF nearly everywhere performed a useful pacification role as defenders against VC depredations. The role of the People's Self-Defence Force was, however, interpreted in too passive or static a sense, and was inadequate against the aggressive PLAF. Liaison between all these bodies and the ARVN, lacking a directorate of operations, was sluggish, bordering on the chaotic.

The most significant shift in the people's allegiance towards Saigon had begun in 1968, leading eventually, in the Land-to-the-Tiller Law of 1970, to a genuine Land Reform Act which distributed land away from the landlords. Some 800,000 tenant families benefited, rent payments were cancelled, holdings were reduced from 250 hectares to a maximum of thirty-seven for self-cultivators. By 1972, 1.5 million acres of land had been distributed and, by 1973, tenancy had been reduced from 60 per cent to 7 per cent. A painful class issue had been nearly abolished, farmers grew richer and output increased, all to the detriment of the VC.

By 1971 the RVN was reestablishing control in an almost complete reversal of the commanding position held by the VC in the 1960s. Due to newly improved pacification or 'protection of the people', PAVN/VC attacks had greatly decreased. Schools had reopened. Trade was booming. The agricultural economy, both in production and distribution, had recovered. No one, particularly Bob Komer in CORDS, could guarantee that the RVN's new popularity would survive a new VC drive, or undertake that RVN corruption had ended or, even, that security statistics corresponded to reality. 'The RF/PF receive good intelligence and utilize it effectively; when they know the enemy is coming, they simply withdraw or 'defend in the wrong direction'.' The VC and RVN officials, in other words, had 'arrangements' and the RVN were often in charge only in the mornings, sloping off after lunch.

Without US fire-power, most ARVN formations were no match for tough, hardened PAVN divisions in Pleiku and elsewhere, yet pacification and Vietnamization did appear to be taking hold. This was not to discount botched, evaded actions, desertions, poor tactics, but a balance of forces been attained, and the race between US withdrawals and ARVN improvements was beginning to seem imaginable. Other factors, of course, were more ominous. Saigon, for example, built for half a million inhabitants, by 1972 held four million.

XXXVI
The North Vietnamese
Spring 1972 Offensive

A North Vietnamese offensive for spring 1972 had been agreed as early as 1970 by the 19th Plenum. At that stage, the primary motive was probably to achieve a victory that would lessen Nixon's chances of re-election, thus enabling the DRV to dictate their own terms for ending the war.

In order to be sure of defeating the US and the ARVN, Giap had to demand an enormous share of his country's resources and to accept a halt in economic development and production. For the first time, he insisted on the call-up of factory workers, teachers and students, hitherto reserved from conscription, to man sophisticated Soviet military equipment in operations to include artillery barrages accompanied by tanks.

Skilled technicians were needed. Their possible loss, as future leaders, represented a gamble for the régime that Truong Chinh, with his preference for lightly equipped guerillas, opposed. Le Duan, on the other hand, the proponent of the Tet Offensive, and of armed as opposed to political struggle in the South, acquiesced in the invasion as promising a knockout blow to the DRV's enemies.

Giap himself, whose military reputation had not been enhanced by the battles of 1968 and 1969, had no protector after Ho Chi Minh's death. Although still minister of defence, commander-in-chief and Politburo member, he had been dismissed in 1971 as vice-chairman of the Defence Council. He ranked only fifth – after Truong Chinh – within the council. He needed a major military victory. To lead the invasion, he chose the general closest to him, Van Tien Dung, erstwhile commander of 320 Division in the Delta under French rule.

By 1972 additional arguments for the offensive were that political and economic progress in South Vietnam needed rapidly to be curtailed, that the increased security of the republic should be immediately disrupted, and, possibly, that action should be taken to pre-empt any Soviet or Chinese decision to neglect, even abandon, their Communist ally. The discussion within the Politburo was wide-ranging. 'Conventional' war would impose a heavy drain on

DRV resources, increasing dependence in the civilian and military fields on foreign friends. Dissent might now spread to the 'upper-class' parents of young, drafted echelons. The casualty rate could become intolerable. Internal opposition *could* grow.

At all events, after months of deception by DRV representatives at the Paris talks, Giap broke the unpromising deadlock in the South. 'Protracted war' would now end, in favour of an attempt on the battlefield to overthrow a US president whose re-election might free him from all restraint in the conduct of the war. There was every chance that American combat troops could soon go home. If the RVN could be defeated now, Nixon's chances would be diminished. The Americans had rejected surrender in negotiations. They should be driven to it in battle. No time should be lost in disrupting Vietnamization and pacification or manipulating US withdrawal.

There was no 'intelligence failure' this time. To no one's surprise, the first PAVN troops of Operation *Nguyen Hue*, three divisions with 200 Soviet tanks and many 130 mm guns, crossed the demilitarized zone on 30 March from Laos down the A Shau valley toward Huë. The ARVN fled before them. Two more NVA divisions came out of Cambodia on a line to Saigon, falling upon 5th Division at An Loc. Attacks developed in Quang Tri, Dong Ha falling on 29 April and Quang Tri city on 1 May. The 3rd ARVN Division broke: 20,000 soldiers, deserted by their officers, were killed and wounded in flight southward.

Kontum in the Central Highlands was attacked. The 22nd Division gave under a two-division PAVN attack, but the 23rd and the Airborne relieved it. In Binh Dien, a PAVN division seized a number of coastal positions. South Vietnam was splitting laterally. If An Loc (5th Division) had fallen, the door to Saigon would have been ajar.

President Nixon ordered air strikes to the 18th parallel, and seaborne attacks against North Vietnamese coastal bases. The bombing was hindered by vile weather until 9 April. On 8 May the exceptional order was executed to bomb all military targets in the DRV and to mine all North Vietnamese ports. B-52s attacked fuel storage and power plants in Hanoi and Haiphong in Operation *Linebacker I*, which continued for five months, and was far more damaging than *Rolling Thunder*.

On 11 October the French delegate-general, Pierre Susini, died from injuries sustained when an American bomb destroyed some of the delegation buildings in Hanoi. The centre of the town was bombed that day for the first time since 1967. The Albanian chargé d'affaires was injured, the Indian and Algerian embassies damaged; four French and Egyptian citizens were killed.

Thieu appointed new determined and competent general officers, in particular Ngo Quang Truong, who organized and held a line north of Huë; Kontum and An Loc also held. The PAVN did not, perhaps because of a more stable South Vietnamese defence line, move quickly on from Quang Tri city to Huë, pleading shortage of reinforcements. There was accordingly a lull in the battle. But although Ranger and Marine units eventually saved the day, conditions in Huë had become deplorable, refugees and their babies hurrying down toward Da Nang from Quang Tri. Panic-stricken ARVN soldiers, drunk and half-dressed, fought one another, even set the market ablaze.

Ranger and Airborne units were moved to An Loc. The 21st Division was sent from the Delta to protect Saigon.

ARVN light M-41 tanks were outgunned by Russian tanks. Air-power, rockets and missiles had to be employed to destroy PAVN armour. But the NVA, in their turn, had to face the B-52s, who, in the end, wore them out. By mid-June the PAVN had abandoned An Loc and Kontum, An Loc reduced to rubble after ferocious tank and artillery battles. Quang Tri, also in ruins, was not recovered until mid-September by three first-class ARVN divisions against six PAVN divisions. Years later, the houses there still yawed sideways, without façades, the roads strewn with battered guns and AFVs. At An Loc, detailed plans to move on Saigon were captured from the NVA by an ARVN private soldier. In these battles one whole PAVN division crossed the Thach Han river in twenty-four hours, each man pulling himself across hand over hand on cables.

Fourteen North Vietnamese divisions and twenty regiments, had lost 100,000 men. Although they damaged pacification and increased the number of refugees, they scored no strategic success other than retention of Loc Ninh and Dong Hoi, small rewards for such a price.

ARVN, by determined defence and with American air support, had repulsed the offensive and – to Hanoi's and Washington's surprise – rebuilt their own forces. Vietnamization had not been disgraced, at least on the tacit assumption that American support would continue. But leadership was lacking. General Lam, the corps commander, sat out the battle in Da Nang. Thieu interfered. Reinforcement troops would not obey Giai, the 3rd Divison commander at Quang Tri. Reshuffles by Thieu, except for Truong's takeover from Lam, were not decisive. General Hung at An Loc threatened to shoot his deputy divisional commander in 5th Division.

Despite the relative, if partial, vigour and effectiveness of the South Vietnamese Army, long-term prospects were poor. Continued political and economic corruption amongst senior officers and politicians, social injustice and dependence on the United States hardly provided a basis for determined military and philosophical resistance to an opponent whose stubbornness and determination seemed implacable. However much it had improved, the performance of the South Vietnamese troops was variable, depending greatly on the quality of their officers. They would not have held without US air and naval power or without the deterrent of tens of thousands of US troops still then in-country. North Vietnamese artillery, tanks and men fell, not so much to ARVN infantry, but to the USAF, the 7th Fleet and the 'smart bombs' dropped in interdiction of supply lines and lines of communication. The South Vietnamese people were again conscious that the VC, despite the weight of ordnance, had acquitted themselves well, and that the accelerating US withdrawals might now require a reconsideration of their personal attitudes to the Communists.

Some commentators regarded Giap as having divided his forces needlessly in an almost pan-Vietnam mode, at least into three separate columns. Had he, it was thought, concentrated them in a single thrust, he might have brought about the total collapse of the South Vietnamese armed forces. And whatever the fortuitous political consequences, this campaign had once again been no *military* victory for the general and his soldiers, any more than Tet 1968.

Under pressure, Hanoi agreed to a resumption of plenary talks on 13 July and to a private meeting on 19 July, which, it was hoped, would lead to a political settlement before the presidential elections. At the talks, endless quibbling and prevarication ensued. Lies, abuse and cheating over textual amendments by Le Duc Tho began to fluster and worry Dr Kissinger's Paris delegates.

On 8 October, nevertheless, both sides had roughed out the outlines of a ceasefire agreement, which gave Kissinger much pleasure, and which was eventually signed on 27 January 1973. Le Duc Tho's proposal in October was for an agreement on military questions: US withdrawal, prisoners, no further PAVN infiltration. A ceasefire would take place on signature.

The eventual agreement, bitterly opposed by Thieu and with endless procrastination and verbal games from Tho, had two paralysing central flaws. The first was that, in accordance with Kissinger's assertion that the US had already abandoned the demand, there was no provision for the withdrawal of North Vietnamese troops from South Vietnam. (Kissinger believed that withdrawal could only have been obtained after all-out war, which the United States had already rejected. An 'end' to North Vietnamese infiltration was the best he could get.) The second major flaw lay in the terms of reference for the revised International Control Commission: since they required unanimity, effective monitoring and control were thereby excluded.

And, meanwhile, the PAVN stayed where they were in the South 'in an intricate pattern which had always been the enemy scheme, from which they would break into small units and penetrate the villages and hamlets'.

During the negotiations preparatory to signature, Tho's linguistic tricks, reintroduction of earlier, rejected demands and delaying tactics convinced the Americans that they would either have to apply military pressure or accept an unenforceable peace likely to wreck the republic's prospects.

On 18 December Nixon accordingly ordered a resumption of the bombing against Hanoi and Haiphong on a continuing basis, a massive, devastating campaign conducted almost entirely by B-52s, the only aircraft capable of surmounting the problems of weather. Over thirty were shot down, but 55,000 tons of bombs were dropped, and devastation and ruin brought to the capital. Mining of the ports had been resumed on 17 December. The 'Christmas bombing' lasted for twelve days, to a chorus of journalistic and Congressional hysteria and moral indignation. The East German and Hungarian diplomatic missions were hit, but the industrial suburbs were so heavily bombed that thousands of people camped out in the streets of the so-called '*quartier diplomatique*' in Hanoi. The bombing stopped on December 30. Negotiations reopened in Paris on 2 January.

While the bombing had been in progress, a senior member of the National Liberation Front had been negotiating secretly through General Tran Van Don – one of the leaders of the coup against Diem and a capable soldier – with President Thieu. The NLF intermediary proposed that South Vietnam should be partitioned, the Republic in control south of Quang Ngai, and the Front controlling north of that province. (The offer was allegedly specific that the NLF, *not Hanoi*, should be the ruling authority.) The proposal was put to Washington by Don; the Nixon administration predictably did not comment.

On 2 January also, the House Democratic caucus in Washington, without any provision for a ceasefire, voted to cut off all funds for military operations in Vietnam, Laos and Cambodia. The Republican caucus voted similarly on 4 January. Neither vote caused Hanoi to postpone the resumption of talks. The remaining days until 27 January were spent in redrafts and in incorporating President Thieu's additional points, such as formal recognition of the Saigon government as the legal government of South Vietnam.

Kissinger congratulated himself on the prohibition of further PAVN infiltration and an accord on the return of prisoners; in addition he had been able to 'win' unrestricted US military support for the ARVN, a proper definition of the demilitarized zone and an undertaking by both parties not to exploit Laos or Cambodia as military bases or jumping-off points. He also claimed to have received assurances from Peking and Moscow that Chinese and Soviet offensive military supply would stop.

None of this, in the event, was secured. PAVN infiltration continued from Laos, Cambodia and North Vietnam. New military equipment was installed at North Vietnamese positions within South Vietnam. In response, Nixon was poised to renew the bombing on the scale of December 1972. But, at that moment, 'the floodgates of Watergate opened'. On 30 June Congress cut off funds for all US military activity in Indochina with effect from mid-August 1973. The War Powers Resolution in November had authorized control ('oversight') by Congress over the president's authority to deploy troops overseas, thus eliminating all threat to future Vietnamese aggression and, in the end, all hope for the survival of the republic.

Before Watergate, and before the congressional cave-in, Kissinger thought, or affected to think, that the agreement was valid. The ARVN could have been strong enough to deal with DRV aggression at any level except main-force invasion and assault, at which point Washington's help could have been sought legitimately and successfully by Thieu.

The United States, Kissinger stated, was determined that 'Saigon should grow in security and prosperity, so that it could prevail in any political struggle. We sought not an interval before collapse, but lasting peace with honour. But for the collapse of executive authority as a result of Watergate, I believe we would have succeeded.'

The grisly crew of visiting American actresses, Trotskyists, clerics, black activists, and 'useful idiots' like Bertrand Russell, Tariq Ali and, especially, Ramsey Clark, who found the hygiene in the Hanoi POW cages 'particularly touching', had won a battle that South Vietnam would not have lost. In June and November the United States Congress dispensed with honour. Once more, out of unsuccessful military engagement, Giap was about to secure political triumph.

His cause had been supported by the funding of his country through Swiss and Scandinavian banks; by Dr Cairns' (the Australian Foreign Minister) Congress for International Disarmament and Cooperation, closely linked with the Communist World Peace Council, and thus with the CPSU; by the US People's Coalition for Peace and Justice, a puppet of the Communist Party of the United States manipulating US servicemen and public opinion. And, as was openly acknowledged in Vietnam, 'the anti-war movement in the United States is guided and supported by our DRV delegation at the Paris peace talks'. That support aimed to end US military and, later, economic protection of the RVN, to spread allegations of tyranny against the Thieu régime, to disseminate the lie that the PRG (Peoples Revolutionary Government) and not Hanoi, would be sovereign in South Vietnam, and to pretend that the PAVN only played an insignificant role therein compared with the PLAF.

The propaganda was successful. South Vietnam became, at least for the idle minds who constituted the majority in the world, an international pariah. But a revisionist war crimes tribunal today would have no difficulty in naming the accused: Jane Fonda, Eldridge Cleaver, and the rest of them.

XXXVII
The Consequences of the Peace
Agreement of 1973

General Frederick Carlton Weyand, an outstanding officer of the
United States Marine Corps, to whom reference has already been
made, and the last commander of MACV, said in 1973 that the forces
at Saigon's disposal were capable of

> defending the South Vietnamese from anything but an attack
> of massive proportions supported by a major power. The North
> Vietnamese had been forced to reassess their reliance on force
> as a prime means to political end . . . The Saigon régime had
> become a visibly viable alternative to the political system and
> way of life sponsored by Hanoi. Current South Vietnamese
> attitudes, furthermore, held promise of an eventual end to
> corruption in government . . . If the ceasefire terms were
> honoured, armed conflict could gradually fade away . . . if
> they were not, the US would have to decide on reinvolvement
> and, inevitably, face questioning on the validity of past in-
> volvement.

Weyand predicted that the North Vietnamese would remain in
the South from 1974 to 1978, concentrated in the I Corps zone and
the border areas above Saigon. Judging by the flood of armour,
artillery, anti-aircraft guns and men crossing into South Vietnam,
they could probably mount an offensive by 1974. The result would
depend on Thieu's skill in attracting domestic and international
support, reducing corruption and improving military leadership, and
on a continuation of adequate levels of US military and ecomomic
assistance.

Neither he nor anyone else, before or after Phuoc Binh, forecast
the forthcoming 'attack of massive proportions'.

The general severely criticized deteriorating standards of maintenance in ARVN and SVNAF. Only if the South Vietnamese could
improve their maintenance without US assistance, could their Air
Force, in particular, fill the gap caused by the superior accuracy and

rate of fire of the PAVN's Soviet 122 mm and 130 mm artillery over the ARVN's US 175 mm.

The four South Vietnamese corps commanders were now patriotic, competent and well motivated. There were able divisional commanders but most staffs were weak, failing especially to grasp the need for 'maintenance and logistic discipline'.

In the spring of 1974, after the Tet Festival (New Year) of the Tiger, some very senior political and military cadres met at 33 Pham Ngu Lao Street in Hanoi. Le Duan and Le Duc Tho presented the October 1973 Resolution of the 21st Conference of the Lao Dong Party Central Committee: 'Coordinate military and political strategy with diplomatic . . . fighting while talking.'

The Paris Agreement was regarded by these leaders as a great victory for the DRV. The 'US imperialists' had left Vietnam, 'forced to respect the principles of independence, sovereignty, unity and territorial integrity'. Their military invasion had ended, and the right to self-determination had been granted. The United States was obliged to recognize two governments, two Armies, two zones of control and more than one political force: Saigon's, Hanoi's *and* the 'third force'.

Revolutionary warfare was the course adopted, an offensive strategy, with administrative control and loyalty of the people as principal goals. 'Campaign 275' would fall into three phases. The first was to be the liberation of the Tay Nguyen, or Central Highlands, beginning with an assault on Ban Me Thuot. It would then be the turn of Huë, Da Nang and the coastal areas of central Vietnam, concluding with the 'Ho Chi Minh Campaign' to liberate Saigon/Gia Dinh, and the remaining provinces, thus securing victory.

General Van Tien Dung, Giap's chief of staff and former commander of 320 Division, was appointed 'representative of the Central Committee and of the central command', in general charge, and in direct command during the Ho Chi Minh Campaign. (Giap was minister of defence and secretary-general of the Central Military Committee). He had with him the famous General Dinh Duch Thien, now seventy, who had miraculously supplied Dien Bien Phu, and his own subordinate in 320 Division, Le Ngoc Hien.

In 1974 the ARVN numbered 710,000 men, with greatly increased quantities of armour and aircraft supplied by the United States after the Peace Agreement of January 1973 to match those continually delivered to the North by the Communist states, China, USSR, North Korea and Eastern Europe. Saigon also disposed of a million and a half civil guards. In '36,000 operations' ARVN had begun to thrust into the liberated zones, exploiting up to 60 per cent of its main-force units, controlling 75 per cent of South Vietnam's territory and 85 per cent of the population. The southern Air Force now comprised over a thousand aircraft, the third largest in the world. Hanoi suddenly saw the North Vietnamese position in the South as threatened.

The NVA began to plan a major offensive. In the meanwhile they took Thuong Duc in Zone 5, Dac Pek in the Central Highlands, and other district capitals, some near Saigon, in a series of operations in the summer and autumn of 1974 known as 'strategic raids'. The general staff accordingly concluded that 'our [Hanoi's] fighters' ability was superior to the enemy's'. The PAVN could now 'wipe out the enemy, liberate people and hold territory', not just mount hit-and-run guerrilla actions.

In preparing the offensive, Giap established a number of mobile corps commands: infantry, artillery, tanks and SP guns. Stocks of provisions, ammunition and weapons were accumulated in the 'deep forests' of Tay Ninh, Binh Long and Phuoc Long provinces. Good roads were built, many running off a new main road east of the Truong Son mountains, the section between Quang Tri and eastern Nam Bo stretching to a total length of 20,000 kilometres of track, supporting a network of 5,000 kilometres of pipeline to fuel the new trucks and armour. Ten thousand vehicles used the route. Telephone lines now linked Hanoi with points as far south as Loc Ninh. Routes 7, 14, 21 and 19 were newly extended to the Ho Chi Minh Trail.

PAVN casualties had been high during the 'strategic raids' but, unlike the ARVN's, they had been replaced. The PAVN and PLAF now had strategic positions and stockpiles linking North with South. Locally and internationally, *matériel*, propaganda, and 'friendship' support for the cause had grown. Opposition was intense within the US to any further participation in the war although the Politburo was uncertain whether the United States government under President Nixon would react by sending American troops back to Vietnam should the military situation warrant it.

The answer to this conundrum was supplied, in Hanoi's opinion, when General Tran Van Tra, formerly commanding the VC in the Delta and Saigon commander during Tet, scored a major victory at

Phuoc Binh, near the Cambodian border, about seventy-five miles north of Saigon, and capital of Phuoc Long province. Using two PAVN regiments with T-54 tanks and 130mm guns, he caused losses to the ARVN of 4,000 men, two C-130s and 300 guns. The road to Saigon had been cleared by January 1975; Thieu declared national mourning, closing cinemas, bars and nightclubs.

Despite justified cries of pain and rage from Thieu, all Kissinger said was, 'This is not yet *the* all-out North Vietnamese offensive'. A nod was as good as a wink to a blind mule. At a Politburo conference between 18 December 1974 and 18 January 1975, the decision to mount Campaign 275, starting with the assault on Ban Me Thuot earlier proposed, was confirmed. The Central Highlands was to be the main battlefield, developing eastward on Routes 7, 19 and 21, and south down Route 14.

General Van Tien Dung had been a textile worker, and a prisoner of the French. He escaped his guards in September 1941, thus incurring the suspicion of the Communist Party, and was only welcomed back by the Party three years later. In the meanwhile, in the guises of carpenter and of Buddhist bonze, he had allegedly 'carried out anti-colonial acts independently', presumably on behalf of other political groupings.

He remembered also, from the French empire, his days in the Delta. Here in his peasant's clothes, through the thick mud along the dykes and beside the bamboo hedges of the Ninh-Binh region, or in a bamboo boat with the waves slapping on the gunwales, he had split his groups into small units by day, sinking and hiding his boats under water. He had commanded the famous 308 and 320 Divisions with distinction, 308 Division contained the Hanoi regiment which had left Hanoi in rags and tatters in 1946 after the French had reassumed control of the capital.

Now he addressed the First Army Corps at Ninh Binh, this short, stocky, loyal *compagnon de la route*:

'For thirty years our land has taken up the gun, yet still the disc of our moon is split in two . . . The rhythm of the corps must now blend with the rhythm of the South . . . I hope the corps' battle drums will throb and the trumpets of victory sound in time with the symphony of the whole Army and people. Can all your musicians here do that? If so, the conductor will raise the baton . . .' His congregation responded: 'We can do it, we can do it.'

His opponents had suffered 170,000 deserters. US aid had fallen from the 1972/3 figure of $1,026 million to $700 million in 1974/5; ARVN's mobility had decreased by 50 per cent and its artillery fire-support by 60 per cent from consequent shortages of gasoline and shells. Aircraft sorties had correspondingly diminished. The Army had had to shift its methods from armoured and deep penetration helicopter attacks to defence. 'Thieu was forced to fight a poor man's war.' Saigon in 1975 nevertheless disposed of 1,351,000 troops, 495,000 in main-force units, 475,000 regional troops and 381,000 militia, thirteen main-force divisions and eighteen ranger groups.

The ARVN in I Corps mustered five divisions, four Ranger groups, five armoured regiments, six tank and armoured-car patrols with 450 'vehicles', 100 fighter aircraft, 420 heavy guns.

II Corps consisted of two divisions, seven Ranger groups, 380 heavy guns, 480 tanks and armoured 'vehicles', 140 fighter aircraft. III Corps had two divisions, seven Ranger groups, 370 guns, 650 tanks, 250 fighters. IV Corps comprised three divisions, 380 guns, 490 armoured vehicles, seventy fighters and about 600 ships and boats.

These totals were formidable, but the PAVN was growing stronger and even better equipped, trained and motivated.

Dung flew to Dong Hoi, near Giap's natal village, then took a motor boat up the Ben Hai river marking the frontier of North and South Vietnam. The day was bright but strangely cool. Army girls cheerfully greeted their commander: 'Where are our letters from home?' they cried. Dung ordered a distribution of Tet hair slides and had thousands of cigarettes given to the Army truck drivers, arms nonchalantly out of their cab windows.

He was able to confirm to Giap (code name Chien, 'Battler' Dung's code name being Tuan, 'Excellent') that 'A 75 detachment' had been despatched to the Central Highlands to direct the campaign now set for March. Dung had, as a measure of deception, sent off all his Tet cards beforehand as well as routine messages of congratulation on the Soviet, Albanian and Mongolian Armed Forces Days which would take place *after* his departure from Hanoi. His objective, agreed with the Politburo, was to take Ban Me Thuot and Tuy Hoa, then the highlands and the whole coastal plain from Binh Dinh to Huë and Da Nang before the rainy season at the end of May. In 1975, using this region as a springboard, the next offensive was to bring about the collapse of the Saigon régime through diplomatic, political and military means.

The keys for Giap were 'daring, boldness, surprise through movement security', and incessant diversions to persuade the enemy that the attack would be against the northern highlands, whereas Dung would strike in the south. 'Only daring will bring surprise, enthusiasm, fervour, determination, endurance, whatever the danger or hardship. Lightning speed, more lightning speed; boldness, more boldness.'

Saigon was about to discover that the régime's earlier seizure of territory occupied by the North Vietnamese not only reduced resources, but would bring down retribution. The Communists recreated their material strength and quintupled their transport, radio, petroleum distribution and telephone networks. In General Dung's words: 'Strong ropes inching gradually, day by day, around the neck, arms and legs of a demon, awaiting the order to jerk tight and bring the creature's life to an end.'

In the Central Highlands, Saigon deployed the 23rd Division, seven Ranger groups (ten regiments) and four tank groups scattered over the five mountain provinces. This force eventually faced the 10th, 316th, 320th and 968th PAVN divisions. It also 'confronted' the strategic and tactical errors of both the South Vietnamese president and the commander of Military Region 3, Brigadier Pham Van Phu. Thieu did not believe that the North Vietnamese could take and hold large towns, while General Phu thought that Kontum and Pleiku would be the PAVN's targets. At those points he therefore concentrated his strike forces, so that North Vietnamese superiority at the actual target of Ban Me Thout itself was five to one in infantry, 1.2 to one in armour and two to one in artillery.

And whereas North Vietnam could fight an offensive war for twelve, even twenty-four months, the ARVN desperately lacked gasoline, spare parts, ammunition. Fixed-wing and helicopter missions were further severely reduced against all targets, including the huge PAVN supply dumps. The Delta river fleet ran out of fuel. Whole battalions exhausted their ammunition stocks in battle and either surrendered or were cut to pieces. Artillery fire, once at a hundred rounds per gun a day, was cut to four. Meanwhile, the Ho Chi Minh Trail and its outlet roads looked even more like a super-highway than a 'trail', while the NLF busily destroyed the republic's infrastructure.

On the other hand, the PAVN lacked experience and expertise in tank warfare and in artillery, armour and infantry cooperation; some training was inadequate in all ranks. Relations between political commissars and commanding officers were occasionally imperfect; arms supply from the Socialist countries was erratic; the North Vietnamese often discounted the ARVN's qualities. All these factors marginally diminished the advantage gained by the increase in PAVN numbers in the South and the hundreds of medium tanks now deployed there.

XXXVIII
Giap's Battering Ram

Ted Serong, once an Australian brigadier, in January 1975 an *éminence grise* in President Thieu's administration, recommended that, since the central highlands and central Vietnam had been rendered indefensible by US defection, they should be abandoned. The rest of South Vietnam would then be held by force of arms south of Quang Ngai (a proposal resembling that of the NLF intermediary quoted earlier), or, at worst, north of Ban Me Thuot. Negotiations should not be with Hanoi, but with the Provisional Revolutionary Government (PRG).

Thieu delayed a decision.

Outside the pretty French provincial town of Ban Me Thuot, surrounded by coffee and banana plantations, lay dense primary jungle alive with antelope, elephant, leopard, panther, tiger. In longhouses, Rhade mountain-men dwelt, sometimes loyal to the government and sometimes to the Viet Cong, fighting well for either, particularly for Australian mentors. The streets of the little hill town were lined by flamboyants planted by the colonists; it was a sleepy, bourgeois place.

Dung waited in the green jungle outside the town. Under the *khooc* trees, dry fallen leaves covered the ground like a golden carpet. When he trod on them, they exploded like rice crackers. Around his encampment, elephants roamed in herds of forty and fifty, pulling down the communication wires. The forest around the bunkers and the camouflaged wooden huts reverberated with his generators.

Since the ARVN were occupied with Kontum and Pleiku, the larger capitals to the north, 10, 320 and 968 Divisions opposed only one regiment of 23rd Division and three weak regional battalions. 316 PAVN Division, also, was on its way to Ban Me Thuot in 500 trucks. Dung passed them *en route*. 'The road to the front at that time of year was very beautiful.'

Various diversions, including one by 968 Division, convinced the ARVN that Pleiku was the North Vietnamese target, but a wounded PAVN officer gave the game away on capture by the southerners. Discovering this at 02.00 on 10 March, Dung quickly blocked all roads in and out of Ban Me Thuot, attacking with artillery, tanks and sappers (*dac cong*, who had blown up aircraft on airfields, including Dien Bien Phu, all over Indochina, and sunk an aircraft carrier), all in blitzkrieg mode, with prisoners of war in the front line. As Pleiku airport was under heavy fire, Phu could only fly in 500 reinforcements, not nearly enough to prevent the fall of the town next morning in the PAVN type of operation called 'lotus blossom' or 'exploding-from-within'. Dung next proposed – and Hanoi immediately agreed – the seizure of Pleiku, Kontum, and then the drive south.

After the battle, more than 300 monks, soldiers and civil servants were tied up in the market and shot by the North Vietnamese, their families dragged out of town and murdered in the trees at the sides of the road. Neither here, nor in any of the other cities taken, was there any question that the administration should be in local hands, whether NLF or PRG. The PAVN, with its iron fist, ruled as military governors.

All South Vietnamese efforts to retake the city failed. Without Ban Me Thuot, and now that 316 Division had arrived in the area, Thieu at last decided to evacuate Pleiku and Kontum. He did so not with the aim which Serong had proposed in January but to save the rest of the Rangers and 23 Division, helpless without US supplies and without those B-52s which changed every battle, but no longer – the South Vietnamese Air Force instead bombed from C-130As at 15,000 to 20,000 feet, 'mini B-52s'.

Evacuation by air was impossible. Routes 14 and 19 were cut. Thieu also remembered that it was on Route 19 that the French 'Korea' battalion, Mobile Group 100, had been exterminated in 1954. Route 7B had a wretched surface, but over 100,000 civilians and soldiers on foot, bicycle, cart or truck proceeded painfully down it from 15 March, attacked all the way in the blazing sun, taking terrible losses. (The Montagnards escaped into the forests.) Many thousands were killed, as many captured, far more wounded by mortars, recoilless rifles and 'friendly fire' from South Vietnamese fighter-bombers. There they were left to die. 'Bodies were scattered along the road, burning with the trucks . . .' The line of misery stretched back for miles in the heat and dust, fleeing the dreaded Tonkinese. Fifteen PAVN Molotova trucks drove fast into the crowd, killing and maiming.

Tens of thousand of survivors took to the jungle, pursued

remorselessly, starving, unarmed, often dying of thirst, drowning in the rivers under broken bridges and wrecked culverts, or massacred by their northern compatriots of 320 Division. Six ARVN Ranger multi-battalion units, three armoured regiments, much armour and artillery, were completely destroyed. Old men, women and children died in thousands, 'their bloodstained feet worn through to the bone . . . in all the years of war, there had not been so much personal disaster and tragedy'.

At their destination in Pham Tiet, the survivors chose to vandalize President Thieu's ancestral graves.

Brigadier Phu's new II Corps headquarters were at Nha Trang, defended by naval 76 mm and 122 mm guns. He soon fled thence to Phan Thiet via Cam Ranh Bay, only 250 miles from Saigon, taking the remnants of his staff with him, the Nha Trang garrison having broken long before the arrival of the 10th PAVN Division advancing down Route 21. Cam Ranh's defences faced the bay, not the land. And 968 Division was on its way along Route 19.

In central Vietnam, the collapse became catastrophic. General Ngo Quang Truong, commander of I Corps, was, in Sir Robert Thompson's opinion, 'one of the finest soldiers in the world', proven as a divisional commander in Huë at Tet in 1968, later retaking Quang Tri with three divisions against six PAVN, as corps commander during the 1972 offensive. At Thieu's orders, however, he had had to transfer the Marines from the border province of Quang Tri to positions west of Da Nang, where they relieved the Airborne. The latter prepared to move to the Central Reserve in Saigon, primarily as a praetorian guard.

Quang Tri was abandoned. In panic, 130,000 inhabitants fled down Route 1 to Huë, around which the North Vietnamese stranglehold had been almost completed by December 1974. Panic spread and the people of Huë then evacuated Gia Long's capital, where General de Courcy had landed ninety years before, by sea or trekking down the Da Nang road to the Pass of Clouds. In Da Nang, there was no one to receive them, nothing to eat, no medical care, no accommodation all the barracks pulled down when the Americans left. In any case, there were not enough boats to carry them on. 'Hundreds of bodies were washed up on the shore'.

Giap and the Politburo, seeing these evacuations, estimated that Thieu was preparing to defend at least Saigon, Da Nang and the

Delta in order to achieve Serong's compromise. They now resolved to seize Saigon before the May monsoon.

Although in the second week of March Colonel Cao Van Dong's Regional Forces in Military Region 1 had destroyed five VC battalions, the whole central front began to unravel. What was left of the gallant 1st Division started to break up, the men terrified for their families, who, as in most ARVN units, accompanied them, rendering manoeuvre almost impossible in mass main-force action. Thieu told Truong in his I Corps headquarters at Da Nang to hold Huë à tout prix. Da Nang, incidentally, now contained 800,000 people, later to become one million, with shelter for only 450,000.

One source has asserted that the Huë commander, General Thi, on his own initiative disobeyed orders to defend the city, which promptly fell. (Another report said that in a high-grade muddle Truong himself ordered it to be abandoned.) Thieu thereupon accused Truong, who was at Da Nang, not Huë, of breaking his word. The president and his best general never spoke again. Truong at last realized that Thieu had, all along, determined to give up central Vietnam to the northerners. He 'retreated deep into melancholia, speaking little to his staff and not at all to his troops, all of whom were in urgent need of his leadership'.

At that point, the destruction of the 1st Division proceeded further and, on the sand dunes south of Huë, the men were trapped between the sea and the NVA artillery. Dung ordered General Le Trong Tan, formerly chief of staff to COSVN, to take command at Da Nang, having already started to move the PAVN's 30 mm artillery towards the city. Most of the remnants of 1st and 2nd Infantry Division fled or were eliminated. Mutineers near Da Nang attacked the defending 3rd ARVN Division outside the town, which, under pressure from a seaborne PAVN force and two other columns approaching from the west, surrendered or ran. The Marines refused to obey General Truong, intent only on escape by air or sea, looting and killing refugees who stood in their way. Women and children once more drowned, died of exhaustion or wounds, or were trampled to death. Some perished from drinking sea water. Others were too weak to climb aboard the rescue ships.

Da Nang, South Vietnam's second city, was really taken from within by Dung's 5th Column, even before his divisions launched the main attack. The great harbour had become a PAVN possession by dusk on Easter Sunday of March 1975, the other South Vietnamese forces – 3rd Airborne Brigade, 40th Infantry Division, a Ranger battalion – defeated within the town by 10 PAVN Division. 10, 316, 320 Divisions, now organized in III Corps, with I Corps recently arrived, began to roll south to Saigon from across the border. ARVN 1st, 2nd and 3rd Divisions scarcely existed any longer. Only 4,000 Marines escaped, and they never fought again. Poor General Truong got away in a ship which also evacuated the staff of the consul-general of the United States at Da Nang.

In Cambodia, the Khmer Rouge, *not* the North Vietnamese, had overrun Phnom Penh by 16 April and Pol Pot's terrible killings began, a severe discouragement also to the crumbling South Vietnamese régime. The kingdom of Laos fell to the Pathet Lao in December 1975, the king 'abdicated' and went to a 're-education' camp where he eventually died. In January 1976 a People's Republic was declared in Vientiane. Although with less frightful consequences than in Cambodia, the Communists had thus taken over in Laos also, securing totalitarian rule throughout Indochina.

Thieu intended to hold the line at Phan Rang, south of Cam Ranh bay. General Weyand, now US Army chief of staff, who had been sent by President Ford to examine the situation, reported that if America were to despatch arms and equipment to the value of US $700 million the ARVN could probably defend until the monsoon. As a veteran of the Tet offensive in Saigon, he also believed that the PAVN must at all costs be prevented from bringing their main divisions into the vicinity of a capital vulnerable to attack from innumerable canals, rivers and roads.

In 1975 General Dung had at his disposal five Army corps of three divisions each, plus artillery and armour, with two more divisions in reserve, a total of 153 battalions, as opposed to the seventeen VC and PAVN battalions under Giap's control at Tet in 1968. He feared that Thieu was seeking to concentrate his troops at Phan Rang in order to achieve a military position from which to negotiate a partitioned Vietnam. It is interesting that, according to Denis Warner, the NLF were *still* negotiating through General Don, born in Bordeaux and a French citizen, for a third-force government under the PRG, 'a non-Communist state with respect for private property and no policy of reprisals'. The NLF's alleged thesis was that a settlement must be achieved quickly if Saigon were not to endure bloody conquest.

In these circumstances the Lao Dong Politburo could not permit the republic anything other than crushing *military* defeat, before the rains. The customary rumour ran, nevertheless, that a *coup d'état* had taken place in Hanoi, and that Giap had fled to Moscow.

The three PAVN divisions, 2, 304 and 325, forming II Corps took little more than two weeks to reach Bien Hoa (MR3) on 12 April along 900 miles of coastal road, crossing six rivers and fighting on the way. After II Corps took Phan Rang, where Thieu had hoped that General Nghi and the 22nd ARVN Division would stand, IV Corps (6, 7 and 341 Divisions) began the assault on Xuan Loc. This small provincial town between hills, among rubber estates, was the key to Saigon. The three PAVN divisions were fiercely opposed by 18 Division under General Le Minh Dao, trained at the US Staff College, with F-5, C-130 and A-1 air support from Bien Hoa. The division, without families, fought well, allegedly aided by 'asphyxiation' bombs of huge power ('daisy-cutters'), which eliminated oxygen in the area of explosion. This terrified IV Corps troops, who thought them nuclear weapons.

The division, after severely mauling these PAVN divisions, was much reduced, but was thought by the American Embassy to be holding the enemy. However, 5th and 25th Divisions were cut off at Lai Khe and Tay Ninh respectively; 5th ARVN was later destroyed by PAVN's I Corps, and the headquarters of 25th Division, facing 70, 320, 316 and 968 PAVN, was overrun by armour at Cu Chi. III Corps, victors of Ban Me Thuot, Huë and Da Nang, comprising 10, 320 and 368 Divisions, with I Corps took Dong Du, Cu Chi, Lai Khe and Bien Hoa. 7 Division among others continued to batter 18th ARVN at Xuan Loc where the garrison had once been commanded by General Patton's son, and with II Corps tanks took Vung Tau, Long Thanh and Ba Ria.

On 21 April, just as President Thieu resigned, General Le Minh Dao led what was left of his gallant, stubborn 18th Division out of Xuan Loc, a living demonstration that the ARVN could fight with aggression and courage.

PAVN I Corps, which had been reinforcing dykes in North Vietnam, had left Ninh Binh on 25 March, reaching their southern positions 2,000 kilometres away about three weeks later, after an astounding forced 'march' described by Dung:

Hundreds of thousands of vehicles sped southward, bumper to bumper. On some sections of the road, where the dust churned up by their wheels decreased visiblity, our vehicles turned on their headlights and blared their horns repeatedly. The long trail of dust did not settle on the durian and coconut trees, on the manioc fields, the paddi, the pepper plantations. It snaked through the dense jungles of the central highlands, passed through the green pastures of Bu Prang and entered the bamboo forests in Bu Giap Map.

The passage has a faint echo of John Masters' panegyric to the old Indian Army in Burma going down to the attack for the last time.

Vehicles captured in the South *en route* were pressed into service with prisoners at the wheel – armour, buses, cars, lorries, PAVN trucks; the coastal navy and the Northern Air Force also played a transportation role.

The leaders started to gather in the South. Pham Hung, now in charge of COSVN, met Dung at Loc Ninh. In the 1930s, he had been imprisoned for his share in the murder of a French colonial official and was later elected to the Central Committee of Politburo of the Lao Dong Party. Tran Van Tra, once commander against the French in Cochinchina, now military commander in the South, a former assassin under Nguyen Binh, was present. Le Duc Tho, Kissinger's loathed and devious opponent, senior member of the Politburo and former secretary-general of COSVN, was hurrying down from Hanoi to exercise ultimate supervision over both Pham Hung and General Dung, and to preside over final victory. Le Duc Tho, the poetaster, dashed off a verse at this point:

> As the sun rises over the Loc Ninh jungle
> I hear the call of the black cuckoo
> Harbinger of the rainy season.
> All night not a wink of sleep,
>
> Counting the raindrops,
> Worried about our soldiers,
> Wallowing along endless muddy tracks.
> After the tanks, the artillery,
> Still no news from either,
> Though the Front urgently needs both.
> Rain! Please stop
> So the tracks may dry and firm up,

And lead us to our goal.
In this historic battle,
The first shots are being fired.

Only Giap was absent, under medical treatment for cancer in
Moscow, a tumour which must have been benign: he survives,
nineteen years later, and, indeed, in a few days arrived in Saigon.

The Northerners and their puppets had a total of twenty-four
divisions under arms nationwide, 150,000 men in the South itself,
together with armoured, rocket and artillery units. They had no
combatant Air Force worth the name, but their ground combat
forces at the end of March were, according to General Weyand,
superior to the republic's in a ratio of three to one. The republic, of
course, disposed of over a thousand aircraft, including 300 badly
maintained fighter-bombers and plenty of helicopters, now short of
fuel and ammunition. The ARVN had no staff system and an officer
corps notable less for military qualities than for financial and
political support for Thieu.

Reinforcements for the beleaguered city could not come from
ARVN 7 and 9 Divisions in the Delta, since Route 9 was cut before
Saigon and before Military Region 4, where three more ARVN
divisions were waiting. Nor, because 316 Division barred its path,
could 25 Division get through from Tay Ninh to the capital.
Highway 4 to the Delta was barred by regional VC. The headquarters of III Corps abandoned Bien Hoa. PAVN II Corps had
already taken Ham Tau, 100 miles to the north on the littered road.
Only the 4,000 wretched Marines who had fled from Da Nang were
now at Vung Tau (Cap St Jacques), at the mouth of the river which
was soon to be seized by II Corps; the Saigon river was therefore
also 'inaccessible' to the relief forces. The Dalat road, and Routes 13
(north), 17, 21 and 22 (north-west) were all cut. Tan Son Nhut, the
main airport, had closed under bombardment. IV Corps was
destroying the ARVN at Xuan Loc. Admiral Cang's sailors and
some regional forces could only hold PAVN 5 and 7 Divisions for a
short time at Ben Luc.

The trap had closed: Saigon was isolated by land, sea and air.
Some 150,000 North Vietnamese in sixteen divisions were outside
the city, the special sappers (*dac cong*) and a fifth column thousands
strong within, all facing a few thousand almost exhausted defenders.

Thieu was a brave but not a great soldier, whose power to appoint senior officers was constrained by his chief aide, General Quang and, according to Lartéguy, by the latter's Communist wife. Thieu had been and remained a genuine, if corrupt, nationalist, but now he resigned in favour of the vice-president, Tran Vu Huong, 'an old, poetic ancestor-worshipper', himself flying off to 'freedom' with up to fifteen tons of jewels, ceramics, gold, pictures and jade.

Huong prevaricated but soon transferred the little authority left him to General Duong Van Minh, 'Big Minh', who had led the coup against Diem. Minh was an orchid grower, tennis player, expert on tropical fish, an indecisive conciliator, a Francophile. All he could do for his country now was to save as much of the capital as he could. Although there was nothing else he could manage once Xuan Loc had fallen, this at least he accomplished.

Henceforward Saigon was continually battered by North Vietnamese shells and rockets. Smoke and dust rose in the humid air while the alarm bells of the police, ambulances and fire engines began their hysteric caterwauling. On 27 April the British embassy closed – prematurely, according to the more stalwart members of that mission – staff departing by air for Singapore. Thousands of Vietnamese also packed their bags and abandoned their homes for evacuation points selected by the American embassy. Formal last-minute unions took place between clerks and GIs and, typically, prostitutes, later dubbed 'marriages of inconvenience'.

Junior American employees were each permitted to include eight Vietnamese on personal lists for immigration into the US, in exchange for large sums in cash from each refugee, usually Annamite or Cochinchinese *poules de luxe* and their families. Meanwhile, in Indochina as a whole, 10,000 French also had at last to reconsider their future: planters, missionaries, selfless doctors and nurses, leftist teachers as selfish and insensitive as the doctors were altruist, little businessmen, Eurasians vulnerable to bureaucracy and contempt.

At 10.15 on 30 April, because resistance would have caused up to half a million South Vietnamese dead and destroyed the greater part of Saigon, Minh capitulated. He now commanded perhaps only 2,000 armoured troops and parachutists, who had fought stubbornly to the end, with bayonet and rifle butt, against over 100,000 North Vietnamese. The 'little Red warriors' from Hanoi had thus conquered Saigon, not liberated it, themselves armed for foreign conquest by foreigners – Chinese, Russian, East European. But there had been no popular uprising. The smiling, Marxist revolutionaries had, in the end, won a victory which was only military.

The 122 mm and 130 mm guns became silent. Dung had himself ordered his artillery to cease fire in order to encourage the Americans with their 5,000 Vietnamese collaborators to flee as fast as the helicopters would carry them. Perhaps he wished also to avoid intervention by B-52s. Since President Ford had failed to persuade Congress even to fund Weyand's proposal for resupply, there was little chance of that in this beastly, degrading fall of the curtain.

Van Tien Dung, Army commander, smirkingly referred to 'the tragic defeat of the US imperialists, who had used 60 per cent of their entire infantry force, 58 per cent of their naval forces, 50 per cent of their strategic Air Force, fifteen out of eighteen aircraft carriers, 800,000 US and more than one million ARVN troops . . . they dropped ten million tons of bombs and spent more than 300 billion US dollars. The end result of all this was that the United States ambassador had to crawl on to the roof of the embassy to escape'.

The 'green men' from the North, although for the time being tolerant and kind after some relaxed days of brutal looting, imposed their own order on the town. Loud music was played endlessly over the tannoy. All the petrol pumps were closed. The bo-dois cooked their rice in front of the Presidential Palace and put up their tents in the Botanical Gardens. Women were enjoined to refrain from Western dress, tee-shirts and jeans. Traffic, except leaving or entering Saigon, was much reduced in the streets. Criminals were sentenced, even shot, at the place of their crime. All bars and restaurants were ordered to be closed. The vile, ubiquitous 're-education' campaign was yet to begin.

Five Soviet tanks were found to have been destroyed by a bazooka.

Saigon died: Ho Chi Minh City was born.

After elections to the first Pan-Vietnam National Assembly on 25 April 1976, Giap retained his posts of minister of defence and commander-in-chief of the armed forces, adding that of deputy prime minister in charge of science and technology.

It was in that capacity that he addressed the Fourth Congress of the Lao Dong Party at Hanoi:

The industrialization of our country will be successfully carried out and a new Vietnam, with a modern industrial and agricultural structure, will be born. Our Vietnamese landscape will be transformed and future generations will live a happy and civilized life, finally able to enjoy the beauties of this landscape under a clear sky and pure atmosphere, with its generous mountains and seas, its luxuriant vegetation and beautiful summer nights.

Alas, under the system for which he had conquered all his enemies, none of these things could happen and none of them did.

XXXIX
What Might Have Been

The immediate reasons for Giap's last victory, at Saigon, were several.

Brigadier Serong's January recommendation would have involved the evacuation of zones I and II and the retention by ARVN of only zone III round Saigon and zone IV in the Mekong delta. Most officers on the general staff were convinced; Thieu resisted the proposal.

But on 11 March Thieu told his generals at a luncheon in the Independence Palace that 'we certainly cannot hold and defend all the territory we want'. He proposed 'redeployment only to those populous and flourishing areas that were most important', III and IV Zone, containing rice, rubber and manufacturing plant. He did not, however, precisely advocate evacuation of I and II zones, only to 'hold territory up to Huë and Da Nang', or, at worst 'Chu Lai, or Tuy Hoa'. Immediately, he advocated holding Ban Me Thuot in the Central Highlands as more important than Kontum and Pleiku. But Ban Me Thuot was then within twenty-four hours of capture by Van Tien Dung's forces.

His II Corps commander, as has been said, had failed to understand that the town was Giap's principal target. After it fell, the 'redeployment' proposed by Thieu, which should have been executed, if at all, when Nixon fell in 1974, became the bloody, panic-stricken rout from Pleiku and Kontum. Ban Me Thuot, because of chaotic administration, refugees, cut roads and the defeat under disgraceful leadership of 22, 23, 41 and 42 South Vietnamese Divisions, could not be retaken. The Airborne Division had been reassigned to Saigon; the Marines and 3 Division 'gave' at Da Nang and Phuoc Tuong respectively, the 3rd Division attacked by mutineers from a training camp.

The chairman of the joint general staff at Saigon, General Cao Van Vien, was exceptional in believing that the redeployment should not have been attempted at all and that, if the ARVN had stayed where it was, General Dung would not have been able to mount an offensive in II Corps as violent as that in I

Corps. At least he could not have built on his victory in Ban Me Thuot.

Colonel Van Cao Dong, commanding the Regional Forces in I Corps, which had earlier destroyed the five Viet Cong battalions, believed that the move of the Airborne Division to Saigon and that of the Marines to Da Nang had been tactically inept as well as over-hastily carried out. Quang Tri, whence the Marines had been withdrawn, had fallen because of the panic caused by their departure. The Marines accomplished less than nothing at Da Nang.

The ARVN had been trained by the United States to conduct its operations with full artillery and air support. The failure of American resolution and the consequences of Watergate resulted in a reduction of aid and resupply which broke the capacity of the ARVN to resist. The United States did not fulfil Nixon's many promises to Thieu that his country 'would respond with full force should the settlement be violated by North Vietnam'.

The ARVN's position was defensive and entirely dependent on America. In May 1974, Senator Edward Kennedy's amendment cut a further US $266 million from the military supplemental aid bill. By January 1975, apart from congressional action, world inflation had grossly reduced the value in Vietnam of the US aid package. The price of imports had soared. US spending in-country had greatly fallen. Food prices had risen by 313 per cent and all other items by 33 per cent between January 1971 and September 1974. ARVN pay, already derisory, had been even further devalued.

The South Vietnamese had neither the air nor the ground fire-power, because of inflation and the US refusal to supply fuel, parts and replacements, to mount a counter-offensive. The entire ARVN could expend only the amount of ammunition hitherto held by one US division. Across the whole spectrum of supply, the South had enough for three weeks' intense combat, against several months' for the PAVN. The PAVN, furthermore, could apply their share at a single point, not dissipated in penny packets everywhere.

The only subject for speculation, therefore, is whether the South Vietnamese could have held and prospered even in the little rump state to which they had considered moving, without the support which US legislators wrenched away. Because of their own indecision, mistakes and inadequate military leadership, even that option may not in fact have been open to them. Nevertheless, in its concept of an enclave strategy – the revived Gavin Plan – around the

Mekong delta and close to presumed US aircraft carrier support, it was the plan which the North Vietnamese Generals most feared. Against that possibility, Hanoi greatly increased PLAF and PAVN opposition to pacification in the Delta and, by rooting their forces there, committed sufficient strength to defeat Thieu's attempts at control.

President Thieu's intransigence had defeated other counsel. After 11 March, when Ban Me Thuot fell and the panic was allowed to grow, the collapse may have been irretrievable.

As for the United States, it is plain that American public opinion will always demand rapid resolution to military conflict, or withdraw its support. When the US goes to war henceforward, it will do so in maximum strength and purpose, do successfully what it sets out to do, and get out when the task is over, an assessment ratified by the events of the Gulf War.

The method by which that aim could not only have been accomplished in Vietnam but which, as early as 1965, would have pre-empted further North Vietnamese prosecution of the war in South Vietnam, was to have mined Haiphong and other Vietnamese ports, and, by aerial interdiction on the frontier in the north-east quadrant, to have prevented any significant quantities of war material from entering the DRV by sea, rail or road. This strategy, long before construction of the Ho Chi Minh Trail or PAVN intervention through Laos and Cambodia, would have cut off at *source* the capacity of the DRV to make war in the Republic of South Vietnam. The later proposal, that of the artificial 'barrier' right across Indochina, including Laos, could have been a *pis aller*, eliminating the Ho Chi Minh Trail and thus the DRV's ability to support the Viet Cong. Kissinger, indeed, later came to believe that Laos was a better place to defend Indochina than Vietnam; it was a country hostile to Vietnam and its guerrilla strategy, affording terrain for the sort of conventional war for which the US Army had been trained.

To neglect these targets was to ensure that war equipment would enter the country to be disposed of by a multitude of routes, including the Ho Chi Minh Trail, far more difficult to detect than at Haiphong or the 'marshalling yards'.

The naïve alternative, the 'gradualist' campaign of bombing *within* the DRV, (*after* the arms had arrived there) produced horribly increased casualties on both sides and did not decisively damage a virtually non-industrial state. It also gave the DRV 'time to shore up its defences, disperse its military targets and mobilize its labour force . . . It also violated the principle of mass and surprise.' (When, as has been said, the wraps were temporarily taken off *Rolling Thunder* in 1967, Hanoi was brought to its knees, a posture ignored or not willingly observed by Washington.) But the gravest consequences of this failure to take early, drastic, aerial action against the entry points were the despatch of an American Expeditionary Force of nearly 600,000 men, the deaths of 50,000 US citizens, civil dissent in the United States and the temporary collapse of Western strategies worldwide.

But, 'Lament no more. These things are so.'

Once the Americans, through mistaken fear of potential Chinese and Soviet reaction, had failed to close the logistic gates, other weaknesses supervened. The first, to which reference has been made, was the absence of any objective more concrete and less negative than keeping South Vietnam 'non-Communist'. Its corollary was the military's incomprehension that they now faced a war in which 'the Vietnamese Communist generals saw their armed forces as instruments primarily to gain political goals, whereas the Americans saw theirs as instruments to defeat enemy military forces, the concept of attrition'. As Edward Lansdale, earlier the victor over the Huks in the Philippines, remarked of Vietnam: 'One fought battles to influence opinion in Vietnam and in the world, the other fought battles to finish the enemy, keeping tabs by body-counts'.

After Diem's murder, no successful political alternative was found to Hanoi's national Communism. The RVN was a relatively free country, but it was formalist, corrupt, military-dominated, without adequate administrative or democratic accountability. Even after land reform, it lacked popular legitimacy.

Political and military leadership in this culture were gravely inadequate. The corruption and lethargy of some senior civilian and military leaders were so glaring as to deprive the régime of the legitimacy that Hanoi had earned in its bestial and restricted way. And, apart from the final US failure to supply ammunition, fuel, spare parts, guns and armour, ARVN training was insufficient, and maintenance – because of shortages of technical and management personnel – dangerously weak in communications, in the air and on the ground.

In the imbalance between the lassitude of South Vietnam and the militant nation to the North, mobilized in the presentation of values which, however disagreeable or positively immoral, were at least temporarily shared, the United States declined to intervene. From anti-colonialist and anti-imperial inhibitions, Westmoreland and his successors refused, unlike Templer in Malaya, to impose that unified command which would have enabled the ARVN to avoid its grosser mistakes and correct its more contemptible evasions.

The dilemma between attrition and pacification was never solved. Search-and-destroy operations were nearly always successful. But they often weakened pacification operations in the villages and regions, coastal or otherwise, in which the Viet Cong infrastructure and inspiration for insurrection resided, not in the mountains and forests where battles and attrition took place. ('Search-and-destroy', with concomitant fire-power, had similarly adverse effects on the hamlets which they needlessly destroyed, and the refugees they created.) The war should also have been fought in the villages, where popular allegiance to the RVN could have been gained and secured, as well as through military destruction of the PLAF and PAVN in response to the challenge offered by Vo Nguyen Giap.

Giap said: 'For us, you know, there is no such thing as a single strategy. Our is always a synthesis, simultaneously military, political and diplomatic, which is why the Tet offensive had multiple objectives.' Most, if not all American officers believed that the United States had 'won' at Tet in February 1968. Perhaps only Robert Komer understood: 'Hanoi was far wiser than we in seeing the struggle as essentially a seamless web, a political, military, economic, ideological and psychological conflict.' All the rest of them could only see the military battle, not even that very clearly.

During a conversation in Hanoi in April 1975 between Colonel Harry G. Summers and Colonel Tu of the PAVN, the American said 'You know you never defeated us on the battlefield?' The North Vietnamese colonel pondered for a moment: 'That may be so', he replied, 'but it is also irrelevant'.

The defeat of aggression from outside the country, not civil war, was the condition of Vietnam, but was subordinated by the Americans to the false 'excuses', of counter-insurgency and to Sir Robert Thompson's strategy of building a South Vietnamese nation. The military objective – the strategic offensive to defeat the North Vietnamese aggressor – was diluted in favour of 'nation building', a task not for American soldiers, but properly for the South Vietnamese.

XL
'Beat Not the Bones of the Buried . . .'

On Christmas Day 1978, following a plan devised and monitored by Giap, the North Vietnamese under General Le Duc Anh invaded Cambodia. The People's Republic of Kampuchea was proclaimed. The mass killings of city-dwellers and the educated were halted. Despite continued dry-season fighting between the PAVN and the Khmer Rouge, the new government was able to rebuild at least part of its agricultural economy in areas not occupied by Pol Pot's troops.

On 17 February 1979 China, Pol Pot's ally, decided to 'teach the Vietnamese a lesson'. The PLA with 300,000 men, 1,000 tanks and 1,500 heavy guns invaded Cao Bang province, where they had threatened the French in 1950. This time they took Langson, but withdrew with heavy casualties after some weeks' fighting. Although, according to one observer, they had largely destroyed the six northern provinces, wrecking the apatite mine and killing 250,000 cattle, they had also learned lessons from the masters of guerrilla and conventional warfare. They might have done better had they not made clear that their objective was limited – that they would not attack the Red River delta – like Mao in India in 1963. In July the 'pro-Chinese' Communist dignitary, Hoang Van Hoan, defected from Vietnam to China.

At the Fourth Congress of the Lao Dong Party in 1976, Giap's standing in the Politburo had declined from fourth to sixth. In 1980 he was replaced as defence minister by his friend and pupil, Van Tien Dung, and in 1981 was demoted from first to third deputy prime minister. At the Fifth Congress in 1982, allegedly because of disagreement with the 'dogmatism' of the general secretary and other apparatchiks he was removed from the Politburo. He emained until 1991 on the Central Committee and as vice-premier for science and technology, president of the commissions on these subjects and on demography and family planning, and as deputy-chairman of the Council of Ministers. He attended the funeral at Vientiane of the Lao president in November 1992. As plain General Giap, he visited China in April 1993.

He continues to wear his general's dark green uniform with red tabs and four gold stars, his hair as white now as the snow in the old sobriquet 'Volcano under Snow'. He still receives visitors in the official guest house, Jean Sainteny's former residence, and continues to live with his wife in his charming French colonial villa, often attended by children and grandchildren in that comfortable house with its memories, treasures and busts of Marxist leaders. His French, with the curious Vietnamese nasal twang, remains fluent. He has a car, an 'ADC' and a personal doctor.

He is an icon, one not *much* exhibited to foreigners by an administration seeking to advertise its peaceful image and minimise its violent past.

'Sweet Chucks! Beat not the bones of the buried; the sweet warman is dead: when he lived, he was a man'.

Hundreds of thousands of those who fought with Giap are buried, and many of those against him. Giap himself will die. So let the sentence be an epitaph for him and for all those who perished in the wars of Indochina.

Appendix A

A captured document of 1948 described the Viet Minh Regular Army (*Vo Quoc*) as organized in divisions of three regiments each; regiments consisted of three grouped battalions; battalions of three companies; companies of three sections; sections of three fighting groups and, finally, fighting groups of thirteen men each. A political commissar was appointed to each section commander, whose duties included 'stimulation of patriotism and of loyalty, the organization of propaganda, supervision of military affairs and the elimination of slack and doubtful personnel'.

'Quasi-military units' included guerrillas and irregular formations, each of men from all strata of society.

The *Tu Vé* (militia or 'home guard') were drawn from young men and women over the age of seventeen whose duties included defensive street fighting, transformed when required into guerrilla action. They were organized into units of three people (home), nine (street) and proportionately larger groups for neighbourhood and locality order of battle.

Anti-parachutist units were organized into command groups (ten men), reconnaissance section (thirty), destroyer section (thirty), security section (thirty). The reconnaissance section established the location of the landing, the destroyers killed the parachutists. The security section isolated and surrounded the landing zones and supported the destroyers. The numbers and strengths of these anti-paratroop units varied according to the terrain suitable for drops in each province.

'The most likely time' for attack by paras was between sunrise and sunset, since visibility rendered attack by night almost impossible. The timing of such attacks was usually predictable, preceded as they were by three to four days aerial reconnaissance. Units lit big bonfires to frighten off the attackers, sounded tam tams, lit pagoda torches, yelled loudly in series. The *Tu Vé* would feign attack, then really attack and encircle, with knives and sharp bamboo, supported by the mob armed with spears and pointed sticks.

The Free Corps, or Chung Fong, were drawn from 'soldiers prepared to die and obey all orders, to observe strict discipline, keep secrets, accumulate knowledge, lead, command, recruit and stimulate the population through propaganda. Dismissal would be the consequence of disobedience, flouting regulations, idleness, misconduct, dishonour or three absences from meetings.' The *Chung Fong* was directed by an autonomous group commanded by its chief under the regimental commanding officer. One hour's weekly instruction was devoted to political education; each action was followed by sessions of autocriticism and lessons for the future.

The People's Army or *Dan Quan Viet Nam*, included all armed groups of the population together with the regulars, *Tu Vé*, and guerrillas who were ordinary civilians when not in action. Several guerrilla sections were formed in each provincial sub-prefecture, consisting of the chief of section and his political assistant (both elected), medical orderly, signaller, liaison and supply representatives.

Three to five sections formed a company, with much the same categories of personnel – on a larger scale – although here the company commander and his assistant were appointed, not elected. The company also contained an 'espionage squad'.

Ban Cong Tac (Committees of Action in the Common Interest) were secret units in Cochinchina, especially in the Saigon/Cholon areas, whose duties included assassination and sabotage. Each unit included thirty men divided into sub-committees with sections or groups each containing several squads of three to five men, each group unknown to the others. Weapons included pistols, automatic pistols, grenades and sabotage equipment.

Suicide Squad 'volunteers' were units of 100–200 men in one or two companies, each of three to four sections, drawn from convicted criminals. The sections were: Sacrifice (Kamikaze), Shock, Destroyer, 'Red Cross' and supply. Equipment could include a sword, three grenades, two bottles of crêpe rubber and petrol, three bottles of sulphuric acid and petrol, three strips of inflammable linen.

The fundamental principles of unconventional warfare were:

Pretend to strike in the east, but attack in the west.
Attack the weak points.
Respond to the enemy's attack by silence.
Attack when the enemy is tired.
Scatter before the enemy in small groups, then reassemble.

Use pretty girls to seduce, steal, spy, create quarrels between individual soldiers, murder.

If the enemy advances, fall back; if he retreats, advance; if inactive, harass him, cut off his supplies, set the people against him. If he weakens, attack.

Monsieur Coste-Floret, minister for the colonies in 1948, said that French casualties from September 1945 to June 1948 numbered 8,000.

Many of these units and tactics were first employed in Mao's Stage One, 'Mobilization of the Masses', called *pourissement* ('rotting') by the French. The means to destroy government included assassination of officials, teachers and other colonial government employees; theft of land from landlords for redistribution; illicit taxes; also the raising of militias, welfare, 'consciousness raising', nationalism. Stage Two involved the use of regional forces raised from the militia against communications and French posts in ambush and other mode.

Appendix B

From *La Dernière Hauteur* by Huu Mai
(Foreign Languages Publishing House, Hanoi 1964)

On the hillside by the command post, Assistant Chief of Operations Thinh climbed the beaten earth steps, cut and battered by incessant marching feet.

He looked towards Giap's straw hut. In the east, the sky was still an indeterminate grey-brown. The general should still have been sleeping at this hour. Thinh started to move silently towards the underground Operations Bureau when an animated voice called: 'Thinh, come here a minute.'

Giap, preoccupied, was sitting at a rustic table on a long bench made of a male bamboo trunk split in two. 'What's going on now?' thought Thinh, as he took his stand and waited.

'Did you have time yesterday to check the details of the tunnel with the prisoners?'

That was it! Fortunately he *had* had time.

'I interrogated each one separately: all their statements agreed.'

'They confirmed that the gallery has not been arranged with battle in mind?'

'Yes.'

'Did their answers correspond to the bricklayers'?'

'Roughly.'

'What do you mean, roughly? Did they say how many rows of bricks there were?'

Thinh was uncomfortable. After the fighting on Eliane, Giap had become increasingly fidgety about this tunnel which blocked his advance. The prisoners' statements had been carefully noted. They all referred to underground compartments with brick walls, a sort of cave covered with a layer of earth thick enough to resist a 155 mm shell, simple ordinary shelters against artillery and, not, as one might fear, an underground network. Before the revolution, the colonialists had dug cells into the hill for political prisoners. The Japanese had reinforced them to form anti-aircraft shelters. All the garrison had done was to reoccupy them.

Giap was sceptical. The fighters themselves believed that they were dealing with a solid artefact erected with a view to combat. Giap insisted that the T'ai bricklayers should be interrogated. One did a maquette of the galleries. The evening before, when the commander of the Truong Son Division proposed to dig a sap to blow up the whole thing, Giap told Thinh to find out the thickness of the walls and a general plan of the field-works from the other prisoners.

'I didn't think of asking them how many rows of bricks there were,' replied Thinh. 'But they all thought that the walls, at their thickest, measured about 50 cm.' He could see, in Giap's drawn features, the same scepticism as before.

'It still isn't very clear,' said Giap. 'According to the mason, the gallery walls are thicker.'

'Yes, slightly.'

'How did you put the question to the mason?'

'I told him that the matter was extremely important, that the tunnel had posed enormous difficulties during the assault. I asked him to remember all the details of how he built the walls. I told him our lives hung on his answer . . .'

'You'd have done better to have said less.' Giap shook his head. 'It would have been quite enough to ask him just to remember the details of the masonry. He's a good fellow, you could have trusted him. But precisely because you insisted too much on our problems, there was a risk that he might exaggerate the strength of the gallery.'

A smile suddenly illuminated his face, a smile without reservation, which swept away dark thoughts.

'Do you think that the tunnel really isn't a redoubt?'

'Absolutely.'

'It still presents difficulties. The enemy could still fall back and use their artillery against our men when they go into the attack, and then counter-attack. What do you think of the Truong Son proposal?'

'In my view, if we can't get rid of the position, it's for a variety of reasons and not just because of the tunnel. No one has said that we can't blow up that gallery.'

'What do the sappers think? Can they dig a sap until just below the gallery?'

'I asked them. They said that it wouldn't be easy.' Giap said nothing. Knowing that hasty advice didn't please him, Thinh respected the silence which established itself between them.

'What do *you* think?' asked the general. Then, doubtless because of his collaborator's indecision, he developed his own point of view.

'We're ready to blow up the vault. It's less terrible than it seems. Our last check had several reasons. Is it true that our sapper comrades aren't sure of being able to get the sap immediately under the tunnel?'

'That's what they say.'

'They must get on with it, give all they've got to the division. That shelter's *got* to blow.'

Giap paused again.

'If the sap doesn't reach the exact site of the works, if it explodes a bit to one side, it will still be useful. Nor must we forget the other preparations, above all the trenches which absolutely must have the standard dimensions. Eliane I must be cut off from the Central Sector.'

Thinh felt a great weight fall from him.

'Well, Comrade General,' he said in a burst of enthusiasm, 'we'll fix it so that we can give the sappers confidence.'

'Good. Tell them to see me before taking station. Let the orderly bring some rice soup.' When Thinh got up to take his leave, Giap stopped him.

'Stay for a bit. Bring another bowl,' he said to the orderly. The general poured the soup into both bowls. Thinh, still standing, declined the invitation until Giap added: 'Dong doesn't come until 08.00. We've got time. We can go on talking.'

Spoon in hand, Thinh forgot the bowl of soup steaming in front of him. He had learned Giap's habits during all the years that he had served with him. Once in full swing, the general never stopped. He weighed all questions, looking for contradictions, hitches, obstacles . . . his staff were used to fielding unexpected questions. Their responses were always heard attentively, especially when they were at variance. Giap liked 'objections', however absurd. They obliged officers to be exact, concrete, to make up their own minds. His nature drove him to argue. He didn't like 'trenchant' views, or the idea that anything was settled once and for all. His method, although sometimes causing trouble and apprehension in his staff, was a stimulant. It kept his juniors on their toes, forcing them to extend themselves.

'Help yourself,' ordered Giap, 'while it is still hot.'

Thinh was on guard, in waiting, like a scout on the look-out.

'When you interrogated the prisoners in these last few days, did you notice anything strange?' Giap measured him. 'I have heard of a general who had the habit when campaigning of placing before him the most recent photograph of the opposing GoC. You mustn't think it was simply a dilettantish pleasure, frivolous game. He believed that he could thus grasp the state of his adversary's spirit and so frustrate his plans. I don't think a simple portrait is enough to penetrate the enemy's psychology. One must keep really close to him, follow minutely the evolution of his morale. Prisoners' behaviour often offers an excellent test. One prisoner certainly isn't enough, but several interrogations will produce details about the enemy in all the phases of action. You know what I mean? I need light on these points.'

Thin had to concentrate and consider.

Giap said, 'We have foreseen several eventualities. The enemy can reinforce so as to hold out longer. He can send in a few fresh parachutists, but only a few; we must know the state of French reserves. They could drop behind our positions and cut us from the rear areas; but they don't really have the strength for that. Or they could fall back on Laos. We've thought of that too. If they leave the fortifications at Dien Bien Phu, we'll finish them off even quicker. What other plots has he up his sleeve? Have you sounded out the prisoners? Put yourself in the enemy's place and see what else he could undertake . . .'

Giap picked up his spoon and continued his breakfast. The flame in Thinh's eye betrayed the intensity of his thoughts. Giap made a principle of respecting such moments of intense concentration.

Thinh thought of the prisoners' faces and remembered scraps of confession. Perhaps such rumours had real importance? Who knew? He swallowed a spoonful of soup.

'Comrade General, recently the prisoners have sometimes talked about the possiiblity of massive bombing on the outskirts of Dien Bien Phu. I don't know if the enemy is thinking of something radical. Bombardment, after all, is nothing new. We've had it since the beginning, napalm, HE, AP . . .'

'Do many of them talk about it? In reply to questions or spontaneously?'

'Both.'

'It must be tied in with the Americans.'

Giap was going to say something else. He held back, turned his head to the door. His glance lost itself, through a clearing in the high woods covering the hill, toward the flanks of a mountain fringed with fleecy mist: here and there, through a rent in the fog, could be glimpsed the luxuriance of the forest.

Appendix C

These extracts from an article by Nguyen Chi Thanh in the October 1963 issue of the Party journal *Hoc Tap* illustrate the views characteristic of North Vietnam's 'extremist' faction:

On revolutionary spirit:

> A number of comrades have come scarcely to think of revolutionary duties and Communist aspirations. As a result, their struggle spirit decreased and their revolutionary virtues became blurred.

> To overcome erroneous views and develop correct ones we must pay special attention to ideological education and revolutionary struggle . . . All that is needed is that party members clearly recognize their responsibilities and exert every effort.

On economic policy:

> A small number of comrades at a certain point . . . lost confidence . . . and wished to reduce the rate of industrialization. Some comrades even rejected the self-sufficiency policy.

> Each of us must assert his confidence in the party line of socialist industrialization and must not waver while fulfilling this central task. Any hesitation or deviation . . . is harmful to our revolutionary work.

On the war in South Vietnam:

> Some comrades tremble before the fierce struggle in South Vietnam . . . Manifesting their lack of revolutionary consciousness, they did not strengthen their determination to struggle protractedly and fiercely for national unification. A small number of comrades do not trust the fighting methods adopted by the southern people.

On the Sino-Soviet split:

> Our party has the duty to participate in the struggle against revisionism and right opportunism, the present main dangers for the world Communist movement . . . and the revolutionary movement of world peoples.

Appendix D
Translations of French Military Abbreviations

BEP	Foreign Legion Parachute Battalion
BG	Engineer Battalion
BPC	Colonial Parachute Battalion
BPVN	Vietnamese Parachute Battalion
BT	T'ai Tribal Battalion
BVN	T'ai Battalion (Vietnamese Army)
DBLE	Foreign Legion Half-Brigade
GAP	Airborne Battle Group
GC	Commando Group
GM	Regimental Combat Team
RAC	Colonial Artillery Regiment
RCC	Armoured Cavalry Regiment
RCP	Parachute Light Infantry Regiment
REI	Foreign Legion Infantry Regiment
RTA	Algerian Rifle Regiment
RTM	Moroccan Rifle Regiment

Select Bibliography

I am in the debt of those listed below, very deeply to Lucien Bodard's *The Quicksand War*, the most electrifying account ever of jungle and tropical warfare; to Robert O'Neill's brilliant *General Giap*; to Guenther Lewy's *America in Vietnam*; and to everything written by Bernard Fall, especially *Hell In A Very Small Place*.

I have had the good fortune to consult official UK documents in the FO 371, 474, 959, WO 32, 172 and 205 Series of the Public Records Office, Kew, papers in the Centre des Archives de la France D'Outre-Mer at Aix-en-Provence and in the French Military Archives at Vincennes.

Documents from the United States Central Intelligence Agency and Defence Intelligence Agency at Washington DC have been released to the author personally under the Freedom of Information Act, many of them emerging in the public domain for the first time.

The following is a more or less comprehensive list of books to which I have also had access in the course of research.

BAO Ninh: *The Sorrow of War* (Minerva 1994)
BERGERUD E.M.: *Red Thunder, Tropic Lightning* (Westview 1993)
BODARD Lucien: *The Quicksand War* (Little, Brown 1963)
BOUDAREL Georges: *Le Bureaucratie au Vietnam* (L'Harmattan)
———— *Vo Nguyen Giap* (Pall Mall 1970)
BOWMAN John: *The Vietnam War* (Bison Books 1989)
BRAESTRUP Peter: *Big Story* (Westview Press 1977)
BRIMMELL Jack: *Communism in South East Asia* (OUP 1959)
BURCHETT Wilfred: *At the Barricades* (Quartet 1981)
———— *Catapult to Freedom* (Quartet 1978)
———— *Grass Hoppers & Elephants* (Urizen Books 1979)
BUTTINGER Joseph: *Vietnam: A Political History (The Smaller Dragon)* (Andre Deustch 1969)

CAO Van Vien: *The Final Collapse* (CMH Centre of Military History), Washington 1983)
———— *Reflections on the Vietnam War* (CMH 1983)

CAMERON James: *Witness* (Gollancz 1966)
CASH John A *et al: Seven Firefights in Vietnam* (CMH 1970)
CAWTHORNE Nigel: *Bamboo Cage* (Cooper 1991)
CHANDLER D. *The Offensive of 1968* (Yale)
CHARLTON Michael & MONCRIEFF Antony: *Many Reasons Why* (Scolar 1978)
CHEN Jian: *China & the First Indochina War* (China Quarterly 1993)
CHESNEAUX Jean: *Contribution a l'Histoire de la Nation* (Ed. Sociales 1955)
COLLINGWOOD C.: *The Defector* (Harper and Row 1970)
COLLINS James Lawton: *Development & Training of the South Vietnamese Army* (CMH 1975)
COLVIN John: *Twice Around the World* (Leo Cooper 1991)

DALLOAZ Jacques: *La Guerre de l'Indochine* (Seuil 1987)
DAVIDSON P.B.: *Vietnam at War: The History 1946–75* (Presidio 1988)
DEVILLERS Philippe: *End of a War* (Pall Mall 1969)
———— *Histoire du Vietnam 1940–1952* (Editions du Seuil 1952)
DIVILKOVSKI S. & OGNETOV I.: *Road To Victory* (Progress Publishers 1980)
DREYFUS Paul: . . . *et Saigon tombe* (Arthaud 1975)
DUIKER William J.: *US Containment Policy & Conflict in Indochine* (Stanford 1994)
DUNCANSON Dennis: *Government & Revolution in Indochina* (OUP 1968)

FALL Bernard: *Chronique d'une Guerre Revolutionaire* (Pall Mall 1963)
———— *Hell In A Very Small Place* (Pall Mall 1967)
———— *Street Without Joy* (Pall Mall 1964)
———— *Truong Chinh* (Praegar 1963)
———— *Vietnam Regime: Government & Administration* (Cornell 1954)
———— *Vietnam Witness* (Praeger 1966)
FITZERALD Frances: *Fire in the Lake* (Little, Brown 1972)
FONDE Jean Julien: *Traitez a Tout Prix* (Robert Laffont 1971)
FROST Frank: *Vietnam's Foreign Relations: Dynamics of Change*: (Institute of SEA Studies 1993)
FULTON William B.: *Riverine Operations* (CMH 1973)

GALLUCI Robert: *Neither Peace nor Honour* (John Hopkins 1975)
GOODMAN Allan: *The Lost Peace* (Hoover Institution Press 1978)
GRAHAM Andrew: *Interlude in Indochina* (Heinemann 1959)

GREENE Felix: *Vietnam! Vietnam!* (J Cape 1987)
GREENE Graham: *The Quiet American* (Heinemann 1955)
GRO William Le: *Vietnam From Ceasefire to Capitulation* (CMH 1981)

HALBERSTAM David: *Making of a Quagmire* (Bodley Head 1964)
———— *One Very Hot Day* (Bodley Head 1967)
HAMMER Ellen Joy: *The Struggle for Indochina* (Stanford 1954)
———— *Vietnam: Yesterday & Today* (Holt, Rinehart & Winston 1966)
HEDUY Philippe: *La Guerre d'Indochine* (Societe de Production Literaire 1981)
HESS G.R.: *Vietnam & the United States* (Twayne 1990)
HICKEY G.C.: *Village in Vietnam* (Yale 1964)
HILSMAN R: *To Move a Nation* (Doubleday 1967)
HO Chi Minh: *Le Proces de la Colonialisation Francaise* (Eds en Langues Etrangeres 1946)
———— *Oeuvres Choisis du President Ho Chi Minh* (Eds en Langues Etrangeres 1961)
HOANG Van Chi: *Colonialism to Communism* (Praeger 1964)
HOANG Van Hoan: *A Drop in the Ocean*: (Beijing 1986)
HONEY P.J.: *Communism in Indochina* (MIT Press 1963)

IRVING R.E.M.: *The First Indochina War* (Croom Helm 1975)

JOES A.J.: *The War for South Vietnam* (Praeger 1989)

KARNOW Stanley: *Vietnam* (Viking 1983)
KEEGAN John: *Dien Bien Phu* (Ballantine 1974)
KELLEU Konrad: *Conversations with Enemy Soldiers* (Rand 1970)
KISSINGER Henry: *White House Years* (Little, Brown 1979)
KNOEBL Kuno: *Victor Charlie* (Pall Mall 1967)
KOMER Robert: *Bureaucracy at War* (Westview 1986)
KRIEG E.: *La Tragedie Indochinoise* (Eds de St Clair 1966)

LACOUTURE Jean: *Ho Chi Minh* (Seuil 1977)
———— *Vietnam Between Two Truces* (Seuil 1965)
———— *Vo Nguyen Giap* (Pall Mall 1970)
LANCASTER Donald: *The Emancipation of French Indochina* (OUP 1961)
LANNING Michael Lee & CRAGG Dan: *Inside the VC and the VNA* (Fawcett Columbine 1992)

Select Bibliography

LARTEGUY Jean: *L'Adieu à Saigon* (Presses de la Cite 1975)
LE Quang: *Giap:ou la guerre du peuple* (Denoel 1973)
LEWIS Norman: *Dragon Apparent* (Cape 1951)
LEWY Guenther: *America in Vietnam* (OUP 1978)

McCHRISTIAN Joseph A.: *The Role of Military Intelligence 1965–1967* (CMH 1974)
McGARVEY Patrick: *Visions of Victory: 1964–8* (Stanford)
MacDONALD Peter: *Giap: Victor in Vietnam* (Fourth Estate 1993)
MANGOLD Tom & PENYCOTE John: *The Tunnels of Cu Chi* (Random House 1985)
MARR David: *Independence or Death* (Flinder 1984)
——— *Vietnamese Anticolonialism* (California 1971)
MASSIEU Isabelle: *Comment j'ai parcouru l'Indochine* (Librairie Plon 1901)
MATTHEWS Lloyd & BROWN Dale E.: *Assessing the Vietnam War* (Pergamon/Brassey 1987)
MESKO J.M.: *Riverine Warfare* (Squadron/Signed Publications 1985)
MOMYER William: *The Vietnamese Air Force* (Government Printing Office, Washington 1977)
MORRISON Wilbur H: *The Elephant & the Tiger:* (Hippocrene 1971)
MUS Paul: *Ho Chi Minh, Le Vietnam et L'Asia* (Seuil 1971)
——— *Vietnam, Sociologie d'une Guerre* (Seuil 1952)
MYERSON Joel D: *Images of a Lengthy War* (CMH 1989)

NGUYEN Duy Huh: *Vietnamisation & the Ceasefire* (CMH 1979)

O'BALLANCE Edgar: *The Indochina War 1945–54* (Faber & Faber 1964)
O'NEILL Robert: *General Giap* (Praeger 1969)
OBERDORFER Don: *Tet* (Doubleday 1974)
OTT David Ewing: *Field Artillery* (CMH 1975)

PATTI Archimedis: *Why Vietnam?* (California 1980)
PEARSON Willard: *The War in the Northern Provinces* (GPO Washington 1989)
PEDRONCINI Guy & DUPLAY Philipp: *Leclerc et L'Indochine* (Albin Michel 1992)
PIKE Douglas: *PAVN: People's Army of Vietnam* (Presidio Press 1986)
——— *Vietcong* (MIT Press 1966)
Vietnam & the Soviet Union (Westview 1987)

ROBEQUAIN Charles: *Economic Development of French Indochina* (Hartmann)
ROBEQUAIN Charles: *L'Indochine Francaise* (Armand Colin 1935)
ROGERS Bernard W.: *Cedar Falls* – Junction City (CMH 1974)

SAINTENY Jean: *Histoire d'une Paix Manquee* (Amiot–Dumont 1953)
SANTOLI Al: *Everything we had* (Random House 1981)
———— *To Bear any burden* (E.P. Dutton 1985)
SHAPLEN Robert: *Time Out of Hand* (Harper and Row 1969)
SHARP Ulysses S.: *Strategy for Defeat* (Presidio Press 1979)
SHEEHAN Neil: *After the War was Over* (Random House 1992)
———— *A Bright Shining Lie* (Random House 1988)
SHORT Anthony: *Origins of the Vietnam War* (Longman 1989)
SHOWATER Dennis & ALBERT John: *An American Dilemma*: (Imprint Publications 1993)
SMITH Ralph: *History of the Vietnam War* (MacMillan 1983)
———— *Vietnam & the West* (Heinemann 1968)
SPECTOR Ronald: *Advice and Support* (CMH 1983)
SUMMERS Harry: *On Strategy* (Presidio 1982)
SUN-TZU: *The Art of War* (Shambhala Publications, Inc. 1988)

TANHAM George: *Communist Revolutionary Warfare: Viet Minh In Indochina* (Praeger 1967)
TERZANI Tiziano: *Giai Phong!* (Allen & Unwin 1988)
THAYER C.A. *The Origins of the National Front for the Liberation of South Vietnam* (Australian National University 1977)
THOMPSON Sir Robert: *Defeating Communist Insurgency* (Chatto & Windus 1967)
———— *Make for the Hills* (Cooper 1989)
TRAN Van Don: *Our Endless War* (Presidio 1978)
TRULLINGER James: *Village at War* (Longman 1980)
TRUONG Chinh: *The Resistance will win* (Hanoi Foreign Languages Publishing House 1960)

VAN Tien Dung: *Our Great Spring Victory* (Monthly Review Press 1977)
VO Nguyen Giap: *Big Victory, Great Task* (Praeger 1968)
———— *Dien Bien Phu* (Hanoi Foreign 1962)
———— *Military Art of People's War* (Monthly Review Press 1970)
———— *People's War People's Army* (Maspero 1966)

Select Bibliography

_____ *Selected Writings* (Hanoi Foreign 1970)
_____ *Unforgettable Months & Years* (Hanoi Foreign 1974)

WARNER Denis: *Certain Victory* (Sheed Andrews & McMell 1977)
_____ *The Last Confucian* (Angus & Robertson 1964)
WARNER Jayne & HUNT David (eds): *The American War in Vietnam* (SEA Programme, Cornell)

YONAS Marilyn B: *The Vietnam Wars* (Harper Collins 1993)

Infantry in Vietnam – US Army Infantry Magazine
Notre Guerre du Peuple a vaincu la guerre de destuction Americaine: Le Peuple du Sud Vietnam Vaincra (Foreign Languages Publishing House, Hanoi)

Index

Index

Index

Index

Index

Index

Index

Index

Index

Index

Index